# Literature, Partition and the Nation-State

The history of partition in the twentieth century is one steeped in controversy and violence. That history is comprised of both the cold war partitions in Germany, Vietnam and Korea and the colonial partitions that occurred in Ireland, India, Palestine and Cyprus, as British imperial rule contracted in these locations. *Literature, Partition and the Nation-State* offers an extended study of the social and cultural legacies of state division in Ireland and Palestine, two regions where the trauma of partition continues to shape political events to this day. Focusing on the periods since the 1960s, when the original partition settlements in each region were challenged by Irish and Palestinian nationalists, Joe Cleary's book contains individual chapters on nationalism and self-determination; on the construction of national literatures in the wake of state division; and on influential Irish, Israeli and Palestinian writers, film-makers and public intellectuals, such as Amos Oz, Neil Jordan and Ghassan Kanafani. Bringing debates from several different sites in the 'postcolonial world' into dialogue, *Literature, Partition and the Nation-State* is a radical and enthralling intervention into contemporary scholarship from a range of disciplines on nations and nationalism. The book will be of interest to scholars in Cultural and Postcolonial Studies, Nations and Nationalism, Irish Literature, Middle East Studies and Modern History.

JOE CLEARY is Lecturer in English at the National University of Ireland, Maynooth where he teaches Colonial and Postcolonial Literature, Literary Theory and Renaissance Drama. He has published widely on Irish literature and film and on contemporary political and cultural theory in books and journals such as *The South Atlantic Quarterly* and *Textual Practice*.

D1595748

# Cultural Margins

General editor
Timothy Brennan
*Department of Cultural Studies and Comparative Literature and English,
University of Minnesota*

The series Cultural Margins originated in response to the rapidly increasing interest in postcolonial and minority discourses among literary and humanist scholars in the US, Europe, and elsewhere. The aim of the series is to present books which investigate the complex cultural zone within and through which dominant and minority societies interact and negotiate their differences. Studies in the series range from examinations of the debilitating effects of cultural marginalisation, to analyses of the forms of power found at the margins of culture, to books which map the varied and complex components involved in the relations of domination and subversion. This is an international series, addressing questions crucial to the deconstruction and reconstruction of cultural identity in the late twentieth-century world.

# LITERATURE, PARTITION AND THE NATION-STATE

*Culture and Conflict in Ireland, Israel and Palestine*

*Joe Cleary*

CAMBRIDGE
UNIVERSITY PRESS

PUBLISHED BY THE PRESS SYNDICATE OF THE UNIVERSITY OF CAMBRIDGE
The Pitt Building, Trumpington Street, Cambridge, United Kingdom

CAMBRIDGE UNIVERSITY PRESS
The Edinburgh Building, Cambridge CB2 2RU, UK
40 West 20th Street, New York, NY 10011-4211, USA
477 Williamstown Road, Port Melbourne, VIC 3207, Australia
Ruiz de Alarcón 13, 28014 Madrid, Spain
Dock House, The Waterfront, Cape Town 8001, South Africa

http://www.cambridge.org

First published 2002

Printed in the United Kingdom at the University Press, Cambridge

*Typeface* Palatino 9.5/12 pt.     *System* LATEX 2$_\varepsilon$   [TB]

*A catalogue record for this book is available from the British Library*

ISBN 0 521 65150 6 hardback
ISBN 0 521 65732 6 paperback

*For Peter and Mary Cleary*

[M]any novelists, painters, and poets like Manzoni, Picasso, or Neruda, have embodied the historical experience of their people in aesthetic works, which in turn become recognized as great masterpieces. For the intellectual the task, I believe, is explicitly to universalize the crisis, to give greater human scope to what a particular race or nation suffered, to associate that experience with the suffering of others ... This does not at all mean a loss in historical specificity, but rather it guards against the possibility that a lesson learned about oppression in one place will be forgotten or violated in another place or time.

—Edward Said


We can always pinpoint differences, it is the easiest of all scholarly tasks, since everything is always different in some ways from everything else across time and space. What is harder and takes priority is to discover similarities.

—Immanuel Wallerstein

# Contents

# Acknowledgements

This study began as part of my doctoral research at Columbia University, New York. I wish to thank especially my supervisor Edward Said, who was always inspirational and intellectually generous, and my assistant supervisor, John Archer, who offered tremendous solidarity and support. I have also benefited enormously from intellectual exchanges with many friends, teachers, and colleagues in that institution: Joy Hayton, Jean Howard, Qadri Ismail, Zaineb Istrabadi, Siobhán Kilfeather, Colleen Lye, Fenella MacFarlane, Amy Martin, Joseph Massad, Anne McClintock, Rebecca McLennan, Franco Moretti, Aamir Mufti, Rob Nixon, Laura O'Connor, Yumna Siddiqi, Gayatri Chakravorty Spivak and Gauri Viswanathan.

My friends and colleagues in the Department of English at the National University of Ireland, Maynooth, where the project was completed, were equally supportive. I would like to thank them all, and especially Professor Brian Cosgrove who helped me secure a period of academic leave which was invaluable in helping the work towards completion. Very special thanks are due to Seamus Deane, Terry Eagleton, Richard Hayes, Kevin Honan, Jean Howard, Margaret Kelleher, Colleen Lye, Conor McCarthy, Chris Morash, Emer Nolan and Yumna Siddiqi who gave generously of their time in reading, editing and commenting incisively on sections of the work in progress. The scholarship and friendship of the following have been of immense value to me over the years: Kevin Barry, Steve Coleman, Denis Condon, Colin Coulter, Peter Denman, Honor Fagan, Tadhg Foley, Luke Gibbons, James Heaney, Jason King, Heather Laird, David Lloyd, Siobhán Long, Liam O'Dowd, Lionel Pilkington, Seán Ryder, Eamon Slater and Kevin Whelan. The Red Stripe Seminar in Maynooth and Dublin has sustained intellectual comradeship of a very special kind over many years: my thanks to all involved. Thanks too to Isabelle Cartwright and Karen Donovan, and to the staff in Maynooth Library for their unflagging help in tracing elusive articles and books.

Ray Ryan at Cambridge University Press has not only been enormously helpful in guiding this project to publication but a generous supporter to boot. Timothy Brennan and Neil Lazarus offered trenchant criticisms and helpful advice as readers. An earlier version of Chapter Three was published as 'Fork-Tongued on the Border Bit: Partition and the Politics of Form in Contemporary Narratives of the Northern Irish Conflict', *The South Atlantic Quarterly* 95:1 (1996), 227–76. I would like to thank Candice Ward, *SAQ* editor, for permission to reprint it here. David Pickell, generous as always, designed the book-cover.

Finally, my most incalculable debt goes to Gemma Murphy and Conor Cleary. The project has made severe demands on them both at times, but they have been wonderful companions and my strongest support in every way. The work is dedicated, with deepest affection, to my mother Mary Cleary, who first introduced me to the wonders of literature, and to my father, Peter Cleary, who taught me things too valuable to be learned in books.

# Introduction

The idea for this book first began to take shape in New York towards the end of 1989 when I, like millions across the globe, watched the televised images of the extraordinary political upheavals sweeping across the Soviet Union and Central Europe, including the tearing down of the Berlin Wall and the collapse of the German Democratic Republic. The intellectual climate of those months was quickened with a sense that one was watching the human equivalent of a tectonic shift in the settled political landscape of the late twentieth century. For someone like myself who had grown up in the Irish midlands, and who was keenly aware in 1989 that Northern Ireland was starting into the third decade of a long-running war, the sources of which lay in a partition settlement established in the 1920s, the fall of the Berlin Wall, and the subsequent reunification of Germany, provoked a whole series of questions about nation and state formation, state division and the significance of partition. What are the conditions, I wondered then, that would explain why in some situations partitions collapse or prove reversible, while in others they appear to become permanent, and in others still the issue of division or reunification seems destined to remain a matter of constant contention? Is it only the 'Cold War' state divisions such as Vietnam, Germany and perhaps Korea that can ever be reversed while 'colonial' partitions in places such as the Republic of Ireland/Northern Ireland, India/Pakistan and Israel/Palestine are fated to remain immutable? Why, in some former British colonies such as these, did the end of imperial rule culminate in the break-up of the colonial state while in other situations – such as South Africa, say, where there were discontented White and Zulu minorities that might each have pressed for state division – this outcome was avoided?[1]

1

To some, the topic of partition will seem essentially a matter for historians or political scientists, something that has little to do with literature and culture. As the remarkably bitter *Literaturstreit* (quarrel about literature) and *Historikerstreit* (historians debate) that raged in Germany at the time of unification attested, however, this is clearly not the case. As the German controversies illustrated, the empirical events of partition or reunification cannot be detached from the wider contest within German society to make sense of those events, to press them into various kinds of narrative, and literary and cultural production were clearly central to this broader struggle.[2] Nation- and state-building processes are never just political events in the narrow sense; they also entail the construction of national education systems and national literatures, and they always involve cultural struggles to define how national societies understand themselves and their place in the wider world system. In the case of partitioned societies, cultural narratives play a number of very important functions. They represent one of the media through which the trauma of partition is subsequently memorialised and understood by the peoples involved; they can also help either to ratify the state divisions produced by partition or to contest the partitionist mentalities generated by such divisions. Hence, I believe, any serious attempt to wrestle with the larger dynamics of nation- and state-building in partitioned contexts must engage with the ways in which partition is constructed and contested in cultural and historiographic narrative in the societies in question. The ways in which the traumatic events and legacies of partition acquire an imaginative truth for the peoples involved, through these cultural struggles, is the central topic of this book.

When I commenced this study in the early 1990s I was not to know then that the spectre of partition and state division would constantly haunt the years ahead. The nightly spectacle, watched vicariously from a television set, of the horrors involved in the dissolution of the state of Yugoslavia, the partition of Bosnia-Herzegovina, and the ethnic conflict in Kosovo, served as a constant reminder of the dark side to both state-building and state-dividing projects. In the multinational environment of Columbia University, where I first began to work on this study, there were many teachers, friends, classmates and associates who came from places such as Palestine, India, Israel, Pakistan, Sri Lanka, Germany and South Africa which had already been partitioned or which ran some risk of being so in the future. In this milieu, it quickly impressed itself on me that the Irish experience of partition belonged to a much wider twentieth-century history. Anyone familiar with the history of partition could not fail to be aware that the events then underway in a collapsing Yugoslavia – the massacre and rape, the exodus of terrorised populations across state borders, the creation of new national majorities and minorities by ethnic cleansing, the tented cities of refugees that were the inevitable by-product of the drive to create homogeneous national states – were uncannily similar to those that had attended the partition of places such as India and Palestine earlier in the century. In the 1980s, some academics in Northern Ireland, believing that the conflict there was too deeply entrenched to allow for any negotiated settlement, had outlined the case for a repartition that would divide the province into distinct Catholic and Protestant territorial zones.[3] In Ireland, as in other places such as Palestine, India or Israel, then, watching the debacle in Yugoslavia was to some extent like watching a grisly montage of past or possible versions of one's own national history.

For the most part, the partitions mentioned here tend to be studied in isolation, and there has been little sustained or extended comparative analysis of such situations.[4] There are significant differences between all of these locations, of course, but there are many substantive continuities of experience as well that warrant attention. As Robert Schaeffer has noted, most of the major partitions in the twentieth century have occurred in territories previously subject to colonial rule.[5] Ireland, India, Palestine and Cyprus were British colonies; at the end of World War II Korea was a Japanese and Vietnam a French colony. The situations in Germany and China were in most respects quite different to these, but much of China had been annexed by Japan or was under Japanese rule in the period leading up to its division, and Germany was occupied by four military powers when it was sundered. As a general rule, then, it would seem that partitions are most likely to occur where – as a consequence of colonial rule or of total military collapse in times of war – societies have lost control over their own political destinies and are vulnerable to the wills of external superpowers.

This is not to suggest that partitions are simply attributable to the machinations of such superpowers. The partitions in Ireland, India and Palestine all took place at a specific historical conjuncture. In no case did they occur during the long period of imperial rule itself, though the communal antagonisms that would later lead to division were indeed whetted and nursed in the racialised structure of the colonial state, and were often cynically manipulated to maintain imperial rule. The actual partitions, however, materialised in all cases when the moment came for the imperial power to depart and to transfer power to a native élite. These transfers all took place in the immediate wake of major world wars (or inter-imperial wars) that weakened imperial power in the colonies concerned. Ireland, then, was divided in the wake of World War I; India and Palestine at the end of World War II. In each case, the impetus for partition stemmed from a minority community within the colonial state that feared that the anti-colonial national movements about to assume power would imperil their interests and identity. In none of these minority communities – Protestant Unionists in Ireland, Muslims in British India, Zionist Jews in Mandate Palestine – was the idea of partition universally embraced, but their leaderships were willing to contemplate state division where their preferred political goals could not be realised. In short, then, colonial political partitions, despite individual variables and specific circumstances, display elements of a common structural logic. They typically occur in circumstances of imperial decline or contraction, and at a moment that ought ideally to be a springtime of national emancipation. But in a situation where an imperial state, suffering from injured national pride and anxious to salvage as much international reputation as possible, comes into conflict with the antagonistic nationalisms of majority and minority communities within a colony, the political climate thus generated can prove an exceptionally lethal one. All sorts of catastrophe can occur in the veritable witches' brew of clashing nationalisms generated by such conjunctures.

The issue of partition, then, provokes a concatenation of issues directly relevant to the recent efflorescence of writings on colonial and postcolonial societies and on nationalism. Such issues include the nature of the colonial and postcolonial state, the construction of majorities and minorities, and the connections between literature and the nation, culture and the state. The aim of this book is to place the topic of partition on the agenda of these fields of scholarly inquiry, and in turn to draw on such scholarship to open up new ways to think about the contentious histories and legacies of partition.

Though I will refer occasionally to other partitions elsewhere, this book will concentrate, for several reasons, on the political and cultural legacies of partition in Ireland and Palestine. Firstly, in both of these cases the communal cleavages that were eventually to culminate in partition have their origins in longer histories of colonial settlement under British rule. In this respect at least, the histories of both Ireland and Palestine are closer, in some ways, to those of Algeria or South Africa than they are to that of India since the latter was what is termed a colony of exploitation rather than a colony of settlement.[6] The heartland of modern Unionism in Ireland was in Ulster, a region planted and settled in the early modern period by Scottish and English Protestants loyal to the British crown. Confronted with the rise of Irish nationalism in the late nineteenth century, Unionists there identified themselves as the now desperately hard-pressed defenders of British rule in Ireland, and Unionism, as an ideology designed to keep Ireland within the United Kingdom and Empire, was strongly pro-imperialist. Zionist settlers in Palestine depended on the British Mandate to secure their place in that country before 1948. Early Zionist leaders deliberately courted first Ottoman and then British imperial support by arguing that a Jewish state in Palestine would serve Western imperial interests in the region. Although neither Irish Unionist nor Zionist identities can be seen as undifferentiated, both groups were, therefore, much more closely affiliated with the British imperial enterprise in their respective regions than were Indian Muslims. Both perceived themselves as frontier peoples of empire, as chosen peoples who had already made or who would make the wilderness regions they inherited bloom; both were also consistently anxious about their demographic insufficiency vis-à-vis what they deemed the civilisationally backward majority communities that inhabited the same territory as they.[7] Such imaginings shaped a deeply hostile attitude in both communities towards the prospect of sharing a state with the numerically larger Irish Catholic and Palestinian Arab populations, something which, unlike the Muslim League in India, they were unwilling to consider in any circumstances.[8] Interestingly, despite their close ties with and considerable dependence on the British establishment, both Northern Irish Unionists and Zionists showed themselves willing to go to war with the British rather than to chance their fortunes in independent states controlled by the majority communities in the respective colonial units. This in itself seems a telling indication that, in some ways at any rate, the structural dynamics of majority and minority relationships in Ireland and Palestine were somewhat different to those that obtained in India.

Since this book will concentrate on the contemporary legacies and cultural politics of partition, its focus on Ireland and Palestine is motivated also by the fact that these two situations are increasingly associated with each other in both domestic and international perceptions. This is partly attributable to the more or less concurrent development in the 1990s of the respective 'peace processes' in each region under United States stewardship. But identifications and analogies between the two sites have in fact been in circulation for some considerable time and they pre-date these recent developments. The experience of diaspora is absolutely central to Irish, Israeli and Palestinian nationalisms. In each case, moreover, the diaspora communities are indelibly associated with major historical traumas: the Great Famine in Ireland in the 1840s; the Jewish Holocaust during World War II; the Palestinian *nakbah* or 'catastrophe' of 1948. The political weight exercised by the Irish and Jewish communities in America, and by the Palestinian exiles in the Arab and Islamic world, means that these all represent extremely significant versions of what Benedict Anderson has recently termed 'long-distance nationalism'.[9] One of the consequences of these diasporas is that they have helped to keep the profile of the Northern Irish and the Israeli–Palestinian conflicts high on the international agenda, a phenomenon which has, if anything, become even more significant in recent decades.

Within the academic world, the associations between Ireland and Palestine often take the form of specialised counter-insurgency discourses on 'terrorism'. That association has also been disseminated in mass culture works such as Tom Clancy's *Patriot Games*, in which Irish republican and Middle Eastern 'terrorisms' are closely identified, or in newspaper cartoons such as Gene Bassett's 'Who Said There's Nothing to Evolution?', in which IRA and Palestinian militants are constructed as tree-swinging simians that have evolved from their primate ancestors only to the extent that they have now learned to meddle with explosives.[10] Not all of the identifications between the two regions, however, are mediated through external agencies such as these. Republican wall murals in Northern Ireland, for example, have shown Irish and Palestinian guerrillas as comrades in arms. These murals attempt to counter more hostile discourses by representing Irish and Palestinian armed struggles not as kindred 'terrorisms' but as parallel anti-imperialist struggles.[11] In the early twentieth century especially, Israeli Zionists maintained a complex and contradictory identification with both white settler and anti-colonial nationalisms. Zionists watched Irish nationalism, in particular, with considerable interest and frequently asserted similarities between the plight of the Irish under British rule and that of Jews under imperial rule in Mandate Palestine. An early Israeli film, made in 1955, called *Hill 24 doesn't Answer (Giv'a 24 Eina Ona)*, is set during the 1948 war, and tells the story of four fighters – an American Jew, an Israeli-born Sabra, a Sephardi Jew, and an Irishman – assigned to defend a strategic hill outside Jerusalem. The apparently anomalous presence of the Irishman in this narrative is explained by the desire of those who made the film to suggest that the Zionism was not a regressive colonial settler nationalism but a revolutionary anti-colonial national liberation struggle which, like its Irish counterpart, deserved international sympathy and support.[12] There are, moreover, important parallels between Northern Irish loyalist and Israeli Zionist communities, both of whom see themselves as beleaguered peoples living under a constant state of siege in a territory where the Irish or Arab enemy vastly outnumbers them.[13] Both peoples also see themselves as threatened, Troy-like, by 'the enemy within': that is, by those untrustworthy Northern Irish nationalist or Israeli–Palestinian minorities whose real allegiances are presumed to be with the enemy-states or enemy-peoples across the border. And in both instances these threats are conceptualised not simply in political but also in demographic terms.

While cross-cultural identifications such as those mentioned above are sometimes rhetorically manipulative, designed to represent a particular community as 'progressive' and its antagonists as 'reactionary', there are still, despite manifest differences between the two regions, sufficient structural similarities between the situations to give some weight to the analogies. In different but connected ways, the histories of modern Ireland and Palestine belong to a wider history of British imperial expansion and contraction. In the late nineteenth and early twentieth century, it was the most conservative and most pro-imperialist sections within the British establishment that expressed the strongest opposition to Irish Home Rule. For this section of the British ruling élite, in which individuals such as Lord Salisbury and Arthur Balfour were leading figures, Irish nationalism constituted a threat not only to the territorial integrity of the British state but to the long-term stability of Empire. The close kinship and political ties between the Ulster Unionist leadership and the pro-imperialist wings in both the British Conservative and Liberal parties secured Unionism invaluable political support within the most influential circles in the British administration. This support was to prove crucial not only to the eventual implementation of partition in Ireland in the 1920s, but to helping Unionists secure the military and financial support that made the new Northern Irish state viable. It was to this same pro-imperialist cohort in the upper echelons of the British establishment that the Zionist movement would appeal to secure British backing for its ambitions in Palestine. The Balfour Declaration of November 1917, with its promise that Britain 'views with favour the establishment in Palestine of a national home for the Jewish people',[14] was to become the charter for Zionist settlement in Palestine under the British Mandate, putting Jewish and Arab national ambitions on a collision course that would also culminate in partition. Moreover, as the military historian Keith Jeffrey has noted, after 1907 the Royal Irish Constabulary (RIC) Depot in Dublin was a training centre for colonial police in the British Empire, a function later taken over by Northern Ireland's Royal Ulster Constabulary after partition. When the RIC were disbanded in 1922 after the Irish War of Independence, significant numbers of that force (including the Irish Chief of Police, General Sir Henry Tudor), transferred to the Palestinian Gendarmerie. In the autumn of 1922, General Tudor, having assumed command in Jerusalem, reported to his old friend and new political master, Winston Churchill, that Palestine was 'a rest cure after Ireland'.[15]

In more recent times, possibly the most significant structural parallel is the virtual collapse of the original partition settlements in both Ireland and Palestine since the end of the 1960s. These settlements disintegrated for very different reasons. Israel's seizure of the West Bank and Gaza after the 1967 War effectively abolished the division of historic Palestine established after the 1948 War. In Northern Ireland, the state borders remained in place, but the civil rights movement and the subsequent republican paramilitary struggle led to the collapse of the Unionist state established by partition and compelled the British government to resume direct control of the province. In both instances, the breakdown of the original partition settlements gave impetus to a protracted new stage of inter-communal contest, to the struggles generally referred to nowadays as the Northern Irish 'Troubles' and the 'Israeli–Palestinian' conflict.

Since it deals with quite recent materials, one of the challenges with which the present project has had to contend is that the situations in Northern Ireland and Israel/Palestine have been changing rapidly in recent times, and indeed are still evolving at some pace. Antonio Gramsci's concept of the 'interregnum' is possibly one of the more useful ways in which to conceptualise the long decades of uninterrupted turmoil in each region since the late 1960s. For Gramsci, the concept of the interregnum refers to those periods in which 'the ruling class has lost its consensus, i.e. is no longer "leading" but only "dominant", exercising coercive force alone'. In such periods, Gramsci argues, 'the great masses have become detached from their traditional ideologies, and no longer believe what they used to believe previously'. What constitutes the crisis in such periods, he continues, is the fact that 'the old is dying and the new cannot be born; in this interregnum a great variety of morbid symptoms appear'. For Gramsci, the disruptive energies of the interregnum have positive as well as negative potential. Indeed, the crucial question, as he sees it, to be asked of such periods is: 'Will the interregnum, the crisis whose historically normal solution is blocked in this way, necessarily be resolved in favour of a restoration of the old?' His somewhat hesitant answer to this question is that while a complete restitution of the old order is unlikely (the clock, so to speak, cannot simply be reset to exactly where it was before the interregnum), its general reconstruction cannot be ruled out. It is always possible, he surmises, that 'a "new arrangement" will be found' that reconstitutes the old order, even if in a reformed or some more 'jesuitical' manner.[16]

The respective 'peace processes' advanced in Northern Ireland and the Middle East since the early 1990s clearly constitute a watershed development; they represent an attempt to bring an end to the preceding interregnum by constructing new arrangements. The ambition, in other words, is to move towards the establishment of new state arrangements that will secure sufficient consensus from the two antagonistic communities to enable an exercise of power less dependent on military force and repression. The historical test that will be posed to these new arrangements is: To what extent will they enable new and more emancipatory political relationships to emerge between the peoples involved? Or will they simply amount to elaborate and, to recall Gramsci's terms, more 'jesuitical' reconstructions of the old order that serve only to maintain the old imbalances of communal power that obtained before the interregnum?

A comparatist study such as this has its inevitable restrictions. The subject of partition is always bitterly controversial; the scholarship on it is sometimes intensely polemical and always connected to some extent to wider political struggles within the societies in question. Moreover, the collateral issues that bear on the topic are manifold, and the literatures on partition are in numerous different languages. Hence no individual can expect to master all of the sets of issues involved, and a comprehensive comparative cultural analysis of partition in several different sites is a task that would properly require a whole team of researchers. While I suggested earlier that the situations in Ireland and Palestine may correspond more closely in some respects to each other than they do to India, this is not to say that the differences between these situations and India's are in any way categorical or absolute. The dilemmas that led to and have followed from the partition of India can help scholars to rethink the Irish or Israeli–Palestinian situations

in instructive ways, and it would be useful to add India to the compass of this study were there but 'world enough and time'. Some of
the finest literature on partition, and some of the most innovative historical research on the topic, has been written by writers and scholars
of the Indian subcontinent. While Irish and Middle Eastern historiography continues to be dominated by the 'high' politics of partition,
South Asian historians have begun to investigate the issue from the
perspective of those 'below' as well. In so doing, critical new insights
on the communal violence that accompanied partition, on the specific
experiences of women, and on the role of literature in constructing collective understandings and representations of the traumas involved
have been opened up. This South Asian scholarship is immensely suggestive to those interested in the history of partition anywhere, and,
it is my hope that this study can contribute to the wider debates that
that scholarship has stimulated.[17]

With regard to the question of language, the most obvious restric-
tion to this study is my own lack of proficiency in Arabic and Hebrew.
This has required me to work with these literatures in translation,
something that inevitably places many matters beyond my compe-
tence. Nevertheless, a very considerable body of scholarship on the
Israeli–Palestinian conflict exists in English, and English frequently
serves in the region as a neutral language through which Arabic and
Hebrew speakers and scholars communicate with each other. It is also
the case that in Israel/Palestine, as in Ireland, a considerable body of
literary and intellectual work is written not only with domestic national audiences in mind but out of a concern to explicate the crises in
these regions to wider diaspora and international audiences. English
is the medium through which much of this cultural traffic and exchange usually passes, and it is therefore a revealing medium in its
own right. While there are many ways in which a general work such
as this must yield to the specialist in individual national literatures,
the value and justification of the broader perspective adopted here is
that it can help to open up wider sets of theoretical issues and relationships. Comparative literary studies in the humanities is one of the
few ways through which literary developments can be studied in a
manner not restricted to or determined by a national frame. Yet comparative literary study in the modern university has also always had a
decidedly Eurocentric bias, with the unfortunate consequence that the
scholarly infrastructure available for conducting comparative cultural
analyses across 'postcolonial' countries in different geo-cultural regions such as Ireland and Palestine is still rudimentary. But a start,

however modest, has to be made, and my hope is that others, better equipped than I, will be stimulated and provoked to venture more comprehensive studies of the kinds of issues addressed here.

As befits a study of partition perhaps, this book is divided into two sections. Part I is comprised of two chapters that offer general overviews of the Irish and Israeli–Palestinian situations. Chapter One examines some of the complex theoretical issues that the partitions in Ireland and Palestine provoke with regard to the issue of national self-determination. It argues that while the state divisions in question helped to secure self-determination for some groups, they did so at the expense of the self-determination of others. Partition is often defended by its advocates on the basis that it is the only practicable solution in situations where two antagonistic national groups with conflicting aspirations to self-determination inhabit a shared territory. The strategy's major deficiency, however, is that in regions where the peoples concerned are geographically intermingled, the attempt to manufacture ethnically homogeneous states, or states with secure ethnic majorities, cannot be accomplished without extraordinary communal violence. This violence does not end with the act of partition: violence is not incidental to but constitutive of the new state arrangements thus produced. Chapter Two shifts attention to the cultural politics of partition, and investigates some of the ways in which literature can be used either as a means to consolidate or to contest the official state cultures and partitionist mentalities that emerge in the wake of partition. Beginning with a brief overview of recent debates about the functions of literature in the two Germanys in this regard, the chapter suggests that the processes of state estrangement, or mutual distancing, elaborated in the aftermath of partitions can usefully be grasped in terms of a recurring dialectic of tradition and modernity. The partitioned states, in other words, usually attempt to legitimate themselves on the basis that they represent a more felicitous marriage of the traditional and the modern than the rival-state across the border, which is usually deemed to represent the worst elements of both. The main body of this chapter will be concerned with specific elaborations of this dialectic in Ireland and Israel/Palestine.

Part II is comprised of three chapters that move the study from a general to a more particular focus. Chapter Three undertakes a close analysis of the genres of the romance-across-the-divide and the 'Troubles thriller' as they have emerged in Northern Ireland in recent decades. In these narrative paradigms, I will contend, the Northern Irish conflict is consistently constructed as an 'internal' issue to do with communal sectarianism, thus occluding the many ways in which that conflict is also connected to the construction and character of the wider state system in the British and Irish archipelago. Chapter Four undertakes a close reading of some of the novels of the leading Israeli writer, Amos Oz. An influential public intellectual in Israel, with an international reputation as an outspoken dissident, Oz has consistently argued that a territorial separation of the Israeli and Palestinian peoples offers the only viable solution to their predicament. This chapter examines the ways in which Oz's novels represent the struggle between the two peoples, and argues that in his fiction, as in his writings as a public intellectual, Oz's critique of Israel's treatment of the Palestinians operates within narrow and conservative limits. Finally, in Chapter Five, I offer an extended study of Ghassan Kanafani's remarkable novel, *Men in the Sun*. This novel is an imaginative response to the disaster that the 1948 partition represented for Palestinians and it attempts to convey some sense of the extraordinary dilemmas with which Palestinian nationalism has had to wrestle ever since. The subject of *Men in the Sun* is the destitute condition of a stateless people in a world of nation-states. Its compelling treatment of that condition, it will be argued, means that it continues to speak to the current situation in Israel/Palestine where the fate of the Palestinian refugees has been reduced to an object of barter by the Oslo Accord. Moreover, at a moment when many in the West are celebrating the 'borderless world' that contemporary globalisation is supposedly bringing into existence, Kanafani's work might be regarded as one of the indispensable texts of our times.

*Part One*

## Chapter 1

# Ireland, Palestine and the antinomies of self-determination in 'the badlands of modernity'

I

The subject of partition receives little attention in the remarkable corpus of writing on nations and nationalism that has emerged over the past two decades or so. In the now canonical works of Benedict Anderson, Ernest Gellner, Eric Hobsbawm, Etienne Balibar and Immanuel Wallerstein, Tom Nairn, Anthony D. Smith, Miroslav Hroch and Liah Greenfeld the topic never emerges as an issue for serious reflection. More surprisingly perhaps, it is also ignored in the more influential works on anti-colonial and postcolonial nationalism – such as those by Partha Chatterjee, Homi Bhabha, James M. Blaut and Basil Davidson – that have emerged in the same period, and only in John Breuilly's brief survey of Indian nationalism in *Nationalism and the State* does it receive any consideration.[1] The tendency to bypass the topic in these studies is curious since partition has played an important role in the annals of British decolonisation especially, and because it raises serious theoretical questions about the nature of postcolonial state formation, state division and nation-building.

One of the reasons why the subject of partition tends to be bypassed in contemporary studies of nationalism, it would appear, is that it is taken for granted in most of these works that the newly independent postcolonial states inherited the territorial boundaries of the colonial states that preceded them. In Benedict Anderson's *Imagined Communities*, the single most influential work on nations and nationalism in recent times, this continuity between colonial and postcolonial state borders is axiomatic. Comparing twentieth-century anti-colonial nationalisms in Asia and Africa with eighteenth-century Creole nationalisms in Latin America, Anderson writes: 'In considering the origins of recent "colonial nationalism", one central similarity with the colonial nationalisms of an earlier age immediately strikes the eye: *the isomorphism between each nationalism's territorial stretch and that of the previous imperial administrative unit.*[2] Going on to contemplate the means by which the 'imperial administrative unit came to acquire a national meaning', Anderson attributes central significance to the colony-confined bureaucratic pilgrimages that shaped the careers of both the earlier Latin American Creole élites and those of their twentieth-century native Asian and African counterparts. He asserts, therefore: 'Out of this pattern [of restricted pilgrimages or colony-confined career routes] came that subtle, half-concealed transformation, step by step, of the colonial-state into the national-state, a transformation made possible not only by a solid continuity of personnel, but by the established skein of journeys through which each state was experienced by its functionaries.'[3]

When Anderson writes of 'the isomorphism between each nationalism's territorial stretch and that of the previous imperial administrative unit' or of the evolutionary 'transformation, step by step, of the colonial-state into the national-state', his statements command the authority they do because they seem accurately to describe the experience of most of the previously colonised world. In South America, Asia and Africa, the great majority of independent postcolonial states have indeed assumed the inherited boundaries of the previous colonial units. The experience of Sub-Saharan Africa especially seems to underwrite the trajectory from colonial-state to nation-state that Anderson ascribes to the colonial world in general. The imperial partition of Sub-Saharan Africa in the late nineteenth century carved that continent into colonial states that largely disregarded precolonial patterns of ethnic and political organisation, requiring local communities radically to adjust their concepts of social space. Nevertheless, the emergent postcolonial African nation-states have generally retained the old colonial frontiers and have attempted to nationalise the multiethnic communities within the erstwhile colonial territorial units.[4]

At the same time, Ireland, India and Palestine, to mention only the most obvious cases, clearly do not fit into the model of postcolonial nation-building and state-formation described here. In these situations, as elsewhere, nationalist anti-colonial independence movements did indeed anticipate that the new nation-states would inherit the territorial stretch of the existing imperial administrative unit, but in each case such expectations were eventually to be frustrated. In these countries, the majority nationalist movements within the colonial state found themselves confronted by a minority opposition movement that commanded sufficient popular support and political influence to compel the territorial sub-division of the imperial administrative unit. Anderson's *Imagined Communities* neither invites us to ask nor provides us with the theoretical equipment to consider why territorial cleavages of this kind should have happened in some colonies and not others.

It might be argued that Ireland, India and Palestine are simply aberrations and that even if they do not conform to Anderson's model neither do they seriously trouble its overall validity since it accurately captures the general, even if not universal, pattern of development from colonial-state to nation-state in the old European empires. When one reads his chapter on twentieth-century anti-colonial nationalism with Ireland, India or Palestine in mind, it soon becomes apparent, however, that matters are more complex than this allows. When Anderson contemplates nationalism in the colonies he does so more or less exclusively in terms, firstly, of the indigenous native élites (conceived as quite a cohesive bloc) and, secondly, in terms of the majority nationalist movements that opposed the imperial power in each unit. When he deals with either the Latin American Creole nationalisms that won their independence in the early nineteenth century or the later twentieth-century anti-colonial indigenous nationalist movements (and he stresses only the similarities between the two phenomena), Anderson makes almost no mention of either loyalist nationalisms within the settler colonies or what might be called minority or sub-nationalist movements within either set of colonies. Consequently, his conceptual scheme makes little provision for the fact that the imperial powers could sometimes manipulate minority sub-nationalisms within the colonies to frustrate majority demands for independence or for the fact that minority nationalist movements could sometimes on their own account pose serious difficulties for majority nationalist movements.[5]

Moreover, as his consistent emphasis on the bureaucratic pilgrimages of native functionaries in the imperial administration system makes clear, for Anderson the shaping of national consciousness and identity is something essentially conducted by the nationalist élites. While its importance is not to be underestimated, Anderson's exclusive focus on this class nevertheless causes him to underestimate the extent to which subaltern classes could sometimes provide important initiative and momentum for nationalist struggles against imperial rule and the extent to which the need to mobilise such classes could constrain the political options open to the élites. Even if the leading role of the élites is accepted, therefore, Anderson's work still seems largely indifferent to the ways in which struggles between different classes can infuse the prescriptive content of nationhood with conflicting aspirations.

What I am suggesting, then, is that the processes by which the nation is imagined, national struggles mobilised, and the colonial-state transformed into a nation-state do not simply follow the smoothly evolutionary top–down trajectory that Anderson implies. Such processes are much more sharply contested – in class, ethnic, regional and religious terms – within the colony than his conceptual scheme allows, and these contests have important consequences for the social character or ideological content of the nationalisms that emerge. Only if we take account of the complex articulation of nationalist struggles with those of other social movements, and of the ways in which the latter were often inflected in terms of class, religious or regional loyalties, can we begin to understand why in some situations – such as Ireland, India and Palestine – the territorial borders of the colonial state did not become those of the nation-state, or indeed why in others – as in some African states today – inherited colonial borders continue to represent serious obstacles to ongoing projects of nation-building. Instead of the relatively steady élite-controlled 'transformation, step by step, of the colonial-state into the nation-state' that *Imagined Communities* assumes as normative, a greater appreciation of the significance of rival subnational movements within each colony would allow us to begin to understand why in some colonies communal cleavages should have resulted in territorial division while in other situations where communal or regional cleavages were no less acute – cases such as South Africa, Nigeria or Lebanon for instance – partition was avoided.

The aim of this chapter is not to trace the history of partition in Ireland or Palestine since the historical literature on the events that culminated in partition in these countries is already vast.[6] The chapter will assume some general familiarity with these histories, and will concentrate instead on some of the common theoretical concerns prompted by the issue of partition in these regions. I want to begin in the next section, therefore, by contesting the stubbornly popular thesis that it is the strength or virulence of ethnic nationalism in Ireland and Palestine that accounts for the original partitions there and for the subsequent conflicts that have persisted since then. Nationalist and liberal commentators, who otherwise recognise little in common, share the assumption that the conflicts in question can be ascribed to the persistence of aggressively chauvinistic and illiberal ethnic nation-alisms, but this, I want to suggest, is drastically to over-simplify and mis-identify the issues involved. For the rival communities in Ireland and Palestine, I will suggest, the real dilemma was – and still remains – how to exercise conflicting claims to national self-determination in conditions where the national communities involved are territorially interspersed. Since this dilemma poses serious problems for civic or liberal as well as ethnic nationalisms, it is misleading to isolate eth-nic nationalism as the prime root of political conflict in such circum-stances and to proffer civic nationalism as the benign alternative. In both Ireland and Palestine, the original partition settlements in 1921 and 1948 respectively failed to come to grips in a just manner with the conflicting claims to self-determination asserted by the communities involved. In the final section of the chapter, the degree to which the current 'peace processes' in these regions recognise and attempt to remedy the intrinsic deficiencies inherent in the original partition set-tlements will briefly be assessed.

## II

What kind of a political phenomenon is partition? Perhaps the most useful definition is Stanley Waterman's: 'Partition can be said to have occurred when two or more new states are created out of what had previously been a single [administrative] entity and when at least one of the new units claims a direct link with the prior state.'[7] The manner in which links between newly created states and the older pre-partition territorial units continue to be expressed after partition varies from one situation to another. In some instances one or more of the new states have claimed to be the sole legitimate successor to the territory of the divided administrative unit and have asserted con-stitutional title to that territory: examples include the Irish Republic, West Germany and the two Koreas. Though the Palestinians did not control any of Palestine after 1948, their national charter claimed title to the whole territorial stretch of pre-partitioned British Palestine, and Israel, too, has always regarded the areas of historic Palestine beyond its official state boundaries as 'lost' territories to which it has powerful claim. Even in cases such as India and Pakistan, where partition was accepted as irreversible, or that of East Germany, where a commitment to reunification was eventually abandoned, the new states have usu-ally claimed to embody the best traditions of the older pre-partitioned unit.

The issue of state division, however, always involves matters of *national identity* as well. Where one of the new states claims continuity with the older pre-partitioned territorial unit, this creates the dilemma as to how the national community is to be defined in such circumstances. Should 'the nation' in the wake of partition be reformulated to include only the population resident within the territory that the state in question actually administers? Or, should the state continue to define 'the nation' in terms of the wider trans-border community and/or territory that it also claims as 'its' own? If, as a consequence of partition, a section of the national community finds itself resident in the state across the border, then what obligations to support and protect the interests of that extra-state section of the nation should the 'parent' state recognise? For minority national communities stranded in states on the 'wrong' side of the partitioning border, there is also the question of how to reconcile commitments to the state in which they actually live with commitments to their ethno-national kin in the 'parent' nation-state. Partition, in short, entails a reorganisation of political space that invariably triggers complex reconstructions of national identity within and across the borders of the states involved. Further distinctions might be made here between imposed partitions that divided relatively homogeneous nations along ideological lines as a direct result of Cold War rivalries (as in Germany, Korea or Vietnam) and those implemented to resolve communal conflicts within ethnically heterogeneous colonial states at the moment of the transfer of imperial power (as in Ireland, India and Palestine). Although such distinctions are vital, the dilemmas concerning definitions of citizenship and the reconstruction of national identities that emerge in the wake of both Cold War and post-imperial partitions nonetheless share important similarities.

The strongest and most common defence of partition in the colonial situations that will concern us here is that which contends that in situations of acute inter-communal conflict partition represents a 'best-worst solution' since it is the only alternative to the greater evil of total ethno-nationalist civil war. The assumption, as D. L. Horowitz characterises it, is that, '[i]f it is impossible for groups to live together in a heterogeneous state, perhaps it is better for them to live apart in more than one homogeneous state, even if this necessitates population transfers'.[8] For its advocates, then, in a situation of violent ethnic conflict partition represents the only humane means of intervention available since its aim is to separate the conflicting groups into ethnically homogeneous states that would eventually, it is assumed,

*The antinomies of self-determination*

be created in any event through bloody war. From this standpoint, an imposed partition, conducted under superpower supervision, has at least the advantage that it delivers in a more controlled manner what inter-communal war would otherwise deliver in any case. Where the territorial intermixing of the peoples involved renders a complete separation of the ethnic groups into homogeneous states impossible, the assumption is that borders can be redrawn or population transfers conducted in ways that reduce ethnic minorities to such a small proportion of the 'core' state population that they can no longer be construed as a serious political threat to the states in which they find themselves.[9]

It is imperative to recognise that the principle that subtends partition as a political policy – though often decried by nationalists as an imperialist desecration of 'the nation' or a grotesque violation of the national territory – is, philosophically speaking, impeccably and even dogmatically ethnic nationalist. After all, those who advocate partition as a solution to supposedly intractable ethno-national conflicts operate on the inpeccably ethnic nationalist premise that nation-states should be ethnically homogeneous or should at least have clear ethnic-majority groups exercising sovereignty over their own delimited territory. In other words, advocates of partition share the ethno-nationalist assumption that geographically interspersed communities with different national affiliations represent an impediment to secure nation-building and are inherently conducive to political instability. From this perspective, the range of options available in such situations is narrowly limited: there is a simple choice between nationalist homogenisation through the cultural assimilation of minorities or the territorial division of ethnic communities into separate states, something which also produces another nationalist homogenisation though by different means.

In effect, therefore, partition has always represented an attempt to engineer, usually in an extremely compressed period, nation-states with clear and decisive ethnic majorities in precisely those situations where ethnically intermingled populations were least amenable to such results. Not surprisingly, therefore, the attempt to implement partition has invariably been accompanied by various forms of ethnic cleansing, forced population transfer and coerced assimilation – all in the name of producing the supposedly normative conditions of liberal democratic nationhood. In India and Palestine and in contemporary Yugoslavia, humanly catastrophic population transfers and expulsions have gone hand in hand with the policy of partition.[10]

21

In most instances the conflicting communities have been so inter-mixed, however, that partition could not finally deliver the 'clean cut' it was supposed to do. Even where massive population transfers did take place, the post-imperial partitions have always left substantial national minorities stranded on 'the wrong side' of the new state borders, and these have continued to be a source of both domestic and interstate conflict. The loyalties of communities such as Northern Irish Catholics, Israeli Arabs or Indian Muslims to the states in which they resided were from the outset deemed highly suspect. In times of aggravated conflict between the divided states, these communities are still regularly viewed as 'fifth columnists' whose real allegiance is to the enemy-state across the border, and they can therefore serve as 'hostage communities' to be punished if that enemy-state is deemed to pose a threat. Since the assumption that subtends partitionist thinking is that ethnically homogeneous states will be more stable than ethnically heterogeneous ones, the policy tends to see 'minorities' in an intrinsically negative light as a problem that has somehow to be resolved. Hence after partition Northern Irish Catholics or Southern Irish Protestants, Israeli Arabs or Indian Muslims found themselves locked into states defined overwhelmingly in terms of the nationality of the majority groups. For nearly all of these communities, the struggle to undo the negative consequences of this majoritarian legacy is still ongoing.

For a variety of reasons, then, the utility of partition as a problem-solving device is questionable. In the situations listed above, the actual settlements have provided potent material for ongoing conflict. Far from bringing an incipient or ongoing civil war between populations to a decisive end, partition has generally served rather as a watershed, as a decisive realignment not only of the communal forces but of the very terms of that conflict whereby what was a smouldering 'hot' civil war between populations is afterwards resumed – in slower gear as it were – as a more cautious and protracted 'cold' war between and within states. Moreover, once they have been established, the new state regimes on both sides of the partitioning divide have often relied on whipping up fear of the external antagonist across the border to maintain domestic control at home. In many divided states, the incumbent regimes have continued to be, to paraphrase Perry Anderson, torn like Buridan's ass between contradictory desires to undermine their rivals and to avoid precipitating their ultimate collapse – lest doing so might unleash an accelerated process of change that would also undermine their own position.[11] In many instances, this unspoken collusion of interests between rival state regimes can constitute a major obstacle to any kind of reconciliation between the divided peoples involved.

Most contemporary theorists stress that nations and nationalisms are not elemental or primordial givens, but that they have emerged, rather, in response to relatively recent historical conditions. Nevertheless, despite considerable academic agreement on this point, it still remains the case, as Ernest Gellner has rightly remarked, that '[t]he most widely held theory of nationalism' continues to be 'the one that believes it to be not merely the reawakening of cultures, but the re-emergence of atavistic instincts of *Blut und Boden* in the human breast.'[12] The resilience of this particular conception of nationalism, which conceives of the phenomenon not as a response to modernity but as the unfortunate persistence into the modern of a recalcitrant pre-modern tribalism, is clearly attested by the dominant conception of recent events in the Balkans. During the past decade the conflicts in that region have been repeatedly characterised as the return of repressed ethno-national hatreds. Checked for decades by the authoritarian communist regimes in the area, so the argument runs, the instinctive age-old hatreds between Serbs, Muslims and Croats soon ran amok once the old authoritarian regimes collapsed after 1989. Closely associated with this 'return of the repressed' view of nationalism is the manichean conception that that there are essentially two kinds of nationalism – a good civic kind and a bad ethnic kind – that promote two corresponding understandings of nationhood. From this perspective, the good civic conception of nationhood is based on common citizenship and the bad ethnic kind is based on common ethnic descent. Hence the customary distinction between the aggressive and illiberal ethnic nationalisms, supposedly characteristic of the 'badlands of modernity' such as the Balkans or Ireland or the 'Third World', and the saner civic nationalisms of the industrially developed world, which are identified with the democratising and unifying projects of the progressive middle classes.[13]

In essence, the arguments developed about the Balkans in recent times reiterate those deployed in earlier decades to legitimate the partitions of Ireland, India and Palestine. In these situations, too, it was widely believed, the ethno-national animosities, nurtured over centuries, were so intractable that partition represented the only practicable solution to the dilemmas involved. From this perspective, the authoritarian British imperial regime in these areas, like the Communist ones in contemporary Eastern Europe, had at least served to check the seething ethno-national animosities within the colonies, but when the departure of the British became imminent the usual mechanisms of restraint dissolved and violent ethnic nationalist conflict inevitably ensued. The manichean distinction between ethnic and civic nationalism described above – which holds that some peoples have developed a tolerant civic nationalism that others patently have failed to do – is expressed, for example, by Reginald Coupland, in the *Palestine Royal Commission Report* in 1937. Coupland was Beit Professor of Colonial History at Oxford with expertise in British Commonwealth affairs, especially nationality conflicts in South Africa and Canada, and he was also an informed student of the partition settlement in Ireland. He went to Palestine as a member of the Royal Commission under Lord Peel to investigate possible solutions to the communal conflict there in the wake of the Arab Revolt, which had begun in 1936. While there he became committed to the idea that partition represented the only viable solution to the conflicting claims of the Jewish and Arab national movements. In the Peel Commission *Report*, Coupland argued that 'where the conflict of nationalities has been overcome and unity achieved – in Britain itself, in Canada, in South Africa – one of the parties concerned was English or British, and ... where that has not been so, as in the schism between the Northern and Southern Irish, or between Hindus and Moslems in India, the quarrel, though it is centuries old, has not yet been composed'.[14] In Palestine, he contended, because of the immense differences between a traditional rural Arab society and a modern European urban Jewish one, 'the gulf between the races'[15] was so vast as to make compromises of the kind between, say, the British and French in Canada impossible.

For Coupland, then, the English or British possess a temperamental capacity to live harmoniously with other races in heterogeneous societies.[16] On the other hand, the 'schism' (the suggestion of fundamental religious divergence is telling) that divides communities in Ireland, India or Palestine suggests that these peoples lack the tolerant capacity to construct viable common nationalities in the way the British and Afrikaner settlers in South Africa or the British and French in Canada had done. What is occluded here is the fact that the structural hierarchies of communal domination and subordination between Catholic and Protestant in Ulster or Jew and Arab in Palestine might be quite different to those that existed where two different settler groups, such as the French and British in Canada or British and Afrikaner in South Africa, shared a common supremacy over the natives. In short, the *structures* of communal relationship are eclipsed here; instead, communal antagonisms are ascribed not to structures of dominance and subordination but to essentialised 'cultural' or 'temperamental' differences. From this it is but a short step to the conclusion that the old available means to resolve such situations is to divide the peoples involved into separate states.

The argument that communal or ethnic nationalist hatreds in places such as Ireland, India and Palestine were so implacable as to make partition the only feasible solution is open to serious theoretical objection on several counts. Firstly, to make communal antagonisms the prime explanation for partition conveniently minimises the role of the imperial powers in determining such an outcome. At the most obvious level, the British imperial state had a long history in moulding ethnic identities and manipulating intercommunal conflicts within the various colonies as a means to maintain its own power. The politics of ethnicity within the colonies, in short, was not an innate or autonomous reality but was largely shaped in its modern form in response to imperial policy. Secondly, British imperial rule within the various colonies rested to a considerable degree on what John Breuilly has called 'collaborator systems' that generally required the co-operation of usually privileged élites drawn from minority communities within each administrative unit.[17] In Ireland, imperial rule depended in the nineteenth century on the co-operation of an élite comprised mainly of Anglo-Irish Protestants. In Palestine, circumstances were somewhat different in this respect, but there the British presented themselves as the special guarantors of the Jewish community in the region. The point here is not to denigrate these minority élites as the witting or unwitting tools of the imperialists. It is to suggest that one of the reasons why the separatist strategies of Ulster Unionists and the Jewish Zionists could develop as successfully as they did was because these groups, despite the fact that they were minorities, already controlled important institutions within the colonies that were developed with British acquiescence or support to shore up imperial control. In short, these institutions were vitally important since they provided minority subnationalist élites, despite their demographic disadvantages, with the instruments that enabled them to resist the majority nationalist movements at the moment when national independence became imminent.

It also needs to be remembered in this context that even if at the actual time of the transfer of power British governments might well have preferred solutions other than partition, in each situation sections of the British establishment had provided crucial impetus to the demand for partition at some point. In the case of Ireland, leading British conservative and imperialist politicians threw their weight behind the idea of partition in a calculated attempt to make Irish Home Rule, viewed by them as a threat to the maintenance of the wider Empire, unworkable. In Palestine, the Balfour Declaration of 1917, which committed Britain to support the establishment of both Jewish and Palestinian national homes in Palestine, set the terms for the conflicting national demands that culminated in the division of that territory. In India, the British division of Bengal in 1905 lent added fuel to communal politics and supplied an important precedent for the later partition of the subcontinent as a whole.

None of this is to suggest that 'perfidious Albion' was the sole or even chief architect of partition in the colonies or that Britain implemented partition in any of these cases simply to suit its own selfish purposes. To suppose as much is to confer on the British a degree of absolute agency that nullifies that of the other parties involved. In the colonies where partition was implemented, there were internal divisions within the British establishments of the day concerning its wisdom, and it is also the case that in some situations the British were more strongly supportive of the policy than in others. On the whole, for example, the level of British support for partition in Ireland seems to have outweighed that for the later division of Palestine.[18] Nonetheless, the general point stands: the role of British imperial power, whether by indirect or direct means, in channelling communal divisions in Ireland, India and Palestine towards state division was by no means the trivial one that a convenient emphasis on supposedly primordial or innate ethno-national antagonisms would suggest. This is not simply an academic matter of correctly distributing historical blame. To lose sight of the role of the imperial powers in moulding communal identities and animosities within the colonies, and in providing the institutions that articulated such identities, is inevitably to distort the way in which we understand such conflicts and the solutions we envision to them.

Secondly, the assumption that it is chiefly the intensity of local communal animosities that determines whether or not partition will emerge as the only viable solution is also open to the objection, mentioned earlier, that in other colonies where disputes have been equally acute this has not occurred. Many examples might be cited: the ethnic disputes that temporarily divided Nigeria; Tutsi and Hutu cleavages in Rwanda in the 1990s; the rival Afrikaner, Inkatha and African National Congress national movements that might well have sub-divided South Africa. It is tempting to surmise in this context that where religious confession was tied to the manufacture of ethno-national identity – as in Ireland, India and Palestine – the communal cleavages would ultimately prove more fractious than their racial counterparts in, say, apartheid South Africa. Nevertheless, the case of Lebanon, which has survived as a single unit despite violent communal clashes along confessional lines, tends to complicate this hypothesis. It may ultimately be more significant perhaps that in the cases of Nigeria, Rwanda, South Africa and Lebanon none of the sub-national movements with secessionist or partitionist intent won the support of major external powers. This is in direct contrast with the Ulster Unionists and the Jewish Zionists since each of these groups has secured important strategic alliances with major superpowers with the ability to enforce a solution. It would appear, therefore, that it is not the strength of ethno-national animosities per se, but rather the extent to which a sub-national movement with separatist intentions can secure external support for its ambitions, that determines whether or not partition will take place. In short, international power politics, and not simply domestic factors, would seem crucial to any understanding of which minority sub-nationalisms are likely to succeed in securing their own state and which are not.

The notion that it is the innate strength of ethnic nationalism that accounts for partition is also open to a third serious objection. One of the most important difficulties with any view that starts from this assumption is that it generally fails to distinguish adequately between the social contents of different nationalist projects. For the most part, once it is assumed that the regressive clash of rival ethnic nationalisms is responsible for the persistent conflicts in Ireland, India, Palestine or the Balkans, then commentators are released from the onerous task of discriminating between the various types of national projects in these regions. In such event, there is no need to differentiate between Irish nationalism and Irish Unionism (let alone between the variant strands of each), between Zionist and Palestinian nationalism, or indeed between Serb and Albanian nationalism in contemporary Yugoslavia, since all are construed as equally violent and destructive. Once it is assumed that these contending nationalisms are more or less the same, or that the differences between various national programmes are simply trivial variations on the same will to power, then this agnosticism tends inevitably to lead to moral and political paralysis. It must be said that many contemporary mainstream theories of nationalism, as well as some theories advanced by scholars on the political left and in postcolonial studies, provide ample support for such agnosticism.[19] Since they start from the dogmatic assumption that all nationalisms are regressive, these theories, to use Erica Benner's terms, 'discourage attempts to draw distinctions' and 'insulate a general phenomenon called "nationalism" from the more specific interests and values and political programmes that make it assume different forms'.[20] In many instances, if these theories distinguish at all between progressive and regressive national movements, they do so only by falling back on the manichean contrast between atavistic ethnic and modern civic nationalism mentioned earlier. The tendency either to see all nationalisms as the same, or simply to divide them into 'civic' and 'ethnic' categories, is completely antithetical to the socialist conception of nationalism developed by Marx, Engels and Lenin. From the activist standpoint of these theorists, it was vital to understand the causes of national conflicts and to discriminate between the different social contents of various nationalist movements: to decide which were generally progressive and emancipatory, which authoritarian and repressive, which contributed to the advance or retardation of domestic and international class struggles. Such tasks were indispensable since only in this way could socialists work towards practical resolutions of conflict or decide for themselves which movements deserved socialist support and which their opposition.

One final objection can also be lodged against the argument that ethno-nationalist ideology and sentiment alone are sufficient to account for partition. Although those who support such opinions tend to be anti-nationalist in intent (since they make nationalist passion responsible for the communal calamities in Ireland, India, Palestine or the Balkans), the argument itself is, ironically, deeply nationalist in its assumptions. By making nationalist passions wholly responsible for such calamities, the argument attributes to national sentiment and to national identity what Erica Benner calls an 'overwhelming magnetic pull' that supposedly overrides all other collective social loyalties and interests.[21] Only nationalists themselves perhaps would grant that national identity could exert such autonomous causal force. A grim fatalism inheres in such notions (whether held by nationalists or their opponents) since if nationalist ideology and sentiment can command such absolute loyalty, then, as Benner observes, 'it is hard indeed to see how such conflicts can be alleviated by the politics of bargaining, compromise, and clear-headed discussion'.[22] Against such views, however, a socialist conception of things would insist that nationalism does not have the absolute autonomy, and cannot compel the unqualified allegiance, such views presuppose. Nationalism should by no means be reduced, as some mechanical versions of socialism suppose, to a mere epiphenomenon of more fundamental class or economic interests. But neither do nationalist sentiments invariably override and subsume all other social interests and allegiances.

In sum, the thesis that partition offers the 'best-worst' solution to situations of seething communal conflict can be sustained only if one starts with the premise that the real nature of the problem is a clash of ethnic nationalisms possessed of such strength and mobilising power as to override all other social considerations and to make all other solutions unworkable. To attribute such autonomous strength to ethnic or any other kind of nationalism is, however, a nationalist fallacy. Once the autonomous strength of nationalist sentiment and ideology is accepted as a starting point for social analysis, then the significance of other factors – such as the role of imperialism in shaping and institutionalising ethnic identities in the colonies, or the different social contents of various national programmes – tends to be underestimated. As a practical policy that starts from an overestimation of nationalist appeals, the chief difficulty with partition is that it takes virulent ethno-national conflict as an absolute given. Consequently, it is designed to restructure political space to accommodate such conflict rather than to tackle or transform the wider conditions that generated it in the first instance.

## III

Communalism or sectarianism, subaltern and especially élite class economic interests, strategic imperial interests – these all contributed to the conflicts that led to partition in Ireland, India and Palestine. In each case, moreover, conservative and regressive forms of nationalism (including the imperialist nationalism of the British) clearly played an important role in setting the terms within which political debate developed. Nevertheless, as argued in the preceding section, it is much too simple to attribute communal conflict and eventual partition to the strength of illiberal ethnic nationalism in these regions. The complex dilemmas that emerged in these situations – which essentially have to do with clashing rights to self-determination and with whether or not minorities within a colonial state are entitled to collective cultural recognition or simply the rights of individual citizenship – trouble not only so-called backward and illiberal ethnic nationalisms but the supposedly more civic versions as well.

As majority nationalist movements in Ireland, India and Palestine mobilised a mass base and moved towards the attainment of political independence, in each case a dissident minority movement also came into existence in tandem with them. Each of these movements claimed that it represented not a religious or ethnic minority but a second and separate 'nation' within the colony whose interests would be negated in any sovereign state ruled over by the majority nationalist movement. Circumstances varied in important ways from one situation to the next, and the kinds of political settlements that the minority national movements demanded also differed. Unlike the Muslim League in India, for example, Irish Unionists did not demand a separate national homeland of their own. Instead, they initially opposed Irish Home Rule and campaigned that Ireland as a whole be retained within the United Kingdom (UK). Only when it became clear that this optimal demand could not be met did Unionists alter strategy and seek instead a partition of the island and accept a Northern Irish state that would still remain an integral part of the UK. In Palestine, on the other hand, though Jewish settlers remained a minority throughout the period of British rule, the Zionist movement claimed all the land of Palestine on the basis of ancient Biblical title. After considerable internal debate and dissent in the 1930s, Zionists reluctantly accepted the idea of partition on the grounds that it at least allowed them to secure a smaller Jewish state rather than none at all.[23]

Nevertheless, though circumstances and ambitions varied, the fundamental dilemma in each situation shared some resemblance. In each case, the majority nationalist movement contended that there was only one legitimate nation within the colonial state, and that its opponents – Irish Unionists, the Muslim League, the Jewish Zionists – represented not a second 'nation' but rather a religious minority.[24] From this perspective, those who belonged to these minorities would be entitled to full civil and religious liberties as individual citizens within a sovereign Ireland, India or Palestine, but not to their own separate homeland. When confronted with the imminent possibility of partition, the majority nationalist movements were willing to contemplate some limited kinds of regional autonomy and self-government to appease these religious minorities (as they saw them), but each remained adamantly opposed to the concept of state division.

The minority movement in each instance, on the other hand, contended that it represented not simply a religious community or an ethnic minority but rather a historically and culturally distinct people with collective national rights. Accordingly, even if its members' individual civil and religious liberties could be protected within the new state (and none of the movements accepted that such protection could reasonably be expected), it was collective self-determination and not individual rights that was essentially at issue. In all three cases, then, the initial dilemma that had to be decided was whether there was 'one nation or two' within the existing administrative unit. Were it allowed that there were two culturally distinct peoples or nations, the issue then became how to resolve conflicting claims to self-determination. Since the communities in each case were not geographically concentrated in separate regions, there was also the complex issue as to how minority self-determination could practically be implemented even were it deemed legitimate. In all three situations, therefore, the antinomies of national self-determination generated not only complex issues of principle but acute practical problems as well.

Liberal political theory seems to encounter some severe difficulties when confronted with such situations. Liberal theory holds as a fundamental principle the idea that the state, and all public institutions, will treat all citizens equally, irrespective of race, sex, religion or other cultural particularities. For liberals, it is only when everyone is treated equally that the basic needs of people, shared universally, can adequately be satisfied. But in order to uphold such freedoms, the locus of rights must be the individual citizen, the bearer of human needs. As Partha Chatterjee has argued, liberal political theory in its strict sense, then, cannot recognise the validity of any collective rights of cultural groups; to recognise rights that belong exclusively to particular groups within the state is to destroy the very principles on which liberalism rests. It follows, as Chatterjee contends, that it is extremely difficult to justify the granting of substantively different collective rights to cultural groups on the basis of liberalism's commitment to procedural equality and universal citizenship. Accordingly, the charge that is made against liberalism is not merely that it forces everyone into a single homogeneous mould, thus threatening the distinct identities of minority groups; it is also that the homogeneous mould of state citizenship itself is by no means a neutral one (whatever the claims to the contrary), but invariably reflects the culture of the dominant group, so that it is not everyone but only minorities that are forced to forego their cultural identities.[25]

This was precisely the dilemma that confronted the minority communities in Ireland, India and Palestine. Mass support for the majority nationalist movements in all three cases came preponderantly, though not exclusively in Ireland or India at any rate, from one ethnic and religious community within the colonial state. For the minority communities, then, even were their *individual* cultural and religious rights indeed upheld by the soon-to-be independent states, they would still have to forego their own *collective* cultural and national identities, and essentially be assimilated into the national culture of the dominant group within the new state. Whether or not an independent united Ireland, India or Palestine would indeed have proved as inimical to the individual religious and cultural liberties as the minority communities claimed is now a matter of polemical speculation. In the strictest sense, the issue is somewhat beside the point, however, since the most important concern for the minority communities was not individual citizenship but the collective political and cultural autonomy of their communities.

Despite the claims of Irish or Palestinian nationalists at the time, it may be allowed that both Ulster Protestants and Jewish settlers in Palestine were not simply religious minorities and that they did indeed constitute, as they themselves claimed, distinctive peoples with a separate nationality to the local ethnic majority.[26] It can also be accepted that both Zionists and Ulster Unionists had some reasonable grounds to fear that their opponents might impose their own cultures on them in the event of independence. Historical instances of attempts to coerce national minorities into the culture of national majorities were common enough to warrant such fears. In both situations, therefore, the minority communities had reason to think that securing their own states would best protect their collective cultural identities and interests.

Nevertheless, it does not follow from this that either Unionists or Zionists had an unqualified right to their own independent territorial states. The difficulty for both of these communities was that even in the regions in which they were most territorially concentrated there were also substantial Irish nationalist and Palestinian communities. A critical impediment to both the Unionist and Zionist demands for a separate state that would allow them to exercise full self-determination was that such states could not be produced without denying the same rights to substantial communities of Irish or Palestinian nationalists. In situations where different national groups are intermingled in this way, and where the national self-determination of one group can only be exercised at the expense of another, most liberal theories of self-determination hold that minorities will have to settle for something less than full self-determination. From this liberal standpoint, then, both Unionists and Zionists could legitimately claim a right to the protection of their distinct national cultures. But given the constraints that stemmed from the geographical intermixing of peoples within the colonial unit in both situations, their demands for autonomy would have to be settled by solutions that fell short of traditional statehood.[27]

In Ireland, things were especially complicated by the fact that the question of whether Irish nationalists or Irish Unionists should be considered the minority depended on how the legitimate unit of self-determination was construed. Since Ireland had been integrated as a sub-state of the UK since 1800, Unionists could argue that the British Isles as a whole (and not the island of Ireland) constituted the natural unit of plebiscite to decide such issues. From this perspective, it was the Irish nationalists that constituted the secessionist regional minority that wished to exercise its own self-determination at Unionist expense. Even if the Unionist argument about the proper unit of plebiscite is accepted, however, their case is still quite weak on liberal terms. Before 1918 at least, the leading Irish nationalist party was not in fact demanding complete separation from the UK or full political autonomy, but only a devolved or limited Home Rule parliament in Dublin. Liberal theory would generally accept that national 'minorities' such as Irish nationalists (defined as such within the context of the British Isles as a whole that is) were entitled to this limited measure of sovereignty. On this premise, Unionists had little grounds to object to Irish Home Rule, even if they had stronger ones to oppose complete independence for Ireland. But Unionists were in fact equally opposed to both. Moreover, since a democratic majority in the UK parliament carried the vote for Irish Home Rule, Unionists could not legitimately claim that their opposition to this measure was justified by the fact that it enjoyed the support of the majority of British citizens. In fact, when the British Parliament seemed about to implement Home Rule, Unionists, with the support of leading British Conservatives, imported guns from Germany and organised on a paramilitary basis to defy the democratic will of parliament. Even were Unionist arguments about what constituted the proper unit of plebiscite to determine self-determination to be accepted, then by most liberal standards of adjudication on such matters, Unionist opposition to Irish Home Rule would have to be deemed contrary to liberal and democratic principle.

From the perspective of the majority nationalist communities in Ireland and Palestine, the existing administrative boundaries of the colonial state comprised the natural plebiscite unit in which to decide the question of self-determination. In Ireland, as already noted, this claim was open to Unionist dispute since the island had been part of the UK since 1800. Nevertheless, it is also the case that after the Act of Union Westminster had continued to treat Ireland as a single and largely distinct administrative unit. There was no equivalent to Dublin Castle (the administrative headquarters of British rule in Ireland) or to the position of the Irish Lord Lieutenant in either Scotland or Wales, for example. Ireland also retained its own legal apparatus and was governed by a separate armed police system. The British Conservative or Liberal political parties had never organised in Ireland as they had done in the other three countries that comprised the UK. Moreover, most 'mainland' British politicians did not seem to regard any part of Ireland, including Ulster, as an integral part of the British State in the same way as Scotland and Wales. This is suggested by the fact that even after Northern Ireland was excluded from Irish Home Rule in the South it was accorded its own quasi-autonomous parliament in Belfast, something which clearly set it at a remove from the rest of the UK state. There is much to substantiate the Irish nationalist claim, therefore, that the administrative boundaries of the Irish colonial state constituted the obvious *historical* (not natural) unit within which the exercise of self-determination should be decided.

Within the respective colonial units, Irish and Palestinian nationalists constituted clear demographic majorities and could on this account claim title to national self-determination as a democratic right. In the 1918 General Election, the first conducted in the United Kingdom of Great Britain and Ireland under rules approximating universal adult suffrage, the two major Irish nationalist parties that supported independence, and opposed partition, won 79 out of 109 seats, over three quarters of the Irish vote. The will of the overwhelming majority of the Irish people within the long-established electoral and administrative unit could not be in doubt therefore. In Palestine, Jews still legally held only 6 per cent of the land of Palestine and accounted for only 30 per cent of the population there in the period before the State of Israel was established. The United Nations (UN) Partition Plan, as David McDowall comments, 'awarded 54 per cent of the land area to the proposed Jewish state, even though Jews constituted less than one third of the population. It was manifestly unjust (and arguably absurd) in its demographic division, since it proposed a Jewish state that would be virtually 50 per cent Arab, but an Arab state that would be no less than 98.7 per cent Arab.'[28] In such context, partition cannot be construed as an equitable attempt to solve conflicting principles. Instead, it arbitrarily tried to manufacture a Jewish territorial majority and in so doing effectively provided the warrant that allowed European Jews, as Edward Said has remarked, to usurp the local Arab inhabitants and kick them out.[29] In both situations, therefore, the absolute will of the majority in the colonial administrative unit was against partition.

Within the terms of classical liberal theory, it is difficult to see that either the Unionist or Zionist case for partition in Ireland and Palestine can be defended. From a liberal standpoint, minority nationalities may be entitled to nurture and protection, but their defence cannot be accorded preference over the political self-determination of the majority. From this perspective, where two national communities are intermingled, the smaller will have to accept something short of its own sovereign political state if that cannot be established without denying the larger group its right to national self-determination also. Effectively, therefore, the establishment of partition assumed that Northern Catholics and Palestinians within the new Northern Irish and Israeli states would be expected to accept their status as minorities and to forego their national identities. They were expected, in other words, to submit to exactly the same fate that Northern Protestants and Jews had refused to accept for themselves. The double standard involved is evident.

The equality of nations and their right to self-determination is also a fundamental tenet of socialist doctrine. In its most fully developed form, as elaborated in the work of V. I. Lenin, the right of nations to self-determination includes not just the right to cultural autonomy but also to full political independence. As in the case of the liberal theories already cited, however, for Lenin recognition of the right of nations to self-determination in principle does not, of course, imply an *a priori* endorsement of secessions and state divisions. This is because it is theoretically impossible to say in advance which solutions will allow for the optimal implementation of such rights in specific situations. Hence, Lenin argues, proletarian socialism 'confines itself, so to speak, to the negative demand for recognition of the *right* to self-determination, without giving guarantees to any nation, and without undertaking to give *anything at the expense* of another nation'.[30]

Both socialist and liberal theories, then, share a commitment to national self-determination; but they differ as to how the criteria by which this principle should be applied is to be determined. From a socialist perspective, national self-determination must be considered not simply in terms of an abstract balancing of national rights, but also with a concern for the ways in which specific national struggles can contribute to the extension of social democracy and political emancipation in each region, something which always has consequences for the advance of local and international class struggles more generally.

From this perspective, socialist support for any national movement has to be contingent on its political character. Since there were undoubtedly reactionary elements in all of the major national movements in both Ireland and Palestine, the task of evaluating their social character is quite complex. In the case of Ireland, Ulster Unionism – whatever its class content, immediate economic interests and more chauvinistic elements – clearly did reflect authentic Protestant fears about clerical or cultural domination in an Irish republic. The uneven development of capitalism on the island had created an industrialised northern Protestant bourgeoisie whose economic interests were tied to free trade with Britain and Empire, and an emergent southern Catholic bourgeoisie that required protectionist measures to advance the underdeveloped southern economy. The labour market in the northern part of the island especially was stratified on a sectarian basis by which Protestants dominated the more skilled sectors of the economy and Catholics the unskilled. To mobilise popular resistance to Home Rule, Ulster Unionists were obliged to appeal to Protestant workers' sense of the innate backwardness of Irish Catholics in general, to construe 'Ulster' as a Protestant province under Papist threat, and to promote a reactionary populist identification with British imperialist nationalism. The defence of the Protestant minority's interests, therefore, was expressed not in terms of some emancipatory project to secure a better society, but in terms of sectarian chauvinism and a rearguard defence of the imperial status quo.

Important strands of Irish nationalism undoubtedly displayed conservative Catholic and ethnically chauvinistic values. Nevertheless, the foundational rhetoric of Irish republicanism, dating back to the period of the French revolution, construed Irish nationality in terms of common Irish citizenship rather than in terms of religious identity or ethnic descent. This republican tradition was also structurally anti-imperialist in disposition, and its mobilising appeal was tied to the struggles by the Irish masses to overcome the oppressive colonial legacies of sectarianism, landlordism and Anglo-Irish ascendancy. While Unionism was subjectively and objectively tied to the preservation of the existing status quo in Ireland, therefore, Irish nationalism, despite its reactionary elements, was structurally predicated on the creation of a new and less oppressive social order.

In the case of Palestine, matters might in some ways seem even more complex since many Jews who migrated to that country did so either because they were subject to fierce persecution in Eastern Europe or, after the 1930s, because they were fleeing the terrors of Nazi genocide. The desperate circumstances that compelled many Jews to move to Palestine makes their situation quite different in most respects to that of Ulster Unionists in Ireland who had long been a politically dominant and economically privileged community. Nevertheless, as the example of contemporary Yugoslavia will illustrate, a persecuted people that flees genocide in one place and is received, whether voluntarily or not, into the homeland of another does not have the right to displace its host community and to establish its own state on its territory. Were the Kosovar refugees who recently fled Serbian persecution into neighbouring states to claim this right, for example, this could hardly be defended. Yet this was precisely what the Zionist movement proposed in Palestine. In order to achieve its nationalist goals, Zionists were prepared to ignore and override Palestinian rights, and to secure imperial support from Britain and the United States (US) by arguing that Israel would serve as a rampart to defend Western imperialism in the Middle East.[31] The plight of the Jews fleeing persecution and genocide clearly demanded urgent and radical means of redress. The decision on the part of the Western superpowers to make Palestine bear the whole weight of this responsibility, and by the Zionist movement to channel desperate streams of refugees into a colonial settler and pro-imperialist nationalist project cannot be considered either progressive or emancipatory in its general tendency. In contrast, the Palestinian national movement, though led in the Mandate period by a conservative and ineffective class élite, was able to advance its cause only by appealing to the interests of the Palestinian peasantry against colonial settler intrusion and British imperial control of the region. Whatever the deficiencies of its mercantile-landlord leadership strata, Palestinian nationalism was essentially an anti-colonial nationalism struggling against the expansion of the Ottoman state, Zionist settler colonialism and British occupation.[32]

For all their undoubted deficiencies and conservative strands, the anti-colonial and anti-imperialist dimensions of Irish and Palestinian nationalism distinguish them from Irish Unionism and Zionism, which were both constitutively dependent on imperialist support and on the promotion of chauvinist attitudes towards the local majority populations to achieve their aims. Both Irish and Palestinian nationalist leaderships were undoubtedly wrong to insist that Northern

Unionists or Zionists respectively did not represent distinct peoples with their own national identities and to dismiss their claims to some measure of collective self-determination on such account. Nevertheless, when compelled by force of circumstance to accept that Unionists or Zionists were entitled to some accommodation on this matter, Irish and Palestinian nationalists both showed themselves willing to contemplate measures of regional autonomy, federalism or confederation that allowed significant scope to Unionists and Zionists to exercise autonomy. In the circumstances, it is reasonable to conclude that the goals pursued by Irish and Palestinian nationalists were more emancipatory than those pursued by their opponents.

In the event, the complex problems that stemmed from the contending claims to self-determination in Ireland and Palestine were resolved by the balance of military force that prevailed in each region and in ways that would satisfy neither liberal nor socialist principle. During the period of British rule in both regions, the two communities most dependent on imperial support, Irish Unionists and Zionists, were able to build up, with tacit British acceptance, strong paramilitary forces. Both of these paramilitary forces were decisive in ensuring not only that partition and not some other solution was implemented, but also in settling how the territory was actually to be divided.[33] In both instances, interestingly enough, these paramilitary forces were mobilised by the local Unionist and Zionist communities to defy the power of the British to decide what their political destiny should be. Despite such defiance, however, neither the Unionist nor the Zionist paramilitary organisations were ever seriously down-faced by the British military. In sharp contrast, the British attitude to the Irish and Palestinian majority nationalist movements was much more determined and draconian. In the years that immediately preceded partition, the British military fought a bitter campaign to defeat Irish separatist nationalism in the south of Ireland. Similarly, when Palestinian peasants rebelled against British rule and the dispossessions caused by Jewish settlement in the Arab Revolt in 1936, this insurrection was crushed by the British with such severity that the Palestinian national movement was still crippled throughout the next decade when the whole issue of partition was decided. In Palestine, the British disengaged themselves before partition was implemented and the country's fate was passed over to the UN. Nevertheless, under British rule the Zionists had developed a highly effective fighting machine based on Jewish defence forces trained by the British during the Arab Revolt, and on Jewish brigades that had served in the British Army during World War II. The net result of British disengagement at that juncture, therefore, was to grant Zionism a decisive military advantage when war broke out following the UN decision to partition the country. In the 1948 war, the Zionists were able to convert their military superiority into real political gains when they seized 73 per cent of the land of Palestine, territory far in excess of that proposed in the UN partition plan.

In short, in neither Ireland nor Palestine did partition produce either equitable or imaginative resolution to the problems raised by the clash of conflicting claims to self-determination. In both instances, complex problems that demanded complex institutional solutions were eventually 'settled' by crude military–territorial dictate. The outcome maximised the power of Ulster Unionists and Zionists in the respective regions, converting what were previously minority communities in the colonial state into new ethno-national majorities with their own semi-autonomous or autonomous states. The decisive objection to partition in each instance, however, was not that the territorial divide was inequitable or the borders badly drawn or unjust – though they were manifestly unjust, and outrageously so in the Palestinian case especially. A more equitable territorial divide and less arbitrary borders might have diminished conflict in both regions. Nevertheless, the more serious objection to partition was – and still remains – that Unionists and Zionists insisted on rights to self-determination for themselves that they refused to extend to others, and that their self-determination was secured in ways that effectively consolidated the colonially inherited domination of one group over another. Thus while Unionists insisted on their right to resist coercion into an all-Ireland Catholic-dominated state and to remain part of the UK, they conceded no such rights to the Irish nationalists within their own boundaries. Instead, they went on to impose, with British support, their own form of majoritarian rule over Northern nationalists on the basis that this was the only way that the semi-autonomous Northern Irish statelet could be safeguarded. Northern nationalists were viewed as actual or incipient enemies to the new 'Protestant state' and were subjected in ensuing decades to various kinds of legal, economic and political discrimination to reduce whatever power remained to them.

In Palestine, Zionists secured the right to exercise national self-determination in an independent Israel, but in the course of setting up this state over 725,000 Palestinians were dispossessed. When the UN voted after the war that these dispossessed refugees be allowed to return to their homes, Israel refused to acknowledge any such right and proceeded to bulldoze most of the Palestinian villages to make sure that there would be no such return. The dispossessed Palestinians were condemned to the condition of stateless refugees. Zionist self-determination, therefore, was achieved at the cost of the absolute negation of the right to self-determination of those that were displaced.[34] Moreover, the approximately 160,000 Palestinians who remained inside the new 'Jewish state' were reduced in subsequent decades by both legal and practical discrimination to a condition of political, social and economic impotence.[35]

The ways in which Ulster Unionists and Zionists, then, established and exercised their self-determination were patently oppressive. In the case of Palestine, the material effect of partition was to consolidate an actively expanding colonial-settler nationalism that aimed to supplant the local inhabitants of the region with Jewish immigrants. In the case of Ireland, its effect was to shore up the longstanding colonially inherited dominance of one section of the population over the other in the northern part of the country at a time when the retracting colonial system was being gradually dismantled on the rest of the island. The actual historical circumstances in the two situations were acutely different in many respects, and the levels of injustice inflicted on the Palestinian people (both outside and inside Israel) have greatly exceeded those inflicted on Northern Irish nationalists. Nevertheless, the structural logic underlying both situations is essentially quite similar. Both Unionists and Zionists refused to accept *any* kind of state arrangement or shared sovereignty that would require them to accept co-citizenship with the Irish or the Palestinians within the administrative boundaries of the old colonial states. They each refused this on the grounds that they were distinct peoples entitled to national self-determination and because to accept anything less might reduce them to the condition of oppressed minorities who might possibly be stripped of their civil liberties as well. By successfully gaining their own states, both Unionists and Zionists secured their own self-determination and avoided *potential discrimination* in the future in states not of their choosing. But in order to shore up their new states each went on to visit on 'its' minorities *actual discriminations* of the type they had claimed to fear in order to promote the case for partition in the first instance.

## IV

States come into being in all sorts of historical circumstances, most involving violence and oppression of various kinds. To say that the Northern Irish or Israeli states came into existence in violent circumstances, or that both have since discriminated against their minorities, is by no means to supply a persuasive case for the armed destruction of either state. What can legitimately be argued, however, is that these states were established in ways that were detrimental to a more equitable and democratic resolution of the complex issue of self-determination for all the peoples in the respective regions. Hence, a critical question that must be asked today, many decades after partition, is to what extent the more liberal elements within Ulster Unionism or Israeli Zionism respectively have shown themselves willing or able to redress the inherited deficiencies in the original partition settlements? To what extent do the respective 'peace processes' currently underway in each region serve to correct the injustices inherent in the asymmetrical application of the rights to self-determination in the earlier settlements?

Today, as in the past, populist Unionism in Northern Ireland continues to construe concessions – whether civil, economic or national rights to Northern nationalists – not as an enhancement of democracy within the province but as an attack on Protestant identity and on the very existence of the Northern state.[36] In the past decade or so, a more self-consciously liberal and secular intellectual stratum has emerged within Ulster Unionism that has attempted to develop a liberal argument to defend the Northern state from the criticisms of its opponents. These 'New Unionists', as they are called, contend that the strongest argument in defence of unionism is that it is premised on a claim to citizenship of the UK, which is, in their view, a multi-ethnic, multinational, multi-faith society. Unionist allegiance to this pluralist British state is, they assert, inherently more progressive than Northern nationalist allegiance to a mono-national Republic of Ireland dominated by one ethnic and religious community. In the words of Arthur Aughey, a leading New Unionist intellectual, 'the identity of unionism has little to do with the idea of *the nation* and everything to do with the idea of *the state*'.[37] For the New Unionism, then, the most positive case for Ulster Unionism is that it is a political doctrine committed not to questions of national identity but to membership of a UK state that guarantees advanced civil and religious liberties to all its citizens irrespective of their nationality. This opens a conceptual distance between the New Unionism and more traditional and populist versions of Unionism that tended to anchor their commitment to liberal values not so much on secular ideas of citizenship as on the notion that Protestantism was intrinsically more liberal than Catholicism.

Nevertheless, there is, as Liam O'Dowd has argued, still some shared ground between 'new' and 'old' Unionisms.[38] For both, Northern Irish nationalists are entitled to full civil and religious liberties as individual citizens, but to qualify they must accept the legitimacy of the boundaries of the Northern state and relinquish their aspirations for a United Ireland. For nationalists to do otherwise is, both hold, to challenge the security of the state and hence to bring legitimate democratic repression upon themselves. On this premise, the Northern nationalist aspiration to a United Ireland and the Unionist commitment to maintain Northern Ireland's already established membership of the UK cannot be accorded the same degree of political legitimacy. To do so would be irrational, the New Unionists contend, as it would accord equal validity to those who would dismember and those who would maintain the existing UK state order. For some New Unionists, the Northern Irish state might accord a de-politicised Northern nationalist *cultural identity* some institutional recognition, thus necessitating some reform to a Northern state which has been since its inception exclusively Protestant and British in its public iconography, symbolism and ceremonial ritual. For others, however, even parity of cultural esteem between Catholics and Protestants in Northern Ireland is suspect: to institutionalise such parity, they contend, would effectively 'hibernicise unionist Ulster,'[39] which would thereby dilute its Britishness and pave the way for Irish reunification.

New Unionists, then, construct Irish nationalism as an illiberal 'ethnic nationalism' and see Ulster Unionism as wedded to the supposedly superior 'civic nationalism' of the larger British state. In so doing, New Unionists distinguish their own good, legitimate and inclusive civic nationalism from the illegitimate and exclusivist variety supposedly endorsed by their opponents. The idealistic assertion that UK citizenship, unlike its Irish counterpart, transcends matters of nationality will, however, stand little scrutiny. Its assumption is that the UK has developed a completely acultural conception of citizenship, or a sharp separation of citizenship from cultural and ethnic nationality. This idealised claim conveniently ignores the ways in which the British state and British citizenship were historically articulated in terms of a common Protestantism and an aggressive and chauvinistic imperialist nationalism, and ignores well documented facts of continued racial stratification, injustice and discrimination within the UK. The assertion that the British concept of nationhood is inherently more civic than the kind developed in the Irish Republic is therefore tendentious. Like their more traditional counterparts, as Liam O'Dowd observes, New Unionists 'consistently demand from Irish nationalists that which they reject for themselves: the separation of culture from politics and the shelving of their national rights and aspirations'.[40]

The British–Irish Agreement, signed on 10 April 1998 and later ratified by separate referenda in Northern and Southern Ireland, attempts to tackle some of the inequalities in the original partition settlement in ways that are more radical than those conceived by the New Unionists. The most significant departure involved in this Agreement perhaps is that it is in essence consociational: it conceives of the two political communities within the North not as Catholics and Protestants or numerical majorities and minorities, but as *national communities* with conflicting aspirations. For Northern nationalists, this represents an advance since it requires Unionists to recognise them as Irish nationalists and not just as Catholics or a minority. In turn, Irish nationalists are required to recognise that Ulster Unionists have their own distinct British nationality and to see them not just as Protestants who might some day become simply a religious minority within a future United Ireland.

The institutional and procedural mechanisms envisaged in the Agreement are complex, and in some instances extremely nebulous, but its essential outline is reasonably clear. Within Northern Ireland, the Agreement envisages cross-community executive power-sharing between Unionists and nationalists within a devolved Northern Irish Assembly. The governing body in that Assembly is to be comprised of ministers appointed by parties on the basis of their respective strength in seats: consequently ministers would be drawn from both nationalist and Unionist communities and government would therefore unavoidably involve cross-community coalition. Veto-rights for minorities or 'parallel consent' measures require both an overall majority of Assembly members and a majority of both nationalist and Unionist members to endorse government proposals. Outside of government, the Agreement also contains measures designed to promote a more representative police force and a Bill of Rights designed to give equal recognition to both national cultures.

Beyond the provisions for power-sharing within Northern Ireland, the Agreement also stipulates the establishment of a North–South

Ministerial Council. This body provides for some limited cross-border co-operation between Northern Ireland and the Irish Republic. It has symbolic importance also as it provides an institutional basis that would link Northern nationalists to the Irish Republic whereas the North had links only with the UK in the original partition settlement. In turn, a British–Irish Council is also to be established, under which all the sovereign and devolved governments in the UK can meet to agree common policies. This proposal is designed to meet Unionists' concerns to counter-balance the North-South cross-border bodies. It also provides a mechanism through which they would continue to be linked to the UK in the hypothetical event that at some future time nationalists became a demographic majority in the North and a vote for unity with the Republic were carried. Finally, as part of the over-all deal, the Irish Republic agreed, subject to the Agreement being implemented, that it would surrender its constitutional claim to the territory of Northern Ireland. In its place, it has substituted a clause which stipulates: 'It is the firm will of the Irish nation, in harmony and friendship, to unite all the people who share the territory of the island of Ireland, in all the diversity of their identities and traditions, recognising that a united Ireland shall be brought about only by peaceful means with the consent of the majority of the people, democratically expressed, in both jurisdictions in the island.'[41] The emphasis on diversity here suggests that were a United Ireland to be attained in the future, Northern Unionists could not coercively be assimilated into a mono-national Irish state; instead, some sort of bi-national arrangement would have to be established.[42]

The British–Irish Agreement clearly aspires towards a settlement along consociational and binational lines designed to avoid the compulsory assimilation of one national community into another – something that might well have been attempted on an all-island scale when the original partition settlement was implemented in the 1920s. Nevertheless, it works within the given state order established in that partition settlement. Under its provisions, Northern Ireland continues to remain part of the UK state, and hence nationalists, in return for the concession of power-sharing within Northern Ireland, must be content with largely (though not entirely) symbolic links with the Irish Republic. Moreover, the actual scope and powers that the envisaged North-South bodies will actually have is not determined by the Agreement itself, and they remain nebulous and minimalist at best.[43] The Agreement attempts, within these limits, the tricky business of balancing conflicting Unionist and nationalist state allegiances. Support for it in the opposing political communities depends to considerable extent on different assessments about where it might eventually lead. Pro-Agreement Unionists hope that it will safeguard the Union; nationalists hope that it may provide the basis for a democratic transition towards some kind of United Ireland over the longer term. Whether the complex cross-communal apparatus it envisages would endure were it clear that historical circumstances were moving matters in a direction incompatible with the longer-term expectations of either community is unclear.

While the complexity of the Northern situation undoubtedly makes it urgent and necessary that the Agreement should attach real significance to the respective political aspirations of both nationalists and Unionists, it would appear to operate on the assumption that these polar nationalisms are largely autonomous forces. Yet, as stressed earlier in this chapter, to suppose that nationalism has such autonomous power is to overestimate its mobilising capacity. Nationalism usually acquires substantive mobilising power only when it is attached to other social struggles, and the different social groups involved in such struggles usually infuse nationalist projects with different social content. The Agreement does not take account, however, of the complex ways in which the Northern conflict has a social and class content that is not wholly reducible to national identities and allegiances. To the extent that it attempts at all to deal with the longstanding economic inequalities between Northern Catholics and Protestants, or between the working and middle classes, the Agreement does so only by providing for legislation against discrimination. History suggests that economic inequality and social discrimination are seldom legislated out of existence, however, and since these are highly correlated to ethnoreligious background in Northern Ireland, nationalism will probably continue to be one of the modalities through which the Catholic struggle against discrimination is articulated. It is not clear, then, that formally balancing nationalist and Unionist state allegiances, however *necessary* it may be, will be *sufficient* to undo the structural imbalances and unequal distribution of power that drive inter-communal conflict in Northern Ireland. Finally, there is the more immediate question as to whether both communities have the same incentive to implement the proposals envisaged in the Agreement. Historically, nationalists have always been the subordinate and Unionists the dominant political community in Northern Ireland. Unionists, therefore, have more to lose in any settlement that equalises power in the region. In the circumstances, it is predictable that to date most support for the Agreement should come from Northern nationalists while Unionists have been more internally divided about its merits and implications.

In Ireland, the anti-colonial struggle in the south was successful and an independent Irish state that extended over two-thirds of the island was formed, though the consequences of partition have cast a long shadow over the political and economic development of the entire island ever since. In Palestine, however, the consequences of partition were much more catastrophic. Over 70 per cent of Palestinian territory fell to the new Israeli state between 1947–9, while Jordan and Egypt annexed what remained. After 1948, Palestine as a defined administrative entity literally ceased to exist. Palestinian problems were compounded when Israel seized the remaining Palestinian lands from Jordan and Egypt in the Six Days War of 1967. In the succeeding decades, Israel established military rule over the West Bank and Gaza and deliberately promoted extensive Jewish settlements in the West Bank especially. These were clearly designed to maximise Israeli territorial gains and to prevent the emergence of an independent Palestinian state on what lands remained in Palestinian possession after 1948.[44] In Ireland, then, partition was immediately detrimental to the interests of only one section of the Irish people, Northern Irish Catholics; in Palestine it has had drastic consequences for all Palestinians. Whether they live within Israel proper, in the West Bank and Gaza, or in the Diaspora, all Palestinians have been adversely affected in one way or another by the dismemberment of their original homeland.

Though commonly compared in the media, there is a fundamental distinction between the British–Irish Agreement and the Oslo Accord, signed between the State of Israel and the Palestinian Liberation Organisation (PLO) in September 1993. The British–Irish Agreement clearly recognises, in principle at least, that the 1921 partition settlement could not adequately address the dilemmas generated by clashing rights to self-determination without at least some alteration to the state system in the region. However constrained the envisaged North–South institutional links, their very existence acknowledges that there could be no purely 'internal settlement' to the Northern conflict. In contrast, the Oslo Accord, which envisages some limited form of Palestinian self-rule within sections of the West Bank and Gaza, assumes that a simple territorial partition can solve the Israeli–Palestinian conflict. In essence, the Accord represents a return to the principle of territorial division and separate Jewish and Palestinian states embodied in the 1947 UN partition proposals. But while the principle might be the same, the crucial difference is that in the interim period Israel has secured control over territory well in excess of anything conceived in the 1947 plan. The effect of the Accord, then, has been to imagine a 'two-state solution' that would ultimately allow Israel, with Palestinian consent, to set aside any obligation to recognise either the borders envisaged by the UN in the 1947 partition resolution or those subsequently defined in the 1948–9 armistice agreements. This effectively gives Israel the opportunity to consolidate by negotiation not only its territorial gains in the 1948 war, but also much of those made by conquest and settlement since 1967.

Were an independent Palestinian state to emerge within the terms of the Accord, therefore, it seems certain that the areas under its control would be so limited and dissected that Palestinian autonomy, either political or economic, would inevitably be chimerical.[45] The major problem with the Oslo Accord, then, is that it uses the illusion of national autonomy to ratify the effective subordination of one national community to another. The attraction of the Accord for its Palestinian supporters is that it seems to allow for the eventual emergence of a 'two-state' solution that would enable Palestinians to exercise national self-determination within at least some small section of historic Palestine. While a fairer division of territory just might render the 'two-state' solution workable, the actual arrangements concerning land and sovereignty that have emerged in the negotiations conducted since the Accord was signed make a travesty of this. Ultimately, however, it may be that, as in the Irish case, it is not simply the actual details of territorial division, but the whole principle of a two-state solution that needs to be questioned.

A key assumption of the two-state idea is that Palestinian rights to national self-determination can be exercised in a small territorial state in the West Bank and Gaza. From this it follows that were the territorial remit of a Palestinian state to be agreed between Israelis and the Palestinian leadership, then the State of Israel would have fulfilled its obligations towards the Palestinian people. But there are all sorts of problems here. First, this supposes that if a Palestinian state emerges, then Israel is automatically absolved of any obligation to deal with the Palestinian refugees displaced in 1948 and 1967, many of whom are still stateless and living in precarious conditions across the Arab world. Israel's refusal to repatriate these recently dispossessed Arabs stands in sharp contrast to the preferential treatment it accords to Jews anywhere in the world. The Law of Return (1950), which gives any Jew the automatic right to settle in Israel, and the Law of

Citizenship (1952), which confers automatic citizenship on any Jewish immigrant who does 'return' to Israel, clearly illustrate the double standard involved.[46] Secondly, since the 1960s there is a growing consensus among Israeli Palestinians that they should be recognised as a national minority within Israel with political and cultural rights equal to those of Jewish Israelis, something that would challenge the present construction of Israel as a Jewish state. A two-state solution seems unlikely, then, to do anything to advance the political emancipation or self-determination of either Palestinians who live in the Diaspora or within Israel.

The Oslo Accord has represented a return to the principle of partition as the best means to solve the Israeli–Palestinian question. Interestingly, the most articulate secular Palestinian opposition to the Accord has also returned to a principle that had been advocated by some British officials in the period before 1948, and that had been taken up by the Palestinian resistance for some time after 1967. For these critics, the best future for Israelis and Palestinians lies not in two separate states but in a single bi-national state.[47] Such a state could be developed along some sort of consociational lines that would require neither community to be either politically subordinate to the other or to forego its own national identity and be culturally assimilated into the other. Given the traumatic legacy of conflict between Israelis and Palestinians, this idea seems to many to be utopian in the most puerile sense of that word. Nevertheless, the history of partition in the region has little to recommend it, and a bi-national state in historic Palestine that would be joint homeland to both peoples may well be the only long-term solution worth fighting for. Moreover, shared citizenship of this kind could help solve the difficulties not just of Palestinians in Gaza and the West Bank but of those inside Israel or in the Diaspora as well. To advance a political strategy along these lines would, however, require that Palestinians completely re-define their struggle so that its goal would no longer be the establishment of a separate Palestinian state. Instead, they would have to recognise that the 1967 conquest has effectively ended partition by reuniting all the territory of historic Palestine under Israeli rule. Instead of attempting to reverse Israeli control over some of that territory, Palestinians would have to re-articulate their struggle as one to secure full civic rights as citizens and full national rights as equal partners in a common bi-national Palestinian–Israeli State. The focus of struggle, that is, would have to shift from the liberation of territory to the establishment of a common state that would grant the most advanced liberties to all its citizens.

## V

Despite the many differences between the two, what links the situations in Ireland and Palestine is that both stem from the antinomies of self-determination where two peoples with different national affiliations are intermingled in the same territory. To attribute the political conflicts in these regions, as so many commentators have done and continue to do, simply to the strength of reactionary ethnic nationalisms in these regions is to simplify the issues involved in ways that are misguided in principle and disastrous in practice. In principle, there can be no democratic reason to oppose the division of one state into two or more new states to accommodate the interests of conflicting nationalities. In situations where the two nationalities involved inhabit relatively clearly demarcated territorial zones, the actual implementation of such division poses few serious problems. But such situations are rare, and in many countries the attempt to devise borders to produce mono-national states is simply not a democratic option. Ethnic cleansing, forced population transfers, the relegation of minorities to second-class citizenship: these are all predictable consequences of attempts to engineer ethnically or culturally homogeneous states in situations where the mingling of peoples is inimical to such an outcome.

Since the late 1960s in Ireland and Palestine, the two communities whose prospects for political emancipation suffered most from the original partition settlements – Northern Irish nationalists and Palestinians generally – have been engaged in a long and difficult struggle to renegotiate the terms of those settlements. However different the actual historical circumstances and conditions, and in many respects the regions are indeed very different, this basic structural similarity connects the two situations. In both instances, the struggles were initially inspired by the progressive political revolutions sweeping the globe in the 1960s. The American Black Civil Rights campaigns had an important impact on Northern Irish nationalists. The Algerian and Vietnamese liberation wars inspired the stateless Palestinians in their struggle. By the mid-1970s, the insurrectionary energies of the previous decade were in recession across the globe, however, and the struggles in Northern Ireland and Palestine have since been pressed in a climate of intense political reaction. The nuclear hostilities of the Second Cold War, the retreat of socialism across the globe, the consolidation of right-wing regimes across Western Europe, and the tightening of American control over the Middle East are only some of the more obvious examples of this reaction. And when that late Cold War period itself drew to a close in 1989, the struggles in both Northern Ireland and Palestine also underwent dramatic transformations.

Waged in this malevolent international climate, the political struggles directed against the original partition settlements in Ireland and Palestine were never in any case philosophically or strategically adequate to the political complexities involved. Faced with the continuous displacements of population and the savage and systemic coercion visited on them by the Israeli state, the Palestinian people have an indisputable right to defend themselves by armed struggle. That said, the struggles waged by the different sectors of the Palestinian people – those in the Diaspora, in the Occupied Territories and within Palestine – have rarely been co-ordinated with each other, and this has undoubtedly been one of the major weaknesses in the Palestinian movement. If Palestinians are to remedy that problem in the future, it is better political and not military strategies that will surely be required. In Northern Ireland, once the civil rights campaigns were launched considerable levels of state violence were directed against nationalists, and long-entrenched in-built Unionist political domination inhibited normal democratic strategies to improve the situation. Nevertheless, the capacity of an armed struggle to solve the Northern dilemma was always dubious, and the militarism of the IRA had from the start the character of a desperate attempt to force a short-cut through a complex situation that would permit nothing of the sort. Though very different organisations in many ways, the IRA and the PLO have both tended to oscillate dramatically between an absolute reliance on militarism, on the one hand, and on diplomatic negotiations with the imperial superpowers, on the other, to advance their causes. Neither movement has displayed much confidence in the development of sustained mass popular movements that would reduce their dependence on either one or the other of these gambits. Despite all the decades of violence and suffering, therefore, the real struggle to overcome the democratic deficiencies inherent in the original partition settlements is still only beginning in both regions.

*Chapter 2*

# Estranged states: national literatures, modernity and tradition, and the elaboration of partitionist identities

## I

In many contemporary theories of nationalism, cultural and communications media are ascribed an important function in developing and maintaining a sense of national consciousness and national sentiment. These theories provide the conceptual basis that can help to explain why the development of a national literature is always an important dimension of the modern state-building project. Like national museums, national broadcasting services, national galleries and national newspapers, national literatures are a stock assumption of the modern nation-state. They serve multiple functions, which extend to both domestic and international audiences. The construction of national literatures usually involves processes of linguistic standardisation and canon selection designed to promote the sense of a shared national culture overarching 'subsidiary' regional, religious, ethnic, gender or class differences. For domestic audiences, therefore, national literatures help to create a sense of a shared cultural inheritance and a sense of a common destiny. In the international arena, they allow nation-states to establish cultural credentials that in turn allow them to secure full political recognition and to compete for cultural status and prestige.

For most contemporary theorists, nationalism is an essential element of modernisation, an ineluctable feature of the transition from agrarian to industrial or from pre-capitalist to capitalist society. Modern industrial or capitalist economies require the state, and the state in turn can operate successfully only if it can develop and be maintained by a common, accessible, written culture. According to Ernest Gellner, 'nationalism is, essentially, the general imposition of a *high culture* on society, where previously *low cultures* had taken up the lives of the majority, and in some cases of the totality, of the population. It means that generalized diffusion of a school-mediated, academy-supervised idiom, codified for the requirements of reasonably precise bureaucratic and technological communication.'[1] In the period before the modern *nation-state*, Gellner suggests, states rarely attempted to impose a standardised or homogeneous state culture on their subjects: instead, complex networks of local groups, sustained by their own locally reproduced 'folk cultures', were the norm. With the coming of industrial modernity and its attendant divisions of labour, these local cultures, he maintains, tend to be subsumed into an impersonal mass society, which makes it necessary for the state to develop some kind of shared national culture and to support the diffusion of literacy to sustain a common medium of communication.

There are several elements in this functionalist account of things that can be disputed. Gellner's insistence that it is modern mass society and the division of labour created by industrialism that generates the need for a common national culture is clearly not tenable for the colonial world where the development of nationalism often preceded the beginnings of industrialisation. Likewise, his suggestion that nationalism invariably leads to the establishment of states – each with a single homogeneous culture – cannot take theoretical account of modern multi-ethnic, multi-language, multi-cultural states.[2] The assertion that the creation of a national culture involves the imposition of a 'high' national culture where before a medley of 'low' folk cultures had co-existed is also questionable. In some situations at least, and especially in the colonies perhaps, the creation of new national literatures has involved the active demotion of what had previously been prestigious 'high' literatures to the status of 'folk cultures'. Nevertheless, while the transactions involved are undoubtedly more varied, complex and politically charged than Gellner allows, many of the processes he describes are indeed a staple of most nation-building projects.

Like Gellner, Benedict Anderson also stresses that the historical emergence of nationalism is bound up with the spread of literacy and education. His account centres on the displacement of older religious or dynastic conceptions of community by the development of modern print capitalism, new modes of transportation and communication, and the cultivation of vernacular languages. For Anderson, it was through media such as the novel and the newspaper that the peoples of the new nation-states first came to see themselves as national communities with a special relationship to a particular territory and as participants in a common purposive national history.[3] Many cultural critics, building on Anderson's work, have noted the correspondence between the rise of the modern nation-state and the rise of the novel form, and have suggested that there are important parallels between 'the modern nation, with its implication of all the people of a territory bound together into a single historical process, and the technique of the major nineteenth-century novels, whose emplotment enmeshes their multiplicity of characters into a single, overarching narrative trajectory'.[4]

In *Nationalism and Literature*, Sarah Corse suggests that the importance of a national literature to the construction of nation-state identity can be observed with particular clarity in the United States (US) in the late eighteenth and nineteenth centuries.[5] By the 1780s, the political autonomy of the US was assured, but American men of letters remained adamant that this was not enough. The new American republic, they insisted, needed to establish itself as a distinct and unique nation as well as an independent state. For the American intellectual élite in this period, the creation of a distinct national literature required above all the creation of a literary heritage that would be distinct from that of imperial Britain. By 1787, as Corse notes, Noah Webster was warning Americans that the 'authority of foreign manners keeps us in subjection'.[6] An 1816 announcement in *The Portico* reiterated the same point more forcefully: 'Dependence, whether literary or political', it commented, 'is a state of degradation, fraught with disgrace'.[7] Throughout the nineteenth century, however, both British and American commentators contended that the US had still failed to complete the task of creating an authentic national literature, its literature being still only a poor simulacra of Britain's. As one British writer in 1831 put it: 'The literary independence of the Americans is far from being so complete as their political, for as yet they possess no national literature and invariably regard ours as appertaining also to them.'[8] Nonetheless, by the end of the century, galvanised by the need to re-establish a common sense of national feeling in the wake of the Civil War, the outlines of an American national literary canon had taken shape. By the 1890s, Corse argues, courses in American Literature, with a recognised set of 'major authors,' were being offered in a broad range of US colleges and universities, though the topic was not fully institutionalised in the more élite universities until the early twentieth century.

Several basic points with wider application might be deduced here. Firstly, the American case suggests that the creation of a national literature is something that evolves quite slowly and that the process is one in which there is an insistent emphasis both on domestic identity (what Americans supposedly share in common) and international difference (the things that separate the US and Britain or Europe). It also indicates that in some instances the anxiety to distinguish a national culture may be most acute precisely where the substantive cultural differences between national Self and significant national Other are least obvious.

The relationship sketched here between the emergence of nationalism, the creation of national literatures, and the transition to modernity (variously conceptualised) is a familiar one in the contemporary theoretical literature on nationalism. What has received less attention, however, is the way in which the self-understanding of modernity has always defined itself in terms of a dialectic between 'tradition' and 'modernity'. It is true that most contemporary theorists share the assumption, usually associated with Tom Nairn, that all nationalisms accommodate both traditional and modern elements. Nairn associates this dialectic with the emergence of nationalisms in the peripheries of the modern capitalist world system where the nationalist élites attempted to emulate the 'progress' of the more metropolitan states but strove to do so in their own terms:

> The peripheric élites . . . had to contest the concrete form in which (so to speak) progress had taken them by the throat, even as they set out to progress themselves. Since they wanted factories, parliaments, schools and so on, they had to copy the leaders somehow; but in a way which rejected the mere implantation of these things by direct foreign intervention or control. This gave rise to a profound ambiguity, an ambivalence which marks most forms of nationalism.[9]

Hence, for Nairn, while the nationalist élites in the peripheries construed themselves as the emissaries of Enlightenment and modernisation, they simultaneously represented themselves as the heirs and guardians to ancient and distinctive national traditions. For him, the determination to marry the traditional to the modern begins with nationalism in the underdeveloped peripheries, but is then later also taken up by metropolitan state-led official nationalisms. This, he concludes, explains the recurrent 'Janus-headed' quality of all contemporary nationalisms.

It might be argued against Nairn's story of origins, however, that this ambivalent dialectic between 'tradition' and 'the modern' neither begins with nor is peculiar to nationalism in the peripheries. This is because the concept of modernity can never exist in pure form since it is always constitutively dependent on some concept of the anti-modern. In other words, in order for the modern to exist, there has also to be an anti-modern against which it can dialectically be defined.[10] What this means is that the conceptual self-realisation and the lived experience of modernity – whether in the metropolis or the peripheries – has from the very outset always operated as a dialectical relationship between 'modernity' and 'tradition,' conceived as a relation between two distinct conditions, two regions, two temporalities, two temperaments.

This dialectic has played itself out in specific locations in remarkably diverse ways. Thus, for example, metropolitan European modernisation was conceived in terms whereby supposedly 'backward' regions – such as the Celtic peripheries in Western Europe or the Slavic ones in Eastern Europe – were assimilated into supposedly more dynamic and advanced imperial heartlands. On a global scale, European imperialism, too, was conceived as a modernising project in which 'modern' Western energy, industry and enlightenment would be infused into colonies where the natives supposedly remained mired in static 'traditional' societies. But the dialectic between tradition and modernity was never simply conceived in terms of a *geographical* contrast between centre and periphery whether defined in domestic terms (advanced England/backward Scotland) or on an international scale (industrious Europe/static Orient). In the colonies, the same dialectic was often transposed onto populations to distinguish between subject peoples. Thus in the white settler colonies, it was the European settlers who were deemed to embody the values of progress and modernity; the slatternly natives who supposedly epitomised recalcitrant tradition. Elsewhere in the administrative colonies, potential allies among the local peoples were categorised as honest, brave, loyal and more 'modern' (or with a greater receptivity to modern values) while potentially oppositional majority populations were considered degenerate, feudal and generally 'backward' in disposition.[11] In summary, the metropolitan characterisation of modernity, whether elaborated in Europe or in the colonies, is always articulated in terms of an evolutionary temporal chronotope that thrives on the distinction between traditional backwardness and modern European progress.[12]

When, in the early twentieth century, legislative democratic institutions began to be formed within the carapace of the hitherto autocratic and racially stratified colonial states, the monopoly of power commanded by the imperialists and their coalition partners was threatened. As the majority nationalist movements moved to take control of the state, the settler or ethnic élites that were once privileged coalition partners with the imperial administration now constituted themselves as the representatives of distinct and threatened nationalities and appealed for imperial protection. Long attuned to seeing the majority population through imperialist eyes as backward, anti-modern and politically incapable, the minority communities sought what remedy they could to avoid submersion into this backward mass that democratisation would ineluctably entail. To compound matters, the subordinate majority communities had usually developed as part of their political self-assertion a cultural nationalism dedicated to the 'revival' of their own ancient languages, literatures and customs. Where the minority communities were concerned, these apparently atavistic and backward-looking cultural revivals – with their attempts to 'recover' Celtic pasts or classical Arab heritages – seemed only to confirm the majority's congenitally anti-modern disposition.

This chronotopic paradigm has considerable importance for the ways in which national literatures are developed since this dialectic is one that can be used to distinguish between regions and communities internal to the state and internationalised to distinguish between one state and another. In the US, to return to this paradigmatically modern instance, the dialectic is played out internally between the North and the South, where in one version the North possesses the rude industry but also the vulgarity characteristic of the modern and the South the grace and charm but also the 'old corruption' characteristic of the *ancien régime*. The distinction reappears, in another variant, in the contrast between a more urban and sophisticated but also more effete East and a less civilised, more violent and lawless, but also more vigorous, West. The dialectic operates within the East itself in terms of the distinction between the 'Boston Brahmin' Anglo-élites and the more recently arrived immigrant hordes. In this case, the established élites sometimes possess an 'old world' charm threatened by the vulgar immigrant rabble. In a counter version, however, they can also be associated with European degeneracy and Asiatic lassitude whereas the new immigrants possess a rude democratic and commercial vigour that ensures that the future is theirs. The same distinction is internationalised in the conventional literary contrast between an old, somewhat sinister Europe and a more callow but also more innocent America. In later writers such as Henry James this crude dichotomy is infinitely modified to the point where it seems about to dissolve yet still remains necessary.

National literatures, however, do not simply articulate distinctions of this sort along the temporal–spatial axis of tradition and modernity; they usually attempt to suture them as well. These sutures usually take the form of some sort of supposedly mutually beneficial trade-offs whereby the best elements of tradition and modernity are wedded together, usually with much mutual congratulation. Thus Eastern civilisation and sophistication is invigorated by rugged Western values, Northern energy and industry refined by contact with Southern grace, and so on. The sutures thus celebrated are usually constructed in literary narrative as victories for civilisation; what usually gets elided are the processes of war, genocide, slavery and exploitation that produced these divisions in the first instance. Moreover, there are always some that cannot be integrated into these compensatory exchanges between tradition and modernity. Walter Scott's Gaelic Highlanders are one such instance in the nineteenth-century British version; in the American versions, American Indians and Negroes are another.

In the case of partitioned societies, the dynamics of nation-state building are not essentially different in kind to those involved in the birth of other nation-states. Nevertheless, because of the incestuous intimacy of their shared geography and history within what was historically the same political unit, the processes of national identity construction and mutual estrangement are undoubtedly different in degree, the pre-partition intimacy of the now divided peoples requiring an even more violent and clamorous estrangement. Each of the newly emergent nation-states typically sets itself the task of mobilising and shaping its own imagined community and providing it with its own distinct historical, geographical and cultural heritage and identity. National educational systems, state broadcasting companies and national literatures are some of the key meaning-generating institutions mobilised to serve this task. In this instance, too, the dialectic between tradition and modernity comes into play. Broadly speaking, each of the two newly partitioned states usually claims that it embodies the most fertile marriage of tradition and modernity while the hated rival state across the border is associated with the most negative elements of both.

As suggested earlier, however, in the colonies the tradition–modernity dialectic was never simply regional but was instead transposed by the imperial administrators onto different peoples or communities as well. In colonial partitions, therefore, the demand for partition is articulated from the very outset in terms of this dialectic. Hence Irish Unionists and Jewish Zionists, and their respective metropolitan supporters, argued that these groups represented modern, industrious peoples with advanced metropolitan credentials, and that they would be utterly compromised were they reduced to a minority within states with backward, anti-modern majorities such as the Catholic Irish or the Palestinian Arabs. In such cases, the cultural distinction between tradition and modernity used by the imperial administration to stratify peoples within the colony was now used to ratify politically regressive partitions and the states thus created were then re-ratified as the manifest realisations of these essentialist differences. To put it simply, the dialectic between tradition and modernity that had its origins in the colonial stratification of populations was instantiated and preserved in the cultures of the rival states that emerged out of partition. In such circumstances, it was inevitable perhaps that the national minorities inside the partitioned states would themselves be construed as the bearers of the 'anti-modern' stigmata associated with the rival state across the border.

It would be a mistake, however, to see literature only as an instrument of state élites. For while it is clear that literature can be used to create new state identities and new partitionist mentalities, it can also be deployed to resist them. Literature can, in other words, be used to assert the existence of shared identities, shared historical experiences, common values and concerns that cut across the state divides imposed by partition. In the nineteenth-century US, as in many twentieth-century postcolonial countries, state independence was secured prior to the establishment of a common national culture. In other situations, however, a strong sense of a common nationality, and the development of a common national culture and literature, were sometimes elaborated well before a subject people secured control of a state apparatus. The German scholar, Friedrich Meinecke, coined the terms *Staatsnation* and *Kulturnation* to distinguish between such situations. For Meinecke, long after its main European rivals, France and Britain, had consolidated themselves as centralised nation-states (or *Staatsnations*), Germany continued to be divided into multiple states, and hence could experience a sense of national unity only vicariously through culture. Throughout most of the nineteenth century, it was not a common political home that brought Bavarians, Swabians and Prussians together, but rather a shared sense of German culture that existed prior to nation-building and in spite of ongoing political division.[13]

In partitioned societies, contradictory commitments to *Staatsnation* and *Kulturnation* usually continue – in unresolved tension with each other – well after state division. While the new states created by partition commonly attempt to institutionalise literature in ways that will consolidate their separate identities, literature can also be used by states hostile to partition as a means of keeping alive some sense of a *Kulturnation* that continues to survive despite state division. Challenges to official state identities of this sort need not, of course, be politically progressive. Some may simply be irredentist or expansionist in tone, some quite conservative if they look only to ethnic bonding as a means to contest present division. But some literature may also be quite radical in its desire to contest the narrowly partitionist mentalities consolidated by state division.

The initial history of partitioned states is invariably one in which the new states display intense hostility towards each other. These hostilities sometimes abate with time, and periods of rapprochement follow in which the divided states attempt to open normal diplomatic, trade and cultural relations with each other while still maintaining a separate existence. Over the longer term, however, the states must ultimately decide between a path that will lead to permanent divergence and separation or one that leads towards some sort of convergence. In the latter case, convergence may be limited (restricted, for instance, to common membership of wider regional organisations) or may lead towards complete reintegration as has happened in Vietnam and Germany. Needless to say, such developments are always intensely political and keenly contested, and all sorts of factors, domestic and international, condition the trajectories upon which particular states evolve. Neither ultimate divergence nor convergence is predetermined, and the modalities of separation or reintegration vary from one situation to another.[14]

This chapter will investigate some of the various roles that literature can play in partitioned states. The general thesis I wish to outline is not a particularly complex one. Literature, it will be argued, can be deployed in ways designed either to consolidate or to challenge partitionist identities and mentalities. Over the longer term, it can serve either to advance the goal of complete state separation and divergence or, alternatively, to promote various modes of convergence and reintegration. It is, it must be stressed, the ways in which either division or divergence are imagined that allow us to distinguish between regressive and emancipatory imaginings. The supplementary thesis I argue here, however, is that in most instances post-partitioned states elaborate their relationship in terms of an ongoing and endlessly malleable dialectic between tradition and modernity. This dualistic opposition is not peculiar to colonial partitions: but in colonial partitions in places such as the Irish Republic/Northern Ireland and Israel/Palestine it is one directly inherited from the colonial era and then transposed into stereotypical state identities, and to this extent it represents one of the ways in which colonial stratifications and antagonisms survive into the present.

In order to elucidate these matters, it will be useful to begin with a short overview of the role that literature played in reconstructing a sense of nationality during the division and recent reunification of Germany. Later, the role of literature in the post-partition periods in Ireland, Israel and Palestine will be discussed. Though the survey begins with Germany, the intention here is not to set up Germany as a template from which current literary relations in other partitioned countries can be adduced. Its interest here is simply that it allows us to assess the role of literature in a situation that has undergone a process involving both division and re-integration. Longer-term developments in Ireland and Israel/Palestine may prove quite different and developments in Germany are patently no index to the future in either region. Nevertheless, even a cursory outline of the German case can elucidate issues that are worked out in variant ways in other quite different situations.

## II

In many respects, the institutionalisation of literature in the East and West German states that emerged in the 1950s quite clearly reflected the wider differences between the two societies. In socialist East Germany (GDR), literary production and the study of literature were politicised in terms of orthodox Marxism and Soviet-style Communism. Literature, that is, was explicitly ascribed the socially activist task of changing social consciousness, and was expected actively to contribute to the development of a new socialist society. Although that state's conception of the role of the writer underwent several shifts between 1945 and 1989, the socially activist task assigned to literature, and accepted by both academics and writers, remained quite constant. This ensured, on the one hand, that the state went to considerable lengths to police literary production. The chief publishing houses in the GDR were state-owned, and the main literary publishing house, Aufbau, was under the direct control of the ruling Communist party, the Socialist Unity Party of Germany (SED).[15] On the other hand, however, the state's activist conception of literature also conferred on the writer and the literary intellectual considerable moral authority.

David Bathrick has argued that in a repressive Communist regime where controversial issues could not be debated in public media such as newspaper or television, literature acquired additional importance since it enabled discussion and reflection, sometimes in coded form, on topics not otherwise discussed. Literature, that is, though constrictively tied to the state, could, so long as it remained 'constructively critical,' also constitute an alternative public sphere to the party and its media.[16]

In capitalist West Germany (FRG), on the other hand, the literary system was tied less to the state than to the market. In the decades after World War II, conservative critics in West Germany urged the creation of a literature that would free itself of politics and be assessed solely on aesthetic criteria. This, it was contended, would allow West German literature to escape the deforming politicisation of art associated with the Nazi period and with the socialist realist aesthetic sponsored in the East. Nevertheless, the need to come to terms with the horror of the Holocaust, to understand how German modernity had issued in such disaster, and to deal with the division of the German people into two states, meant that 'national questions' continued to obsess writers in the Federal Republic also – however much conservatives might decry this. Indeed, many of the state's most internationally distinguished writers – such as Heinrich Böll, Günter Grass and Martin Walser – returned obsessively to national issues in their works. Despite the fact that they assigned different roles to literature, and promoted different aesthetics and different reading practices, in both German states, therefore, literature continued to be charged with political responsibilities, and writers acquired considerable authority as public intellectuals and as the 'moral conscience' of society.

Despite their separate development over several decades, and the mutual hostility that characterised the Cold War period, each of the two states continued to articulate conceptions of Germanness in terms of its different state ideology. Each state went to great lengths to represent its version of German identity as the antithesis to the other, and this process of differentiation was rehearsed in terms of a dialectic between tradition and modernity in which the rival state incarnated the worst elements of both. In its official ideology, East Germany was the direct inheritor of the heroic 'antifascist struggle' in which the progressive elements in German history had finally triumphed over the reactionary elements in its past as well as over the destructive tendencies inherent in capitalist society generally. As such, East Germany split German tradition into 'good' and 'bad' strands, and saw itself as the legitimate heir to all that was best and most progressive in traditional German culture. From such a perspective, West Germany was viewed both as the neo-fascist inheritor of the anti-Enlightenment elements in Germany's history and as a supine puppet state that incarnated the worst elements of American imperialist modernity. In the official ideology of West Germany, on the other hand, the GDR was constructed as the authoritarian and totalitarian successor-state to German fascism, its anti-democratic culture and backward economy cited as evidence of the evils of Marxist social philosophy. From this perspective, the GDR represented a dire example of everything that would be lost if the progressive modern values of Western individualism, liberal democracy and economic enterprise – values West Germany claimed to incarnate – were surrendered. As Alison Lewis has remarked, for each state 'it was always the other side that was seen as heir to the fascist legacy of the Third Reich. Each German nation thus sought to cleanse its national imago of the strains of genocide and mass destruction by projecting these onto the other.'[17]

At their inception, both German states officially aspired to national reunification. The building of the Berlin Wall in 1961, which was soon extended into a fortified frontier between the two states, and the gradual development of different political, economic and cultural systems seemed to indicate, however, that two distinct national identities had permanently consolidated. With the adoption of a new legal code in 1968, and of a revised constitution in 1974 that made no mention of a single German nation, the GDR in particular seemed committed to the development of a separate German identity that would recognise no affinity with its West German counterpart.[18] The commitment to reunification continued to be enshrined in the West German constitution (something that would acquire real importance when unification became an option after 1989). Nonetheless, commentators seem generally agreed that by the 1980s most West Germans regarded East Germany as a foreign country, and there were no political movements in that state actively pursuing unification as a political objective.

Some literary historians have also argued, however, that just at that moment in the 1970s and 1980s when the two political systems seemed to accept that partition had become permanent, German literature moved in the opposite direction and began a process of 'convergence'.[19] The concept of a single German *Kulturnation* transcending state borders was revitalised in this period, partly as a compensatory reaction to the seemingly inevitable dissolution of a common German culture. Moreover, in the hostile climate of the Second

Cold War, which escalated the nuclear threat to both states, the concept of the *Kulturnation* could also be activated to allay inter-state tensions by stressing what the two societies shared in common. For some, like Günter Grass, who declared in 1980 that 'the only thing in the two German states that can be proven to be pan-German is literature',[20] the *Kulturnation* idea was designed not to challenge the legitimacy of partition, but to promote better relations between the two states. For others of a more nationalistic bent, such as Martin Walser, it did serve, however, as an argument against the legitimation of partition, and as a means of keeping open 'the German Question' within the public discourse of the Federal Republic. In the 1980s, several important novels by leading German writers, such as Stefan Heym's *Schwarzenberg* (1984), Peter Shcneider's *The Wall Jumper* (1984) and Martin Walser's *No Man's Land* (1987), directly grappled with issues of German unity and division.

In other ways, too, the argument for a literary 'convergence' in this period seems to have substance. West German scholars such as Hans Mayer and Fritz J. Raddatz, writing in the 1960s and 1970s, had formulated the idea of two discrete East and West German literatures. In the late seventies, however, both scholars retracted their theses. Mayer contended in 1979 that 'there is a movement of convergence in German-language literature of our day'[21] and five years later Frank Trommler asserted that there was only one German literature irrespective of state boundaries. In the same period, several leading GDR writers broke with the dominant socialist realist aesthetic in that state, and began to develop more modernist and humanist literary styles. New works by authors such as Christa Wolf who had made this move became major literary events not only in the East but also the West, and this too contributed to the sense that a common German literature still survived even after decades of division.

The suggestion here is that though they followed separate courses there were nonetheless significant points of rapprochement between the two German literatures, not that literary nationalism or literary 'convergence' somehow paved the way for political reunification in the 1990s. It was patently the collapse of its patron state, the Soviet Union, and its own economic stagnation and political bankruptcy, that ultimately cost East Germany the allegiance of the bulk of its citizens, and which by extension enabled reunification. The trauma of Germany's fascist past had made many Germans, especially liberals and leftists, either uncertain or opposed in principle to the country's moral right to unity and deeply suspicious of what the consequences of an ethnically defined German nationality might mean. Hence some West German writers, most prominently Günter Grass, opposed unity. So too did many leading East German ones such as Christa Wolf, Heiner Müller and others for whom the 1989 uprisings in the GDR represented an opportunity to build a truly democratic socialism in that state. Once unity was achieved, these writers came under savage attack from right-wing cultural intellectuals, Grass because he insisted on warning about the dangers of a strong Germany, the GDR writers because they were demonised as craven apologists for a discredited authoritarian state.

As several critics have argued, the critical fury directed at figures such as Grass and Wolf in the *Literaturstreit* that attended reunification needs to be understood as part of a wider attempt to redefine the role of literature and national culture in the new Germany. The object of the attack on figures such as Grass and Wolf, these critics suggest, was to discredit the tendency of many distinguished left-liberal writers to act as public political commentators on German society. As the *Literaturstreit* developed, the roles of politically committed writers in both the FRG and the GDR were increasingly conflated and then subsumed into a wider attack on the whole notion that literature should have any political role. For conservative critics, as Stephen Brockmann has noted, the political role of literature in the two Germanys 'was a relic from the unhappy authoritarian past, and it should therefore be discarded as writers in both Germanys integrated themselves into a normal western democracy. The essence of true art, they argued, was its autonomy from the competing spheres of politics, morality and economics, and a politically committed art was inartistic and inadequate.'[22]

What emerges from this patently schematic overview of the German situation is that literature can play quite a complex role in processes of division and reunification. In the wake of partition, both German states attempted to harness literary systems to reinforce a sense of their distinct national cultures and identities. But while literature could certainly be institutionalised to such purpose – by way of education systems, writers associations, academies and other cultural institutions – it was by no means reduced to a pliant instrument of the state. For one thing, in its more dissenting and utopian versions at least, it also possessed the capacity to challenge the East and West German states by measuring their actual achievements against their respective commitments to socialism and democracy. Moreover, despite the real differences between the two literatures that emerged in each state, writers in both kept open bonds of solidarity and channels of cultural contact and exchange well after partition and long before political union was achieved.

Over their forty years of existence, the two states did create distinct cultural and national identities, but the events of 1989–90 would also suggest that some overarching sense of common nationality and obligation, however tentative, still survived notwithstanding such difference. Like the US in the decades after the Civil War, the present German state contains two populations with a common ethnicity but with different state histories and different sub-national identities. The *Literaturstreit* that has raged since reunification undoubtedly represents a cultural contest, not unlike that which raged in the United States during the period of Reconstruction, to decide on what terms the re-suturing of those identities will proceed. It is, in other words, ultimately a contest over what the social content or ideological character of the new German nationality shall be.

Just as the dialectic between tradition and modernity provided the terms through which the struggle between the two German states was articulated, it has also supplied some of the key terms through which the contemporary reunification continues to be interpreted and lived. Thus for many West Germans today, Easterners, supposedly long sheltered by a communist system that privileged security over enterprise, lack the entrepreneurial spirit, the managerial abilities and democratic sensibility to function in a modern society, and the financial cost of modernising their backward economy is viewed as an unwelcome burden. From this perspective, the merger of the two states is conceived as one in which the East is the ungrateful beneficiary of Western energy and industry. Since reunification, many Westerners have filled managerial posts in the higher professions and the universities in the East, and Western companies were quick to takeover newly privatised East German firms. The superiority of West German industry and culture was starkly asserted in this take-over, and for many East Germans this 'modernisation' is experienced as a version of West German carpetbagger 'colonisation'. In this dialectic, however, East German economic backwardness can at least be turned to cultural account. Because they remained outside the crassly consumerist culture of West, *Ossis* (Easterners), it is sometimes argued, are less vulgar, less materialistic, than their *Wessi* (Westerner) counterparts. Regarded as bankrupt and worthless by some, East German culture is regarded by others as a remarkable repository of older German values that have supposedly long since disappeared in the West. As was the case in the US during the decades after the Civil War, then, the cultural self-realisation of the new Germany is conceptualised as a complex suturing of tradition and modernity, the integration of their different temperaments and cultural characteristics. That East Germany is the defeated party is beyond doubt; like the American South perhaps it may yet manage to engineer a cultural triumph from its political and economic collapse.

# III

In Ireland, as in other colonial situations, the development of a national literature was galvanised by a struggle for political independence. Though Ireland was incorporated into the United Kingdom after 1800, the Union never won the same popular support there that it did in Wales or Scotland. Any number of circumstances help to explain this: economic lag relative to the rest of Britain; mass immiseration, culminating in the catastrophe of the Great Famine in the 1840s; and the fact that Britishness was defined in terms of a Protestant 'elect nation' constitutively hostile to Catholicism. The enormous population haemorrhages from the Irish countryside that continued for decades after the Famine and the attendant accelerated collapse of Irish as the language of the masses lent impetus to a cultural nationalism that sought to 'recover' and promote a distinct Irish cultural identity. The Literary Revival, in the English language, that developed in tandem with the struggle for Home Rule at the turn of the twentieth century represented an attempt to assert the vitality of an Irish culture generally dismissed as moribund and inferior. It drew many of its leading writers from a section of the Anglo-Irish intelligentsia sympathetic to Irish independence despite its own colonial history, but the mass base for this cultural movement came from an increasingly assertive Irish Catholic middle-class.

As in other colonial situations, however, Irish cultural nationalism was shaped in discursive terms largely set by the colonial context. In the nineteenth century, hostile British representations of the Irish stressed that they were an inferior race naturally given to violence and lawlessness. More sympathetic accounts, rehearsed in the Celticist idiom made fashionable by Matthew Arnold and Ernest Renan, construed them as an imaginative but politically inept and unworldly people – thus lacking the requisite capacities for self-rule and in need of British industry, enterprise and good government. Most versions of Irish cultural nationalism tended simply to invert this conception: the fact that Ireland lagged behind British industrial modernity allowed it to stand for what had been lost in that enterprise, but also to see itself as a refuge for values that could lead to a transfigured future. Irish culture, in short, was defined in terms that insisted on its supposed spiritual superiority to the crass materialism and philistine utilitarianism associated with English industrial modernity.

Though the interests of the declining Anglo-Irish intellectual élite and the emergent Catholic middle classes that shaped this cultural revival were often at odds, both shared a common stress on the anti-modern cast of Irishness. For many of the Anglo-Irish intellectuals, notably W. B. Yeats and Standish O'Grady, modernity was identified with the entrance of the masses into politics and with an attendant cultural coarsening and the destruction of aristocratic value, refinement and heroic sensibility. For the Catholic Church, too, modernity was equated with spiritual decline, moral degeneration and the collapse of traditional authority. The literature of the Revival was remarkable in its refusal of the mimetic codes of British social realism, innovative in its forms, confident in its sense of the importance of its Irish subject matter, and, occasionally, utopian in its social vision. It drew its energy from a wider modernising drive to transform the inherited colonial social structures that shaped Irish society. Nevertheless, the dominant vision of Ireland that emerged was one in which the country was conceived as an outpost of an ancient civilisation threatened by, but heroically resistant to, the corrupting tides of Anglophone urban industrial modernity. The Revival was an island-wide and not simply a twenty-six county phenomenon. But when the Irish Free State was established in 1922, the literature of the Revival was institutionalised as the foundational literature of that state, whereas in the new Northern state the writers in that part of the country associated with the Revival were largely written out of literary history.[23]

The circumstances leading to the establishment of Northern Ireland were quite different. In contrast to Irish nationalism, the aim of Irish Unionism was not to establish an independent nation-state but to keep Ireland within the UK. Once it became clear that some measure of Irish autonomy was inevitable, Irish Unionism contracted to an Ulster Unionism devoted to the establishment of a six-county state in the north-east. Unlike Irish separatist nationalism, in its inception an anti-state movement with a popular mission of political emancipation and cultural 'renaissance', Ulster Unionism was conceived not as a project of social transformation but rather as a 'loyal' counter-revolutionary defence of established Protestant liberties and of British imperial culture in Ireland. In the lead up to the creation of the Northern statelet there was, therefore, no major literary or cultural 'revival' designed to create a new Ulster or Northern Irish identity. Instead, the whole rationale of the new state was identified with the protection of Protestantism and it was the most reactionary elements of British state iconography – the symbols of royalism, Protestant supremacy and Empire – that were appropriated by Unionists as the icons that mortared their sense of Britishness.

Broadly speaking, the contrast between the Southern and Northern Irish states resembled that between revolutionary postcolonial societies that had fought wars of independence from Britain and dominions such as Canada that had a strong sense of attachment to Britain and Empire and only limited aspirations to independence. In Southern Ireland, as in the new postcolonial states elsewhere, the creation of a national literature was deemed an urgent necessity to express a sense of difference to a powerful metropolitan culture and to serve as cultural capital to legitimate an independent state. Like dominions such as Canada or New Zealand, which typically established their own national literatures only late in the twentieth century, the North, anxious to stress its links with Britain rather than its own unique identity, did not 'need' a distinct literature in the same way.[24] Moreover, since 'Irish culture' was associated with nationalism and the South, the very lack of a local literature with national pretensions ratified the North's sense of itself as a hard-headed, industrial enclave in every way different to the agrarian, rural South much given to imaginative vapourings. Instead, Northern identity was conceived as a regional outpost of the transnational British Empire and, later, Commonwealth. The civic and official culture of the new state was overwhelmingly and exclusively British and Protestant. Its state rituals and symbols were based on British state 'high' culture such as royal birthdays and weddings, imperial celebrations and the receipt of titles, decorations and honours. At a more populist level, Ulster Unionism also drew on Ulster Protestantism's heritage of Orange marches, Evangelical missions and commemorations of historic events when the Protestant people had triumphed over foreign enemies and Papist insurrection.[25] This populist heritage was one with little aspiration to securing hegemony or the consent of the subaltern Northern nationalist community; instead of trying to disguise or mystify the violent origins of Protestant supremacy, those origins were constantly commemorated in public parade and spectacle.

Here, the conventional bourgeois bifurcation of history into the different temperaments and temporalities of 'tradition' and 'modernity' plays itself out in the kind of fantastic confusion that sometimes passes for common sense. Southern nationalists, lamenting the loss of the six northern counties, sometimes construed Ulster as the most Gaelic of all of the Irish provinces: the last outpost of Gaeldom to be conquered by England, the place of its most sacred early Christian sites, the birthplace of Irish republicanism. The stress on Ulster's pre-plantation Gaelic past was designed to buttress the argument for reunification but served, of course, to elide the existence of the Unionist population that constituted the major obstacle to this goal. Since they lacked any practical strategy to advance unification, many nationalists consoled themselves, however, by decrying the 'Black North' as a sectarian industrial wasteland inimical to the supposedly edenic charms of the rural South. In Belfast, one commentator observed in 1926, 'you fancy that you are in a latitude more northerly than homely Dublin with its easy air, by as much as Copenhagen, say, is more northerly than a city of Southern France'.[26] For another 'Belfast is an overgrown red-brick manufacturing town. At every turn one is reminded that he is not in polite easy-going Dublin or Cork. The steam and petrol engine burrs everywhere; mammon is discussed in tram and train; the foothpaths are thronged after six with rather well-dressed men and pale girls returning from the mills.'[27] The irony here is that this contrast between a vulgar but brashly energetic urban North and a more sleepy but easy-going rural South is little more than a derivative variation on the 'Little England' paradigm of English identity that emerged in the late nineteenth century. This paradigm – which depicted the rural counties of the south-east as the repository of authentic English values, uncorrupted by either the imperial ethos of London or the industrial blight of the North – was laminated onto the divided Irish landscape where it has retained considerable power as a cultural ratification of partition ever since.[28]

For Ulster Unionists, the new Southern state simply incarnated the stereotypical values long associated with backward Irish Gaels and Catholics: it was conceived as a badly governed provincial agrarian backwater utterly in thrall to the despotic power of the Catholic Church. The qualities of superstition, slatternliness and thriftlessness attributed to the Southern state were also transposed onto the North's subordinate Catholic minority. Fears about the latter's propensity to outbreed Protestants – the reckless fertility of inferior breeds and classes always threatening to swamp their betters – were (and still remain) commonly rehearsed. There was some substance to the negative stereotypes the two states held of the other, but as is usual in such cases the level of self mis-recognition inherent in this dialectic of tradition and modernity was more acute. Objectively, Southern nationalism expressed the interests of the emergent classes of Catholic middle-class professionals and rural smallholding farmers and it was harnessed to a modernising project designed to transform the old colonial state into a politically sovereign and economically self-reliant nation-state. Subjectively, its cultural ideology was predicated on salvaging an ancient Gaelic heritage from the ravages of modernity. Objectively, Northern Unionism expressed the interests of the province's landed and industrial élites and its project was to preserve the status quo that had obtained in the colonial period from the nationalist challenge. Despite this rearguard defence of the old social order against the new, it was Unionism nevertheless which regarded itself as inherently anti-traditional and modernist in disposition.

Even if Ulster Unionism was not a separatist nationalism, however, the new Northern Irish state still needed to consolidate its domestic political legitimacy and its cultural identity as a distinct polity within the UK. Here dilemmas abounded. How was the new state to create its own distinct local identity as a constituent sub-state of Great Britain and at the same time to insist on its absolute difference to the rest of Ireland? The basic tenet of Ulster Unionism was that Northern Protestants did not belong to 'the Irish nation' and that their continued prosperity, civil liberties and religious freedom depended on membership of the UK and exclusion from the alien state and people to the south. Since Ulster had for centuries been administered as an integral province of Ireland and since the geographical area of the ancient province of Ulster was wider than the new six-county state that took its name, the recently created territory of Northern Ireland lacked historical pedigree as a distinct political or cultural space. For Unionists, it was urgent that some such pedigree be produced to legitimate Northern Ireland and set it apart from the rest of the island.

The retention of the old nine-county provincial name (Ulster) as a synonym for the new smaller six-county state indicates how difficult it was to reconcile the twin imperatives of, on the one hand, sacralising the state by rooting its identity in the ancient past and, on the other, asserting its disconnection from the rest of Ireland. While the word 'Ulster' lent the new state a resonance of historical continuity with the remote past, to distinguish Northern Ireland from the rest of the island 'Ulster' was conceived as Protestant and British and its Gaelic and Catholic associations were downplayed or suppressed. At the same time, were it ever to try to win the allegiance of its sizeable

Catholic and Irish nationalist minority, the Northern Irish state would have to incorporate some element of Irishness in its identity. But this, it was feared, would 'hibernicise' Ulster and diminish the absolute distinction between that statelet and the rest of Ireland. In short, Unionists were trapped in a bind of conflicting imperatives: they could assert Northern Ireland's Protestantism and Britishness to accentuate its separateness to the rest of Ireland, but this excluded the Catholic and Irish nationalist minority, and thus deprived the state of the consent it needed to translate political dominance into a more secure cultural hegemony. Geographically, the statelet, defined by its meandering newly created border, lacked the clarity of visual outline conferred by the immutable, sea-given borders of the island of Ireland invoked by nationalists. Historically, Northern Ireland's two antagonistic communities identified with different national narratives and this made it difficult for the state to construct a single popular metanarrative that would appeal to both. Northern Ireland, in short, has always found it difficult to territorialise its history and historicise its geography.

Ulster literary 'regionalism' probably represents the most sustained cultural attempt to 'solve' this dilemma. Literary regionalism was an attempt to provide Northern Ireland with a literature that would be (i) separate from that of the Irish nationalist tradition; (ii) connected to the wider British canon; but (iii) nonetheless distinct from Scottish, Welsh and English literature. As expressed in the work of its most talented advocate, John Hewitt, a poet of Protestant background with socialist sympathies, literary regionalism asserted that a love of the Ulster landscape could be cultivated as an affective sentiment that would bind the peoples of the region irrespective of constitutional or national politics. 'Ulster', Hewitt wrote in 1947, 'considered as a region and not as a symbol of any particular creed, can, I believe, command the loyalty of every one of its inhabitants'.[29] To serve this purpose, however, landscape had to be leached of overt national significance; hence the emphasis on 'region' as a supposedly more intimate and neutral micro-domain below the divisive jurisdictions and fissures of state and nation.

Hewitt's literary regionalism was nonetheless a loaded political construct. His imagined 'Ulster' begins essentially with the Elizabethan plantations and largely elides the pre-colonial Gaelic province.[30] Its geographic emphasis is on the more heavily Protestant region east of the river Bann at the expense of the more Catholic areas to the west.[31] The linguistic and literary inheritance of the region is defined as Ulster Scots rather than Ulster Gaelic, and traditions of

Protestant republicanism and nationalism are downplayed. While the political boundaries and outlines of Hewitt's imagined 'Ulster' remain deliberately nebulous – for him Ulster as a region need not be coterminous with Northern Ireland – the project nonetheless aimed to secure cultural and emotional and ultimately political legitimacy for a more civic version of the Northern state.

The problem with cultural regionalism, however, was that it was a cultural project that sought to attain its political end (the elaboration of a civic unionist identity) by insisting on its apolitical character rather than by harnessing itself to a transformative political project. The literary regionalism sponsored by Hewitt, and taken up to various degrees by other left or liberal Protestant writers such as W. R. Rodgers and Sam Hanna Bell, dissented from both the official 'high' Unionist culture endorsed by the Northern state and from populist Orangeism. Nevertheless, it remained keenly suspicious of Irish nationalism and the sources of Catholic alienation were never systemically or vigorously confronted. At the same time, before the outbreak of the Troubles, the political establishment in Northern Ireland always remained suspicious of literary regionalism, terrified, as Edna Longley remarks, that Ulster 'local' culture, whether Irish or Scots, might always simply be a Trojan horse that would turn out to be a cover for Irish national culture.[32] In the end, therefore, literary regionalism, sponsored by a left-liberal Protestant intelligentsia that never seriously engaged Northern nationalist alienation, and which was also unable to secure the support of the Protestant state establishment, remained the invertebrate project of a small, politically isolated stratum. Nevertheless, the regionalism pioneered by Hewitt and others has survived the period of its genesis. It was taken up in the 1970s, against the background of deepening conflict, by institutions such as the Arts Council of Northern Ireland and it remains important to the 'New Unionist' cultural agenda. Since his death in 1987, Hewitt has been adopted as an icon of a rational, progressive, non-sectarian liberal Unionism committed to the preservation of the Northern state within the UK.[33]

In the South, political independence, soured by the civil war that immediately ensued, led to the establishment of a socially conservative state that defined Irish identity not so much in Gaelic as in Catholic terms. Economic autarky, intended to reduce Irish dependency on Britain, witnessed the creation of several important state development projects, but did not deliver domestic economic vitality. The discrepancy between the Revivalist vision of a renovated Ireland

and the conservative, censorious and economically depressed society that actually emerged after 1922 stamped southern Irish literature with a sense of post-revolutionary disillusion and bitterness that is perhaps its most distinctive quality. A sense of alienation from the Southern state extends across the works of a whole range of southern writers who otherwise shared little in common. For some southern Anglo-Irish writers, many of whom had spearheaded the Literary Revival, the repressive Catholic culture of the new state confirmed their sense of political powerlessness and led them to lament the supposedly superior liberalism of their own 'lost' or threatened Protestant heritage. For the major modernists – Joyce, Beckett and O'Casey – artistic alienation from the 'Irish Ireland' ideal adopted by the new state was accentuated by the physical distance of self-chosen exile in Europe. A generation of socialist republican writers, who had fought in the war of independence and then on the losing side in the civil war, remained at home to become 'internal exiles' within the new dispensation. For these – Peadar O'Donnell, Liam O'Flaherty and Máirtín O'Cadhain – the Free State was conceived as the instrument of a collaborationist neocolonial bourgeoisie that had betrayed the radical possibilities of the revolutionary period. The satirical works of writers such as Austin Clarke, Flann O'Brien, Mervyn Wall and Patrick Kavanagh exploited and excoriated the gap between idealised images of Ireland cultivated by official state culture and the mundane realities of the new society. Writers of a more liberal character, such as Sean O'Faolain and Hubert Butler, became outspoken critics of the cultural provincialism of the new order. A later generation, including novelists Edna O'Brien, John McGahern and William Trevor cultivated a bleak naturalist aesthetic to present an anomic conception of small town and rural Ireland that countered the official pastoral versions of state and Church propaganda. In the period leading up to the formation of the state, writers had conceived of themselves as the heroic creators of the communal consciousness of a new nation. In the decades subsequent to its establishment, the whole function of the writer was re-cast so that writers increasingly saw their role in terms of individual dissent and critique: the artist not as visionary representative of 'a risen people' but as solitary and alienated victim of an arthritic society.[34]

In the late 1950s, the economic sterility associated with the rule of De Valera led to a radical *volte face* in the South that ushered in a new period of dramatic social change. Economic protectionism was abandoned and the country opened up to international (mostly US) investment and communications media. This was followed by political integration into the European Economic Community. The same period saw a gradual, and bitterly contested, disentangling of Church and state, and the emergence of a more secular middle class and intelligentsia. In this charged environment, the sense of alienation that had dominated Irish literature for decades solidified into a wider 'structure of feeling' antagonistic to almost everything identified as essential elements of 'nationalist Ireland'. In this new modernising drive, Catholicism, rural Ireland and anti-partitionist republicanism were increasingly conflated as a malign trinity of recalcitrant 'traditionalism' in Irish society that had stymied economic development and retarded liberal democracy for decades. The new neoliberal modernising discourse that has come to dominate Southern society since the sixties has as its object, as Francis Mulhern has wryly remarked, the creation of a 'really modern Ireland, whose historic other is that surmounted national project now called traditional'. Hence, whereas '[t]he object of De Valera's modernism was "Ireland"; the object of latter-day Ireland, its official good sense, is "being modern."'[35] In this climate, the simultaneous emergence of militant republicanism in the North was interpreted by many as a disastrous resurgence of the regressive and sectarian 'traditions' that the South itself was struggling to dispel. On the whole, the Southern intelligentsia read the Northern Troubles in terms of its own preoccupations with modernisation and with overcoming a conservative Catholic nationalism rather than through any serious systemic or structural engagement with the distinctive material circumstances of the Northern state.[36]

Though motivations and agendas differed, intellectual culture in the South since the outbreak of the Troubles has in some ways converged with Unionist intellectual culture in the North. Whatever their differences otherwise, the new intelligentsia in the South and Northern Unionists shared a common antipathy to militant Irish republicanism, which seemed to represent a traumatic re-visitation of a past that both states desperately wished to leave behind. The extent of this intellectual convergence, though, ought not to be overstated. To some extent, Unionists could interpret the Southern intelligentsia's increasingly critical rejection of 'traditional' Irish nationalism as belated vindication of their own repudiation of that nationalism a century earlier. But as the Southern intelligentsia became more convinced of its own putatively modern, secular, pro-European and post-nationalist credentials, it was also increasingly inclined to see *both* Unionists and republicans in the North as mired in atavistic 'traditions' inimical to its own gleaming modernity. Moreover, as the

South became an increasingly secular liberal democracy, the traditional Unionist claim that a United Ireland would inevitably constitute a Catholic theocracy ('Home Rule is Rome Rule') also became more difficult to sustain.

The decades of the Troubles in the North seem, to some degree, to have created the conditions for the emergence of the distinctive and inclusively Northern Irish literature that the period of Unionist political and cultural domination had never yielded. Since the late sixties, a new generation of writers – among whom poets and literary critics have been most distinguished – from both nationalist and Unionist backgrounds has emerged to international prominence. Whatever their political affiliations, these writers share a common preoccupation with the Northern conflict, setting literature in the North in recent decades at an emotional distance to that in the South with its more de-nationalising preoccupations. By the 1980s, the concept of a 'Northern renaissance', with its deliberate echo of the earlier nationalist Literary Revival in the south, and with its suggestion of a new proto-national literature, had become a matter of some controversy. At its root was the suggestion that the longstanding division of the island into two states was finally issuing in the emergence of two separate literatures.[37]

It would ultimately be simplistic, however, to see the literary 'renaissance' in the North during the Troubles simply in terms of divergence from the South. Though by no means an Irish nationalist cultural enterprise, that 'renaissance' is nevertheless quite closely linked to the nationalist minority's political and cultural assertiveness in this period. Several of its most distinguished poets – Seamus Heaney, John Montague, Paul Muldoon and Medbh McGuckian – are from a nationalist background. Though most of these poets have eschewed overt political commitment, at the level of both form and content their works have often served to excavate links with Gaelic literary traditions and with the wider literary and cultural history of the island as a whole. Hence the body of work they have produced implicitly contests the tendency in earlier Ulster literary regionalism to distance the North culturally from the rest of the island. Moreover, some writers from a Unionist background, such as poet and literary critic Tom Paulin or dramatist Stuart Parker, have attempted to recover the radical Protestant republican heritage of the eighteenth century to challenge orthodox concepts of Northern Protestant identity.

In the field of literary history, the most ambitious cultural enterprise undertaken in recent decades is probably that of the Field Day Theatre Company, a loosely federated Derry-based association of Northern writers and cultural activists. The declared object of the multi-volume *Field Day Anthology of Irish Writing*, assembled under the general editorship of Seamus Deane, was to challenge both narrowly nationalist and narrowly Unionist configurations of Irish cultural history. Since it was island-wide in scope, and since it insisted that despite the state divide the history of the island could still be conceived as a single metanarrative, the anthology was widely interpreted, and in some quarters fiercely resented, as an aggressive example of republican literary nation-building with an anti-partitionist agenda. The anthology was also heavily male-oriented in its selection of modern writers, and drew the fire of many feminists who made connections between its nationalising ambitions and gender bias. The very fact that the anthology was regarded by everyone, admirers and detractors alike, not as a merely belletristic activity but as a charged attempt to harness literature to the purpose of national self-fashioning demonstrated the extent to which literature was still consciously conceived on all sides as a crucial stake in the wider nation- and state-building projects on the island. The anthology's largely negative reception in media and academic circles also displayed perhaps just how difficult it can be to engage in literary nation-building in a late twentieth-century 'postmodernist' context in which canon-building of most kinds, and totalisations of all kinds, are commonly viewed as authoritarian gestures.[38]

In sum, then, the Northern literature that emerged during the Troubles does indeed have its own distinct aesthetic complexion and thematic preoccupations, but this literary activity has not yet been harnessed to any single overarching political agenda, and it cannot easily be construed, therefore, as the emergence of a distinct new protonational Northern Irish literature. The earlier Irish literary 'renaissance,' to which the current Northern one is recurrently compared, had its origins, as already noted, in the political decline of the old Anglo-Irish élite and the emergence of the new rural and professional Catholic classes in the south that created a new state. The contemporary period in the North, in contrast, has been characterised by political stalemate rather than by the emergence of a cohesive and dynamic new class capable of universalising its own interests and channelling social energies into a new state project. The last three decades have witnessed not so much the emergence of a decisive new class configuration in the North as a greater (though by no means complete) equalisation of power between the Protestant and Catholic middle classes and a slightly more even distribution of sovereignty status between Britain and Ireland. Recent Northern literature reflects this tentative balancing act of (a still dominant) Britishness and (a still emergent) Irishness rather than a qualitative break with the inherited cultural discourse of either sectors of the Northern population.

At the time of writing, the division of Ireland into two states has lasted almost eighty years, a period nearly twice as long as that during which Germany was divided. Over that period, the two societies on the island have developed under very different circumstances, and this has undoubtedly left its imprint on literary developments. Separate state broadcasting companies, separate arts councils, separate tourist and heritage industries, condition two different imagined communities, Northern and Southern, that largely correspond to the existing border. Nonetheless, another Irish nationalist imagined community transcending the border has also survived and continues to co-exist, though sometimes not without considerable tension, with the state-defined ones. In the contemporary Irish novel – the form conventionally most closely associated with the construction of national communities – it is notable that there are remarkably few narratives that deal simultaneously with Northern and Southern society. This 'shrinkage' of the novelistic imagination to fit the domain of the states rather than the island suggests that the state divide conditions the imaginative horizons of Irish novelists on both sides of the border, however much nationalists might wish it otherwise.

But even here certain qualifications need to be registered. Because of the Troubles, leading Southern dramatists, novelists and film-makers have attempted some imaginative engagements with Northern Ireland in recent times. Frank McGuinness's *Observe the Sons of Ulster Marching Towards the Somme* (1985), Vincent Woods's *At the Black Pig's Dyke* (1992), Eugene McCabe's *Death and the Nightingales* (1992), Dermot Healy's *The Goat's Song* (1994) and the films of Neil Jordan, Pat O'Connor and Jim Sheridan are notable examples. Although Healy's *A Goat's Song* is a rare exception, it is striking, though, that when Southern writers and film-makers do deal with the Northern crisis their narratives seldom include Southern characters, and that they are almost invariably set exclusively within the Northern state. This suggests that the Northern crisis, when it is engaged from the South, is usually seen from there in hermetically compartmentalised terms: the Northern Troubles, that is, are viewed not as part of a shared history that produced both states, but as a distinct regional problem with which Southerners may engage, but which has still little to do with the South. It would also appear that most of the imaginative traffic between the two states would seem to be between Northern and Southern writers from nationalist backgrounds. The contemporary generation of Northern Protestant novelists has in contrast displayed little interest in the South. In novels such as Maurice Leitch's *Poor Lazarus* (1969) and Glenn Patterson's *Fat Lad* (1992) the Protestant protagonists do travel across the border into the Republic, but the engagement with Southern society remains quite attenuated. In poetry there are, however, notable exceptions to this rule such as the work of Derek Mahon and Michael Longley. In various ways, then, the state division has cut quite deeply into the imaginative contours of contemporary Irish literature, yet the post-partition literary fault-lines do not always correlate tidily with the North–South political frontier.

While partitionist mentalities certainly exist, then, it would be difficult to assert that even after eight decades there are now two separate and distinct Northern and Southern state literatures in the same way that there were distinct East and West German ones during the Cold War. One reason for this is that in the island as a whole the domestic market for literature is too small to sustain major publishing industries. For an Irish writer, North or South, real commercial success and international status is determined by the reception attained in Anglophone Britain and the United States. American and British literary award systems, broadcasting and publishing industries and Irish Studies programmes play a major role in establishing literary reputation and prestige and, by extension, in consecrating domestic literary canons. Consequently, the pressure for writers in both jurisdictions to explicate their societies to British and American audiences is stronger perhaps than the need for Northern writers to engage Southern audiences or vice versa. While this discourages North–South dialogue and reinforces cultural distance on one level, it also contributes to a situation in which the literature produced in both states is commercially marketed, critically interpreted and consumed as regional versions of 'Irishness' rather than as separate national literatures.

The 'Irish Ireland' cultural agenda promoted by the Southern state began to disintegrate in the 1960s and 1970s when the state censorship apparatus established in 1929 was dismantled where literature was concerned at least (censorship was ratcheted up in other areas) and the country was opened up to international markets and media. In roughly the same period, the 'British Ireland' cultural agenda promoted by Unionists also came unstuck when the Northern state collapsed under Northern nationalist challenge and the British government resumed direct control of the polity. The cultural agendas in both states today, therefore, are in a kind of limbo, and the old alliance between culture and the nation-state is arguably shifting to one between culture and the global market.[39] After nearly three decades of conflict, however, the leading Northern nationalist political parties today demand parity of cultural esteem if a devolved government in Northern Ireland is to be re-established. While it is difficult to know what this patently formalist concept (which divorces culture from its social content) would actually mean in practice, it is clear that any renovated Northern Irish state will somehow have to accommodate Irish as well as British cultural nationalism. The attempt by Unionists to construct Northern Ireland as an exclusively British and Protestant society hermetically sealed off from the rest of the island would seem to have little future, therefore, whatever the future of political partition.

## IV

There are two obvious differences between the Israeli–Palestinian situation and the ones discussed so far. Firstly, in the German and Irish situations, the literatures mobilised by the partitioned states were each in the same language. (Despite its obeisance to the Irish language, Irish literature in English has remained the dominant literature in the Southern state.) Hence the scholarly controversies concerning the degree to which state division may be said to have resulted in the creation of one or two German or Irish national literatures. Since the national literatures of the Israelis and Palestinians are usually identified with Hebrew and Arabic respectively, the same types of questions would not seem to apply in this instance. Secondly, in the Irish and German situations, state division resulted in the creation of two rival states whereas in colonial Palestine partition resulted in the creation of an Israeli state that has no Palestinian counterpart to date. The Palestinian situation offers an intriguing example, therefore, of the ways in which a national literature is constructed in recent times by a people – many of whom live outside of the national territory they claim as homeland – without access to its own state apparatus. In this, the Palestinian situation resembles to some degree that of their Jewish national antagonists: in the case of both peoples nationalism has been profoundly shaped by the experience of statelessness and Diaspora, by an overwhelming sense of historical catastrophe, and by the need for return to the ancestral homeland.

The development of modern Hebrew as a national language and literature has been an integral element of the wider Zionist enterprise. Zionism, a national project devoted to the establishment of a modern Jewish nation-state in Palestine, emerged in Europe in the late nineteenth century.[40] Its central tenets were simple: to establish their national autonomy, Jews needed the same things other nations possessed: namely, their own land, their own state and their own language. The proposed Zionist state was intended to serve as the national homeland for Jews throughout the world, though the first waves of Zionist settlers in Palestine were drawn mostly from across Central and Eastern Europe. Yiddish was the prototypical language of the Jewish Diaspora but there were many others including Jewish varieties of Arabic, Aramaic, Greek, Persian, Spanish, French and so on.

As previously remarked, Ernest Gellner has argued that the construction of a modern nation-state has usually required 'the general imposition of a high culture on society' which supersedes the various dialects and 'low cultures' that had previously prevailed. The creation of a national high culture of this kind requires, he suggests, 'the general diffusion of a school-mediated, academy-supervised idiom, codified for the requirements of a reasonably precise bureaucratic and technological communication'. Given the linguistic diversity of the Jewish peoples involved in the Zionist project, the development of modern Hebrew language and literature represents a striking illustration of Gellner's thesis. Because Yiddish was identified as the language of the Diaspora and of religious anti-Zionists, Zionists regarded it as ultimately incompatible with their long-term ideological goals. There was, as Chaim Rabin has observed, an essential difference between the late-nineteenth-century Hebrew revival movement and the language movements associated with European nationalism.[41] In most European cases, and indeed in the Yiddish revival, the object of the language revival campaign was to find a way to lend to the 'low status' but widely spoken language of home and community literary and academic prestige. In the case of Hebrew (as indeed in that of the much less successful contemporary Gaelic revival in Ireland) the task was the opposite: to promote as an everyday vernacular a language not widely used in ordinary life, but whose classical literary status was already clearly established.

Until 1899, secular education in the small Jewish settlements in Palestine was usually in French and religious instruction in Yiddish. From the turn of the century, however, there was a gradual switch in the settlements to Hebrew medium schools (in which all subjects were taught through Hebrew), and kindergartens became the main instruments for developing Hebrew fluency and revernacularisation.[42] The intergenerational transmission of Hebrew therefore was essentially, as is the case with language transmission in many immigrant societies, from young to old rather than vice versa. For Zionism, modern Hebrew would serve as a *lingua franca* that would enable Jews in Palestine to overcome the 'Babel' of languages associated with the Diaspora. In so doing, it would allow for the assimilation of the settlers into a common national culture, distance them from their original gentile cultures, and channel their intellectual and emotional lives into a common Zionist project.[43] Attempts to found a chair of Yiddish at the Hebrew University in 1927 were defeated, and, until quite recently, Yiddish was not admitted to schools or universities or used on radio.[44]

The rich heritage of Jewish liturgical literature and religious philosophy, as well as the multiple European national literatures that had influenced the Jewish writers who settled in Palestine, meant that modern Hebrew literature could draw on an immensely rich palimpsest of foundational sources. Despite its relative novelty as a vernacular, therefore, modern Israeli literature in Hebrew has established itself as a distinct and vigorous national literature.[45] In crudely schematic terms, its development can be divided into a number of phases. In its initial stage, Israeli Hebrew literature was largely involved in the project of taking imaginative possession of what was ideologically the ancient Biblical 'homeland' but which was for settlers newly arrived from Europe a strange and alien landscape.[46] Zionist settlement in Palestine started in the 1880s and accelerated over subsequent decades under the British Mandate. Shaped by a combination of romantic nationalist, utopian, social darwinist and socialistic ideologies, Zionism in Palestine evolved its own distinctive colonial-settler culture. As in other settler cultures, the Zionist conquest of the settled territory was valorised as an epic in modernisation, which would 'tame the wilderness' and 'make the desert bloom'. But it was also conceived as a redemptive process of national regeneration. For the Zionists, the millennia of Jewish existence in the Diaspora were conceived as a relentless process of persecution and as a condition of moral and cultural decline, something that only a return to the ancient homeland and to a robust life of the soil could reverse. In contrast to the supposedly demoralised, effeminate and parasitic Jew in the East European *shtetl*, the new native-born Sabra in Palestine would be self-reliant, manly, independent and well able to defend himself.[47] Migration 'back' to the ancient Biblical homeland was therefore the prerequisite to the Jewish migration 'forward' to modernity, a journey up the evolutionary stream of time for which Jews needed their own nation-state.

The central role of the kibbutz in Zionist mythology may be understood in terms of this chronotopic paradigm. On the one hand, the kibbutzim that marked the outer edges of Jewish settlement were agricultural enterprises and as such represented the redemptive return to the soil that would allow Jews to escape the degenerative consequences of modernity represented by the commercial urban existence of the European *shtetl*. But the kibbutz was also an experiment in socialistic collectivism, and so represented the most utopian and advanced aspirations of the Zionist project. The kibbutz, in short, exemplified both the past-oriented return to the native soil and the future-oriented utopian leap into modernity intrinsic to the whole Zionist project. Although the majority of Jews in Palestine continued to live in urban areas, in the literature, cinema, folksong and school curricula of the pre-state *Yishuv* and of the subsequent Israeli State, the kibbutz was assigned a pre-eminent symbolic role in the national narrative.[48] The principle themes of Hebrew writing in this early settlement pre-state period shifted from the travails of the European Diaspora to the struggle to establish a new society in Palestine. The literature valorised and criticised the new society, attempted to detemine the nature of its future direction and development, debated its relationship to other centres of Jewish existence, and wrestled with the internal tensions of the Zionist enterprise.

In a later epic or heroic phase, Israeli Hebrew literature represented the struggle to build the Israeli state in a manner that underlined its revolutionary nationalist character and its supposedly anti-imperial disposition. The genocide of the Jews in Europe, the War of Independence, and the creation of the State of Israel in 1948 were the dominant experiences that conditioned the canonical writers in this period.[49] Because of Zionism's socialistic tendencies and sympathies with the Soviet Union in this period, much of the canonical novelistic literature in this phase, written by authors such as Moshe Shamir, S. Yizhar and Aharon Megged was influenced by the Russian social realist aesthetic. The rugged young native-born Israeli Sabra, depicted as an heroic or tormented visionary pioneer, emerged as the central figure in this literature. Many of the major writers in this period had direct links with the Israeli establishment and with the kibbutz movement. Their novels frequently express an idealised love of soil and landscape, contemplate the self-sacrifice demanded by the Zionist imperative, and struggle to convert Zionist dream into reality.

In the period since the establishment of Israel, however, the heroic and utopian conception of the Zionist project, and the socialist realist aesthetic, have been critically undermined and displaced. Since the 1960s, an anti-heroic and more existential and introspective aesthetic, one ostensibly less concerned with the collective Zionist epic and more so with the individual travails and quotidian stresses of daily life within Israeli society in a state of war, has dominated canonical Israeli literature. This 'state generation' is associated with several of contemporary Israel's most distinguished writers such as Amos Oz, A. B. Yehoshua, Yehuda Amichai, Amalia Kahana-Carmon, Nathan Zach, David Avidan, David Grossman and Yoram Kaniuk. As Israel became increasingly integrated into the world of global capitalism and more reliant on American political and economic support, it shed much of its earlier socialistic tendencies. The gradual shift away from socialist realism and from Zionism's collectivist ethos towards more 'modernist' and experimental literary currents and towards the celebration of more individualistic concerns has undoubtedly reflected this wider ideological reorientation. But this larger aesthetic transmutation also reflects the characteristic sense of post-revolutionary *tristesse* and disillusion with the heroic nationalist narrative that pervades many national literatures in the post-independence period, including Irish literature as argued earlier.[50]

Despite its internal diversity, capacity for self-criticism and many distinguished achievements, modern Israeli Hebrew literature is nevertheless intrinsically tied to the hegemony of the European or Ashkenazi Jews. In the pre-state period, the first waves of settlers in Palestine were comprised almost exclusively of Ashkenazi Jews, and their descendants have dominated political and cultural life in Israel since its foundation. In contemporary Israel, Oriental or Sephardic Jews – the majority of whom came to Israel from countries such as Egypt, Iraq, Iran, Algeria, Morocco and Yemen in the 1950s – constitute approximately 50 per cent of the population.[51] Palestinian Arabs with Israeli citizenship make up another 20 per cent. As Ella Shohat has observed, this means that almost 70 per cent of the current population of Israel is of 'Third World' rather than of European background, and Ashkenazi hegemony in Israel is therefore the hegemony of a demographic minority. (The percentage of the population of historic Palestine with 'Third World' background increases to 90 per cent if the Palestinians within the West Bank and Gaza are included.)[52] Seen in this context, the effective establishment of Hebrew literature as *the* national literature of the Israeli state clearly involves something more than a tool of national homogenisation as conceived by functionalists such as Gellner. Hebrew may indeed be a useful instrument of assimilation or homogenisation in Gellnerian terms. But it is also a medium with a distinct social and ethnic content that serves to naturalise the 'Western' character of Israeli society, to overwrite the Arabic associations of the landscape, and emotionally to distance Israeli society from the wider Arabic culture of the region.

In Zionist ideology, the Arab world was conceived to be at a much less advanced stage of civilisation than the Europe from which the Ashkenazi settlers came. In fact, as Ella Shohat remarks, most Ashkenazim had come from East European countries, on the periphery of the world capitalist system, that had entered the process of industrialisation and technological–scientific development roughly at the same time as the Sephardi countries of origin.[53] But since Zionism conceived of the Arab Middle East as a primitive world which would benefit from modern Western energy, the Sephardi Jews who began to arrive in large numbers in Israel in the 1950s were essentially conceived as primitives hamstrung by Oriental 'traditionalism.'

From this perspective, it was essential that the Sephardi Jews be desocialised of their own Arabic cultural heritage and resocialised by assimilation into the supposedly more technologically advanced and 'modern' Hebrew culture of the Ashkenazi. Discussing this, Shohat notes that David Ben-Gurion, founding father of the Israeli State, repeatedly expressed contempt for the Oriental Jews and in one statement insisted: 'We do not want Israelis to become Arabs. We are duty bound to fight against the spirit of the Levant, which corrupts individuals and societies, and preserve the authentic Jewish values as they crystallized in the Diaspora.' Similarly, for Abba Eban, one of Israel's most distinguished statesmen: '[the] object should be to infuse [the Sephardim] with an Occidental spirit, rather than allow them to drag us into an unnatural Orientalism.' 'One of the great apprehensions which afflict us,' he stated, 'is the danger lest the predominance of immigrants of Oriental origin force Israel to equalize its cultural level with that of the neighboring world.'[54] In an epistemic operation resembling that observed in Northern Ireland, the estrangement of Israel from the Arabic Middle East is internally recreated within the nation-state as a temporalised partition between Asheknazim and Sephardim, the latter, like Northern Irish Catholics, conceived in terms of the stereotypical defects of the 'tradition-bound' culture of the wider region.

For the Jewish writers who came to Israel from the Arabic world, therefore, there was little incentive to continue writing in Arabic. It would obviously take time to achieve the skill to write well in Hebrew, but to continue in Arabic was to write in the language of the enemies of the state. Though Arabic is an official language of Israel, Hebrew is the pre-eminent language of its education system, media and mainstream publishing industry. Hence to write in Arabic was also to cut oneself off from the mass of the domestic reading public and to confine oneself to a tiny audience within Israel. Jewish writers in Arabic could still seek a public in the wider Arab world, but after 1948 the hostility there to anyone associated with 'the Zionist entity' limited publication opportunities. Although some of the older generation continued to work in Arabic, most younger writers, therefore, switched to Hebrew. Two of the most distinguished, Shime'on Ballas and Sami Mikhael, both from Baghdad, would eventually write important novels in Hebrew, which dealt with the Jewish enclaves of Iraq and the travails of the Sephardi assimilation into Israeli society.[55] Nevertheless, as Ammiel Alcalay has observed, despite their enormous popularity in Israel, Sephardi writers are seldom translated into other languages that represent Israeli literature to the wider world.[56]

The relationship between the various languages mediated by the Israeli state, then, is not simply one in which one, Hebrew, assumes the functions of a 'high' culture and is elevated above others such as Arabic or Yiddish, destined to remain on (as Gellner would have it) as 'low' or 'folk' cultures. The Sephardis who arrived in Israel had written in a classical Arabic, which had enjoyed in the Middle East the status of a 'high' culture. But in Israel both Sephardi and Israeli–Palestinian literature in Arabic was actively demoted to a 'low' culture – in effect turned into museumised 'folk' cultures and valued essentially for their associations with the past in the hallowed but eviscerated way 'folk' languages tend to be. The literary establishment, in contrast, regards Hebrew as the dynamic 'modern' 'living' language in which the nation works out its destiny.

1948 is for Israelis the inaugural moment of triumph when the homeless Jewish nation finally re-rooted itself in the Holy Land and founded its state. But for Palestinians it is the moment of catastrophe, *al-nakbah*, that uprooted and dispersed them as a nation and consigned them to stateless exile. The conditions in which Palestinians have lived within Israel, in the West Bank and Gaza, and in the rest of the Middle East since then have varied enormously, and the Palestinian literature produced within these different zones displays its own typical preoccupations and perspectives. Hence, as Edward Said observes, '[t]here are many different kinds of Palestinian experience, which cannot all be assembled into one. One would have to write parallel histories of the communities in Lebanon, the Occupied Territories, and so on. That is the central problem. It is almost impossible to imagine a single narrative.'[57]

At the same time, it is precisely the lack of a common political home that has made the construction of a national literature so important to contemporary Palestinians. In the absence of an available nation-state, the development of a national literature has enabled Palestinians to reinforce their sense of themselves as a distinct people and to express solidarity across the disjunctive locales of Palestinian existence in the face of repeated political reversals and calamities. Literature, that is, is one of the ways in which the scattered sectors of the Palestinian people can be imaginatively connected in the here and now even if actual statehood remains constantly deferred.

In the period before 1967, cultural contact between Palestinians in the various sectors was quite attenuated. Palestinians inside Israel, in particular, were cut off from their co-nationals not only in the Diaspora but also in the West Bank and Gaza. They were also stigmatised in the Arab world for their association with 'the Zionist entity' and generally regarded with hostility by the mainstream Palestinian national organisations. Ironically, it was the Israeli seizure of the remaining Palestinian territories in the West Bank and Gaza in 1967 that allowed Palestinians in Israel and the Occupied Territories to re-open contact after two decades. Moreover, since Israel now controlled all of historic Palestine, the Diasporic organisations gradually gained an increased appreciation of the crucial strategic significance of those who still lived within the territorial homeland. In these altered circumstances, the ostracism of the Israeli Palestinians was revoked to some degree, and throughout the 1970s and 1980s national organisations within the different zones of Palestinian existence worked to strengthen the bonds between the various communities. Writers and intellectuals in the Occupied Territories and throughout the Diaspora lands were now published in Arabic journals and newspapers in Israel, and Israeli–Palestinian writers were in turn published across the wider Palestinian and Arab world. [58]

Nevertheless, despite the establishment of such networks, the struggle to overcome sectoral division is ultimately more complicated than simply maintaining cultural exchange across state borders. The deeper divergence stems from the fact that in the different sectors of Palestinian society literature works to quite different ends. For Israeli-Palestinians, writing in an Israeli state that sees Hebrew literature written by Jews as *the* state culture, one of the functions of literature is to contest the marriage of culture and state or, in other words, to dispute the idea of 'one state, one culture.' Israeli–Palestinian literature, developed by leading writers such as Emile Habiby or Anton Shammas, asserts that Israel is a country made up of different nationalities with different cultures, something impeded by the Zionist identification of the Israeli state and Hebrew national culture with Jewishness. For Palestinians outside Israel, on the other hand, literature has been mobilised as part of a wider national struggle, the object of which is to seek a state where the Palestinian nation might be reintegrated. This state-seeking nationalism, which has contracted its territorial ambitions in recent decades to the West Bank and Gaza, aims towards the one-state-one-homogeneous-nation ideal that Israeli-Palestinians reject in Israel. There is, then, a division within Palestinian nationalism as to whether its end-goal ought to be a territorial nation-state in the West Bank and Gaza, which would marry a single culture and state as Israel does, or a two-nation-state across historic Palestine where Jewish and Arab cultures could enjoy equal status. Literature can help Palestinians to maintain a sense of common nationality across state borders, but national literatures are not only about imagining communities. They also involve a struggle for control over how those communities are defined, and it is here that some of the deepest fissures within Palestinian writing emerge.

The condition of statelessness, moreover, is not simply about the scattering of the nation; stateless communities in most instances are also subjected to economic super-exploitation and political oppression. In many areas of the Middle East, Palestinians exist as a subaltern and exploited labour force within states that either deny them citizenship altogether or allow them only the provisional forms of citizenship reserved for non-nationals. Israeli-Palestinians enjoy Israeli citizenship but the definition of Israel as a Jewish state reduces them to second- or third-class citizens and in material terms most occupy the lower strata of the Israeli labour force. In addition, they have reason to fear that they might one day be expelled from Israel and transferred to a Palestinian state – should one emerge – in exchange for Jewish settlers in the West Bank.

One of the most striking characteristics of modern Palestinian literature, therefore, is that it is a national literature that in its characteristic thematic concerns most closely resembles the expatriate or *gastarbeiter* literatures written by migrants working in foreign states far from their own homelands. There is the same constant preoccupation in Palestinian literature with crossing state borders, with encounters with hostile state officials, with the need for documentation, with the ways in which migrant communities are targeted as scapegoats, with the absence of security, with nostalgia for distant relatives, and so on, that characterise *gastarbeiter* literatures generally. This Kafkaesque sense of the enormously oppressive weight of the modern state system pervades contemporary Palestinian literature.

Ghassan Kanafani's short stories, for instance, describe the destitution and trauma suffered by stateless Palestinians in the refugee camps after their expulsion in 1948. Novels such as Kanafani's *Men in the Sun* (1963) or Ibrahim Nasrallah's *Prairies of Fever* (1985) deal with the alienation experienced by Palestinian workers compelled by economic necessity to work in the wealthy Gulf States. In Sahar Khalifeh's *Wild Thorns* (1976) the subject is the daily grind of workers in the West Bank living under the routinised oppression of military occupation or compelled to seek work building up an Israel that is simultaneously systematically destroying their own Palestinian society. Emile Habiby's *The Secret Life of Saeed: the Ill-Fated Pessoptimist* (1974) and Anton Shammas's *Arabesques* (1986) expose the discriminations exercised by the Israeli State against Israeli-Palestinians. In novels written by Jabra Ibrahim Jabra and memoirs by Fadwa Tuquan and Edward Said – all members of the Palestinian high-bourgeoisie before 1948 – the same sense of alienation dominates. In their case, that alienation is conditioned not so much by personal victimisation as by a sense of the powerful systemic interests that work to disable the Palestinian people.

In 1983, Nadine Gordimer remarked that 'the sum of various states of alienation is the nature of South African literature today'.[59] The same might be said of Palestinian literature since the 1948 catastrophe. This is a literature predicated on the desire for a Palestinian nation-state, but the sensibility that predominates is one that insistently registers the oppressive nature of the current state system in the Middle East. While there is a deep desire that Palestinians might find refuge in a nation-state of their own, there is also a countervailing sense that it is the wider nation-state system in the region that is the real impediment to emancipation and that while this larger system remains unchanged a Palestinian state will not really alter matters. Hence the relentless insistence on the way in which the region-wide state system strangulates desire and an almost utopian desire for a non-nationalist Arab unity in Kanafani's works. Hence, too, the determination by Edward Said in *Orientalism* (1978) and *Culture and Imperialism* (1993) to expand the specific 'Palestinian question' into a wider diagnosis of the dynamics of imperialism generally. What one gets in Palestinian literature, then, is both the *gastarbeiter*'s gritty 'ground level' experience of the underbelly of the Middle East state system and, in writers such as Kanafani and Said, sweeping 'bird's eye' overviews that insist that the seizure of state power and the attainment of emancipation are not identical.

In situations such as Germany and Korea, where a single national community is bisected by a Cold War frontier, a typical narrative structure that emerges is one that recounts how families severed by the border seek reunion after periods of separation.[60] The device allows for imaginative exploration of the different ways in which the two severed societies have developed while at the same time telling a story that combines human and national interests. Since 1967, the same device plays an increasingly prominent position in Palestinian literary and autobiographical narrative. Some early examples include Emile Habiby's short story collection, *Six Stories of the Six Day War* (1968), and Ghassan Kanafani's novella *Return to Haifa* (1969). Both describe the traumatic reunions after decades of separation made possible, ironically, only by yet another Israeli victory. In novels which appeared in subsequent decades, such as Khalifieh's *Wild Thorns* and Anton Shammas's *Arabesques*, or indeed in visual documentary versions such as Edward Said's 'In Search of Palestine' (1998), the same device continues to recur.

It is in these narratives of return that Palestinian literature enacts its own distinctive version of the temporal dialectic of tradition and modernity encountered in other literatures. To return to Palestine, the natal homeland, is always in these narratives a pilgrimage to renew contact with a lost past. Sometimes the site of that past – the family home, the village, the ancestral grave, the orchard – has literally been erased or survives only as ruin. But even where the house survives intact, the surrounding Israeli social context serves only to accentuate its foreignness and the *heimlich* still becomes the *unheimlich*. What has dissolved this Palestinian past is an Israeli version of modernisation, which is always in these narratives, understandably enough, a regressive modernity. In most accounts, the pre-partition landscape represents a version of pastoral – with its sedate, sleepy rhythms and soft contours – that is pressed and beaten by Israeli modernisation into a graceless, regimented, standardised modernity utterly indifferent to local texture or temporality. What appears, in other words, is a version of Israeli modernity as the gray tyranny of instrumental reason, blindly indifferent to the human and ecological disasters that secure its triumph. Generally in these returns, the returnee is unable to locate himself in any space or time. The pre-1948 Palestinian past has utterly disappeared or is reduced to a sad spectre of its former self; that past cannot be re-entered. But the returnee cannot find anchor in an Israeli present either because Israel constitutes a bad modernity: a colonial-settler penal colony, a transplanted Europe, a site of transcendental homelessness. The lack of any hospitable temporality to inhabit, the eviction from both past and present, inspires mourning and melancholy – the condition Freud famously diagnosed as one whereby the internalisation of loss signifies a despairing longing for reunification. Separated, then, not only by the manichean segregation of space typical of all colonies, but by a chronotopic partition as well, dialogue or mutual recognition between the returned Palestinian and the resident Israelis is inevitably difficult as a result.[61]

As mentioned earlier, contacts between the various sectors of Palestinian literature have been strengthened since 1967, but this does not seem matched by a corresponding level of imaginative engagement with Israeli society. In the major Palestinian novels that have appeared during this period, sustained explorations of Israeli society are still comparatively rare, though this is less so in the Israeli–Palestinian case. In Habiby's *The Pessoptimist*, for example, the friendship between Saeed, the Israeli–Palestinian protagonist, and Jacob, an Arabic-speaking Sephardi Jew, represents an imaginative attempt to engage with the oppressive ways in which each of these 'Orientalised' communities has been integrated into Israeli society. In Shammas's *Arabesques*, an Arab family saga written in Hebrew, one of the characters is an Israeli writer, Yeshoua Bar-On, a thinly veiled depiction of the internationally distinguished Sephardi Israeli writer A. B. Yehoshua. Through the encounter between the narrator and Bar-On, Shammas explores the hierarchies of power that structure the relationship between Israel's dominant Jewish and minority Israeli–Palestinian cultures. Sustained imaginative encounters with Israeli society of this sort are indispensable if Palestinians are to build the cross-cultural coalitions that might allow for a transformed Israel–Palestine to be built, not in some utopian future, but in the problematic here and now.[62]

Both Israeli and Palestinian literatures have their own distinct problems. In Israel, a prestigious literature in Hebrew has been created. But that literature has been closely wedded to the political, economic and cultural ascendancy of the European Jewish community in Israel, and it has served to underpin the Zionist conception of Israel as an advanced 'Western' society hermetically sealed off from the surrounding 'backward' Arab world. The Ashkenazi-dominated literary establishment there has tried to distance Israeli culture from the adjoining Middle Eastern culture by stressing its European character, just as white South Africans once tried to distance their state from the rest of the African continent or as Northern Irish Unionists have wanted to distance their polity from the island of Ireland. All three states have attempted to assert that they do not really belong to the surrounding environments and that they are really much closer to the putatively more modern culture, temperament and temporality of the European metropole. For Jews from the Arab world, who now constitute a majority of the Israeli population, assimilation into Israeli national culture, therefore, has always entailed devaluation of the Arabic dimensions of their own cultural heritage. Israeli-Palestinians are doubly disenfranchised since they are disqualified on both religious and cultural grounds (as non-Jews and Arab Orientals) from the official national culture. Though there is no automatic correspondence of interest between Israeli-Palestinians and Oriental Jews in Israel, there is a growing challenge on a variety of fronts to the established Ashkenazi bias in national culture and by extension to the Ashkenazi bias in the Israeli literary canon. From a conservative Ashkenazi perspective, this is usually conceived as a lamentable cultural degeneration as Israel, to recall the words of Abba Eban, is perceived to be dragged 'into an unnatural Orientalism'.

To this extent, Israel's cultural dilemma is not unlike Northern Ireland's. In Israel and Northern Ireland, the culture sponsored by the state was designed to estrange it from the contiguous Arab and Irish cultures of the bordering nation-states. But in neither state were Arabs or Irish ever simply beyond the state frontiers, the 'barbarians' were always-already within the gates. The difficulty for both Israel and Northern Ireland, then, is that to grant democratic recognition to the national culture of their minorities, they will also have to re-imagine their cultural relationship to the wider neighbouring regions as well.

A distinctively Palestinian national literature is a more recent historical project than its Israeli counterpart. To many observers, the correspondences between the present Palestinian situation and that confronted by Zionists in the early twentieth century are striking. Two scattered and stateless peoples, it is regularly remarked, have built up national movements competing for the same territory from bases largely outside the proposed national territory. Both assert an absolutely sacred bond with a specific stretch of territory, but in both literatures this vies with a countervailing sense of homelessness and dispossession. As Carol Bardenstein notes, Jewish insistence on rootedness in the Holy Land is both extraordinarily persistent and very precarious. The earliest Jewish narratives, she remarks, are characterised by restlessness, tropes of banishment, settling down, wandering, exile and return. Adam and Eve are banished from Eden; Abraham is told by God to leave his birthplace to settle in Canaan; Joseph settles in Egypt and the Exodus is followed by decades of wandering through the desert. Cataclysmic defeats and dispersal repeatedly interrupt relatively short-lived periods of stability in the Promised Land. The obverse of the obsession with rootedness, therefore, is an anxious sense of just how precarious that rootedness is.[63] Today, however, it is the Palestinians who have become the exemplary figures of statelessness and restless exile. But they, too, insist on their right to return, on their allegiance to the lands from which they have been evicted.

These cultural symmetries between national antagonists are important, but if detached from the underlying structural politics of the historical situation, they can conceal as much as they reveal. When the Zionist movement was launched in the late nineteenth century, much of the world was still under colonial rule and the modern global system of nation-states had not yet been established in the Middle East. It was in this context that Zionists were able to secure alliances with the major imperial powers of the day. In their attempt to build a Jewish state in Palestine, they were not confronting the armed might of an already sovereign Palestinian state but only a comparatively weak, mostly agrarian society, the destiny of which was in Ottoman and then later British hands. In contrast, Palestinians have had to take on an independent state that is the dominant military power in the region and which enjoys the consistent support of the world's major superpower. Palestinians, moreover, have waged their national struggle at a time when the neo-colonial state system in the Middle East has created conditions inimical to the emergence of any new states that might upset the established order. The exilic Jewish past may resemble the exilic Palestinian present, then, but the emancipation of the two peoples from the problematic present must be imagined in ways quite different to the colonialist modernisation strategies by which Zionism attained its goals.

## V

From these surveys a few general conclusions about the connections between nation, state and literature in partitioned societies may be deduced. In the first instance, it should be clear that any comprehensive attempt to investigate these issues needs to advance at two separate (though not finally distinct) levels: (i) the institutionalisation of national literatures by the divided states as part of a wider network of meaning-generating systems; (ii) the responses to political division in individual works and genres inserted into the force-field of these national literatures. Let us deal briefly with each of these in turn.

Partition involves the creation of new state units within what had previously been a single geographical area and state unit. Though new state borders can be drawn up quite rapidly, the divided states cannot usually disentangle cultural identities quite so speedily. It takes not simply time, but important social transformations – the widening of educational systems, the emergence of an indigenous intelligentsia, the creation of reading publics – for new national literatures to emerge. The task of establishing social distance between the newly divided state units, therefore, proceeds over several generations. States that wish to defend and maintain partition will usually attempt to occlude the historico-cultural connections that tie them to the wider territorial unit from which they separated. States that oppose the division of the original unit invariably, on the other hand, construct partition as a lamentable national tragedy and assert ongoing ties to the original territorial unit. Even where states declare their commitment to overcoming partition, the incentive, political will or capacity to do so may be limited. In most instances, the attempt to consolidate the state already established takes priority over declared commitments to reunification.

What I have sought to illustrate here is that post-partition processes of state estrangement are consistently elaborated in terms of a dualistic conception of evolutionary progress divided between the different temporalities and temperaments of tradition and modernity. This chronotopic paradigm defines itself as a dialectical relationship between conditions of 'backwardness' and 'advance', measured in terms of a silent assumption whereby 'true' modernity remains an endlessly deferred condition, always somewhere further up the river of evolutionary time. Imported into the colonies by the twin structures of capitalism and colonialism, this dualistic opposition was initially used by the metropolitan settlers to legitimate their modernising mission, but hidden within it was a history of violence and exploitation central to the dialectic, which was even its dynamic. Invariably, though, it was also taken up by anti-colonial nationalists who accepted the dualistic opposition of tradition and modernity and tried to re-inflect it to their own ends, a process which would see 'modern' European institutions and systems indigenised by revitalised native cultural traditions. Transposed onto peoples as well as regions, the same discursive system was incorporated into the meaning-generating structures of the post-partitionist state orders in Ireland and Palestine. It was deployed by states such as Northern Ireland and Israel to ratify politically indefensible partitions and to estrange them from their 'backward' Irish or Arab hinterlands and their own unwanted Irish or Arab elements. The same dualistic categories have also been used by Irish and Palestinian nationalists to oppositional purpose, but the end-result is usually that the in-built double bind simply tightens. Struggling to outdo each other by being more 'modern,' or by discovering putatively happier marriages of the traditional and the modern than the other can do, the competing post-partition states simply reinforce the colonial-capitalist ideologies of developmentalism and statism used to legitimate the division and stratification of the peoples during the colonial period.

If we turn from literature as institution to individual literary texts, as we will do in Part Two, it should be clear that the relationship between individual literary texts and partition ought not to be conceived purely in terms of texts that deal with the original event of partition or with current state frontiers. Contrary to the view expressed in certain types of 'high' historiography, partition is not simply an episode that happened in 1921 or 1948 that is now over and done with, a thing in the past. The division of a state always has major social consequences that extend over several generations and that reach into many different aspects of political and civil society in the new states. For this reason, 'partition literature' ought not to be restrictively conceived as an independent genre, but as a wider body of works that deals with the multiple collateral consequences of state division.[64]

*Part Two*

Chapter 3

# 'Fork-tongued on the border bit': partition and the politics of form in contemporary narratives of the Northern Irish conflict

In a poem titled 'Whatever You Say Say Nothing', Seamus Heaney has written about the obligatory silences, clichés and canny evasions on sensitive political issues that are a condition of polite social conversation between Catholics and Protestants in Northern Ireland. Such constraints, as well as the ambivalence of Northern middle-class nationalists towards a state in which they have considerable economic investment but little emotional stake ('We're on the make / As ever'), together with their desire to distance themselves from republican militarism, has rendered many, Heaney suggests, 'fork-tongued on the border bit'.[1] The phrase resonates. Read one way, 'border bit' suggests a rote position on a jaded topic, an inherited and automatic rather than seriously considered response to the border issue. But the phrase might as easily suggest that the border has grown deeply into the groove of nationalist self-consciousness; that it is a 'bit' that chafes because, complex sentiments about it having had to be curbed for so long, a language adequate to their expression does not exist. It may suggest, that is, that various modes of censorship, including self-censorship, have generated elaborate circumlocutions that signal positions on the partition question even when they appear to side-step that controversial topic altogether.

The border that partitions the island of Ireland has a long and contentious history. Its establishment between 1912 and 1925 was contemporaneous with the extensive redrawing of international frontiers that followed World War I, when the borders of Eastern Europe were reconstructed to create the states of Yugoslavia and Czechoslovakia and when Britain and France superintended the carving up of the Middle East into the polities of Lebanon, Syria, Transjordan, Iraq, Kuwait and the Mandate of Palestine. All of these frontiers would later generate considerable conflict, and by the end of the twentieth century many of these states would be shattered by communal violence. Unlike other borders redrawn in Europe at the time, the partitioning of Ireland was determined neither by local plebiscite nor instituted under international mediation. Instead, that partition was implemented under the domestic auspices of the British government and was settled along lines that essentially reflected the balance of coercion then prevailing between British forces and Northern Unionists, on one side, and Irish nationalists, on the other. The settlement ratified in 1925 took little account of the interests of Northern Irish nationalists, who found themselves the second-class citizens of a state specifically designed to perpetuate Unionist power. By the late 1960s, the balance of forces obtaining in the early twentieth century had shifted considerably, however, and the 1925 settlement began to come apart under the weight of its own insufficiencies, giving rise to what would become the longest running conflict in contemporary Western Europe.[2]

Given its turbulent history, one of the more remarkable things about this border between Northern Ireland and the Irish Republic is what must be called, for want of a better term, its discursive invisibility. There are numerous ways in which this 'invisibility' is sustained. Since its establishment as a state, the Republic of Ireland has maintained the official fiction that it is Ireland *tout court*. Logo-maps of the Republic usually represent not the twenty-six county territory it administers but the island as a whole. Logo-maps of Northern Ireland, on the other hand, generally represent that state as if 'Ulster' were a separate island altogether rather than one corner of the landmass called 'Ireland'.[3] Both strategies obfuscate the reality of the political border that joins and separates the two states: the border is rendered invisible either to produce a geographical unity or to represent Northern Ireland as a wholly detached space without a contentious land-border at all. For the British, Northern Ireland is, of course, part of the United Kingdom of Great Britain and Northern Ireland, but the idea of 'the island race' is so entrenched in British nationalism that Northern Ireland is rarely considered part of the British 'island story' at all.[4] Paul Fussell writes, with telling parenthesis: 'The British are singularly sensitive to land frontiers because (with the exception of the one embarrassing line separating Ulster from Ireland) they have none.'[5] The structure of Fussell's sentence, not to mention his conflation of Northern Ireland with the larger province of Ulster, perfectly reflects what has been official British policy with regard to Northern Ireland since its establishment: claiming it as an integral part of Great Britain, while simultaneously bracketing it for practical and political purposes as an embarrassingly anomalous 'place apart'. In different ways and for different purposes, then, the Irish Republic, Northern Ireland and the United Kingdom have all striven discursively to occlude the most militarised border in the archipelago.

The 'invisibility' of this disputed border is predicated on and maintained by a complex lamination of social forces since all of the parties involved have had reason to be circumspect about the issue. While 'defending the border' is one of the shibboleths of Northern Unionism, the circumstances of the border's establishment and the coercion needed to maintain it are issues that few Unionists have cared to acknowledge. The insistence that 'good fences make good neighbours' sums up the Unionist line on the border, but Unionists have sound reason not to look too deeply into the history of how those 'fences' were constructed, which would require acknowledging that they owe more to imperial imposition than to democratic values. For Irish nationalists, it has always been easier to invoke the ideal of a 'United Ireland' than to say how a border that the Unionist majority in Northern Ireland clearly wishes to maintain can practically be eliminated. As the existing state institutions on either side of the boundary have come to serve increasingly important functions in the everyday lives of the Northern and Southern populations, the practicalities of reunification have grown more complex and equivocation on the subject more byzantine.

In some respects, of course, the reluctance of many politicians and the intelligentsia to delve too deeply into the question of state borders is understandable. The subject of partition is dangerously divisive; historically, 'the border bit' has been cynically exploited by demagogues on all sides; in many places across the world scholarship on disputed borders has been appropriated for ugly political ends. Nevertheless, reticence and obfuscation do not make problems go away. The twenty-five years of continuous warfare prior to the 1994 cease-fire and the current 'peace process' have in many ways hardened the pre-existing communal divides in Northern Ireland. The emergence of 'no-go' areas, so-called 'peace-lines' that barricade off Protestant and Catholic districts, and territorial markings such as painted kerbstones and mural graffiti, create the impression of a balkanised state continuously on the verge of disintegration. This fragmentation is so extensive that it could be argued that since the 1970s the partition of Ireland no longer stopped at the inter-state border: the militarisation of local territorial boundaries and the increased segregation of its two communities have effectively produced a whole series of internal partitions within Northern Ireland as well.[6] This territorial segregation is most visible and intense in working-class areas. Middle-class residential areas are more intermixed, but the prevalence of separate schooling systems, separate churches, separate cultural institutions and political parties ensure that the communal divide is largely maintained even where residential segregation is not.

Thus while a certain reticence on the border question may appear commendable, there is a darker side to it, one that stems not from restraint but from a highly invested occlusion of the many ways in which the Northern conflict is imbricated in the longer history and wider structure of the British and Irish state system. During the decades before the current peace process, even as they extended their stewardship over the Northern conflict, both the UK and Republic of Ireland state governments gradually evolved strategies and ideologies of containment designed to downplay as much as possible their own involvement in the struggle and to suggest that its roots lay exclusively in the intractable sectarianism of Northern Ireland's hostile communities.[7] This allowed both states to represent themselves as largely disinterested 'external' brokers working to help the two 'internal' communities overcome unfortunate legacies of sectarian bigotry. For the British, this policy, like the original partition settlement, helped to insulate the Northern problem so that it impinged as little as possible on the rest of the UK and so that it did not provoke deeper questions about the whole edifice of that state. Since its physical proximity to Northern Ireland is greater and since it would consequently be much more directly affected should the 'Troubles' dramatically explode, containment has also been the priority of the Republic of Ireland, its constitutional territorial claim to the whole island notwithstanding.

The policy of containment, however, was never simply a military matter. The attempt by both the British and Irish states to try to manage the Troubles in harmony with their own (occluded) interests inevitably conditioned intellectual conceptions of the situation as well. Since 1968 an enormous social-scientific literature has accumulated on the Troubles, making it one of the most written about conflicts in the world. As John Whyte noted in his magisterial survey of this material in 1991, by the early 1970s the intellectual 'dominance of the internal-conflict approach [to understanding the conflict] was assured'.[8] This interpretative model perceives exogenous forces (whether imperialism or wider archipelagic processes of state formation) as being largely irrelevant to the conflict in Northern Ireland. Instead, it diagnoses the sources of conflict in the intrinsic conditions and political culture of the region itself, and hence looks largely to internal solutions as well.

The ascendancy of the 'internal conflict' model in the 1970s and 1980s owed much to the rather crude versions of some of the earlier modes of interpretation it displaced. Nevertheless, the fact that the internal conflict hermeneutic emerged alongside and converged philosophically with the containment policies of the British and Irish states is hardly accidental. What both state policy and this mode of analysis share is the tendency to treat Northern Ireland as a self-enclosed unit of analysis (as though the conflict had little to do with the determination of that unit itself). By separating off Northern Ireland as a discrete unit of analysis in this way, this particular mode of scripting the Troubles at best underestimates, and often ignores, three salient points: firstly, the degree to which the whole issue of state allegiance (as opposed to local sectarian bigotry or communal chauvinism) is fundamental to the conflict; secondly, that the conflict is the product of a historical system of relationships that in its origins and dynamics operates at the level of the two islands; and, thirdly, the degree to which its own interpretative frame predisposes this mode of analysis towards an 'internal settlement' as opposed to one that would entail some more radical reconstruction of the state order in the archipelago as a whole.[9]

Given the tremendous contradictions that stem from the Republic of Ireland's determination to contain the Northern conflict within that state, on the one hand, and its declared commitment to the ideal of unification, on the other, it is not surprising that it is in the Republic that the most fundamental projects of rewriting that crisis have taken place. The concerted militant nationalist campaign in Northern Ireland began at a time when the old nationalist élite in the South was finally replaced by a post-revolutionary generation whose primary commitment was to 'modernising' the seriously distressed southern economy by means of attracting multinational investment. When the militant republicans in the North appropriated for themselves the southern state's revolutionary nationalist heritage, the southern élite accelerated its drive to divest itself of the increasingly embarrassing trappings of its own revolutionary nationalist past. Moreover, the atrocities carried out by the militants in the name of Irish reunification alienated many southern nationalists, ironically widening the rift between North and South that the militants hoped to overcome. It is in this context that the huge volume of 'revisionist' historiography that has dominated academic enterprise in the Republic over the past several decades needs to be understood.[10]

A fundamental goal of this revisionist enterprise is to expose what it sees as the inherently sectarian, violent, irrational and anti-democratic propensities of Ireland's revolutionary nationalist tradition. One of its central thrusts is to displace interpretations of Irish history in terms of colonialism and imperialism because these are deemed to lend themselves to dangerously populist and Anglophobic interpretations of the Irish past and, by extension, to lend credence to the militant republican campaign in the North. The revisionist assault on what it perceives as the simple-minded tendency in Irish nationalist 'mythology' to attribute all the country's ills to the centuries of British rule undoubtedly has its salutary side. But in their anxiety to correct such prejudices, revisionists often seem either to dismiss the issue of imperialism altogether or to construe it as an essentially progressive process of modernisation. Revisionists typically conceive of themselves as an iconoclastic liberal avant garde boldly shattering 'traditional' nationalist myths institutionalised by a conservative state and embraced by a compliant populace. What this analysis misses, however, is the degree to which in critically challenging old orthodoxies the revisionists were in fact uncritically endorsing new ones: the revisionist critique of revolutionary nationalism, that is, has comported comfortably with the southern élite's attempt to integrate the state into the global capitalist economy and the European Union. As an historical enterprise, revisionism is at least as much in service to the state and in thrall to the times as the old nationalist historiography it displaced.

While its critique of 'traditional' nationalism has sometimes been cogent and impressive, the revisionist project's claim to exemplify progressive liberal and democratic values in opposition to the old conservative Catholic nationalism and to illiberal republicanism is questionable. Irish revisionism has sometimes displayed an acute awareness of the artificiality of national identities, but it has had remarkably little to say about the construction or function of national states as political units within a grossly uneven world system. Because it is theoretically indifferent to such matters, its critique of Irish nationalism has always remained a narrowly moral one. For some of its most vocal public intellectuals, revisionism in any event is essentially concerned, as Liam O'Dowd has observed, with redefining the 'Irish nation' in order to make it coterminous with the Southern Irish state – thereby divesting that state of the awkward 'supplement' of the Catholic nationalists in the North.[11]

The later career of Conor Cruise O'Brien, the most internationally distinguished Irish revisionist intellectual, discloses some of the more authoritarian tendencies that lie behind Irish revisionist liberalism. Following his appointment as Minister for Posts and Telegraphs in the Irish Republic in 1973, O'Brien refined Section 31 of the Irish Broadcasting Act that provided for government censorship of the national media and airwaves. As a result of the changes introduced, the most prominent groups excluded from directly addressing the Irish public were the Provisional IRA and Provisional Sinn Féin, but the remit was extended to include any organisation proscribed by the British government in Northern Ireland. This censorship, like the tendency by historical revisionists to construe their mission in terms of an agon between the supposedly neutral and dispassionate 'objectivity' of the professional historian and the dangerous populist 'mythologies' embraced by the indoctrinated masses, displays the same patrician distrust of the Irish public, and the same tendency to conflate criticism of British rule in Ireland with IRA apologetics. Many of the leading public intellectuals who have most loudly evangelised revisionism – including John A. Murphy, Eoghan Harris, Ruth Dudley Edwards and Cruise O'Brien himself – have worked as columnists for the *Sunday Independent*, an aggressively anti-leftist national newspaper that has for decades consistently propounded new right free-market politics. The authentically liberal credentials of many individual revisionists are beyond doubt, but revisionism has been elaborated in such media as part of a broader new right crusade that ostensibly champions individual liberties and freedoms but always at the expense of collective projects of social transformation that might create the kind of world where these would acquire substance for more than a wealthy minority. Revisionism, in short, may well have served as an intellectual arm of the liberalisation of southern Irish society since the 1960s, but while it has displayed a strong (and commendable) secular animus against the conservatism of 'traditional' Irish Catholic nationalism, it has also been deeply complicit with wider international conservative currents.

Until now I have been discussing some of the ways in which the problematic of partition has been refracted in recent political and intellectual discourses in Ireland. I want at this point to consider some of the ways in which that problematic is refracted in Irish cultural narrative. Given the extent to which the North has dominated politics in the South ever since the island was divided, at first glance it seems quite odd that partition is a central topic in only a handful of Irish novels and films, and in even fewer that can be said to have acquired canonical status. In this respect, a contrast with the Indian subcontinent is instructive. The partition of India figures in a good deal of imaginative writing in Urdu, Hindi, Punjabi and Indian-English. This narrative corpus extends across both India and Pakistan and includes not only works written immediately after partition, such as the short stories of Saadat Hasan Manto or the poetry of Faiz Ahmed Faiz, but also an extensive body of contemporary narrative by writers such as Salman Rushdie, Bhisham Sahni, Amitav Ghosh and Bapsi Sidhwa.

In Ireland, however, the events that have dominated cinematic and literary narratives that deal with the country's dramatic early twentieth-century history have been Easter 1916, the War of Independence and the Civil War in the south. Partition rarely looms large in these narratives. Many of the most distinguished literary chroniclers of the early decades of the twentieth century were writers who had actively participated in the national struggle such as Frank O'Connor, Seán O'Faoláin, Seán O'Casey, Liam O'Flaherty and W. B. Yeats. All of these writers, whether Catholic or Protestant by background, are of southern origin, and the geographical imagination of their writing is also distinctively southern. In the period of the independence struggle between 1919 and July 1921 roughly 752 people were killed in Ulster, a greater number than in the rest of Ireland put together. Approximately two-thirds of those killed were Catholic.[12] In the process of establishing the new state, the Northern government financed and then legalised, with sanction from London, several paramilitary bodies that helped to crush Catholic opposition to that state over the next decade. These Northern episodes find little place, however, in the standard 'birth of a nation' type narratives that dominate the literary treatment of the decades leading up to the foundation of the Irish Free State. This lack of engagement with events attending partition might be taken to confirm the revisionist quip that the Ireland beloved by Irish cultural nationalists always had an enormous West Coast and no Northeast corner. The historian Clare O'Halloran goes further and suggests that the lack of a major body of Irish fiction about partition can be taken as evidence that partition was never experienced by the majority of Irish people as a national trauma of any sort. Had it been experienced thus, she surmises, there would be more literary evidence to suggest so.[13]

There are, however, several problems with O'Halloran's conception of what counts as partition literature and of how to read that literature as historical evidence. Firstly, O'Halloran's idea of what constitutes 'partition literature' is very restrictively conceived. In her search for 'partition literature,' she seems to have looked to the novel only and apparently did not consider oral folk culture, popular ballads, the short story, theatre or poetry, for example. Nor does she consider the politics of publication in Ireland in the extremely tense and bitter climate of the 1920s and 1930s. The lack of major literary material on the topic in the decade or so after partition is noteworthy, however, and seems to suggest that the trauma of the Civil War did indeed overwhelm the border issue for southern writers. Other issues may also have been at work. Many nationalists in this early period, North and South, considered the Northern state unviable and consequently convinced themselves that partition was destined to be short-lived. Silence on the border, therefore, may suggest neither acquiescence nor indifference, but rather a stubborn refusal to accept that partition had become an enduring reality. After the death of Michael Collins, and the total failure of the Boundary Commission to alter the border in the South's favour, the newly installed Free State government, moreover, was anxious to distance itself as much as possible from the border issue. Later, successive southern governments lacked serious strategy for attaining Irish unity, and all of these factors may have contributed to the wider evasion of the topic in literature. Even so, it must also be observed that writers in the Free State and what later became the Republic were not all geographically equidistant from or emotionally indifferent to the border. It is significant that one of the earliest novels about partition, Peadar O'Donnell's *The Knife* (1930), was written by a socialist republican who came from an area directly adjoining the border. Even in recent times, the southern Irish writers that have most engaged with the Northern Troubles tend to be those who live in 'the border counties': one thinks here of Eugene McCabe, Shane Connaughton, Patrick McCabe, Frank McGuinness, Darach MacDonald, and many others.

While O'Halloran's general thesis about the absence of a partition literature needs to be modified, then, there is something even more fundamental amiss with her claim that there is 'insufficient literary evidence for any major sense of public trauma over partition'.[14] The assumption here is that the volume of literary response provoked by some historical event is a reliable index as to whether that event constituted an authentic public trauma. By this criteria one might question whether the Irish Famine could count as traumatic since, with few exceptions, that catastrophe does not have a very high profile in 'high' or canonical Irish literature either. The Freudian conception of trauma involves not simply a disturbing episode, however, but one so hurtful that that episode is repressed, so that traumatic experience is always lived retroactively and the original traumatic occurrence displays itself only symptomatically in apparently subordinate, concomitant memories of the original event. Trauma, in this sense, is as much about aphasia as it is about eloquence; it is as much a matter of repression, silence, sublimation and the difficulty of working a hurtful episode into coherent narrative as about speech or literary utterance.[15]

In this context, we might look again to the Indian subcontinent. The partition of India, in which roughly one million people died, and over seven million were displaced across the borders of the two new states, was obviously on a scale vastly different to the Irish experience. The essential differences between Ireland and India may have to do not simply with the scale or the emotional depth of the tragedy, however, but with the ways in which partition has been officially remembered and to what end. The ruling élites in India after 1947 clearly considered partition a great national tragedy and relations with Pakistan continue to be extremely tense to this day. Unlike their Irish counterparts, however, the Indian establishment nonetheless conceived of partition as a *fait accompli* and Pakistan was not regarded as part of India *irredentata*. Border regions such as Kashmir continued to be disputed between the two states, but the larger partition itself was not regarded as reversible. India is a vast multiethnic state, however, with huge regional disparities and the anxiety that further communal struggles might lead to another fragmentation or breakdown of the state in the future has always remained strong. In such a context, memories of partition can serve an essentially minatory function: the catastrophe of 1947 is evoked as the great *Ur*-trauma that serves to remind Indians of the potentially disastrous consequences of further communal conflicts and the secessions and partitions they might still provoke. The memory of partition in this sense can actually be deployed in the service of consolidating an always potentially fissiparous state. In Ireland, in contrast, the newly installed élites never accepted that partition was irreversible, though from the outset strategies to advance reunification were in short supply. In this instance, the memory of partition was an awkward affair to manage, and the whole relationship between cultural memory of the event and the self-preservation of the state was quite different. In the Irish situation, the memory of partition could not be deployed to consolidate the state; indeed it has always served to underline the provisional nature of the existing state order on the island.

In short, for Indian secular nationalists, partition is memorialised as an apocalypse in the past that serves as a warning against another apocalypse in the future if the region's historic communal divisions are not overcome. For Irish nationalists, on the other hand, it was conceived as a tragedy in the past that may one day be reversed when the island has finally solved its historic communal divisions. For O'Halloran, the lack of a major 'partition literature' suggests that the Irish event was never really experienced as a national trauma. It is only when partition is examined not simply as an empirical set of events, however, but in terms of the ways in which it was constituted in the nationalist imagination that one can begin to make sense of the literary response (or indeed lack of response) to the issue.

With the outbreak of the contemporary Troubles in Northern Ireland in 1969, the status of the Northern state established by partition, and the concomitant question of the border, acquired an urgency that it had lacked during the relative calm of the previous decades. As the North exploded into violence in the early 1970s, and as the struggle between nationalists, the British army and Unionists settled into a 'low-intensity' military campaign that would run for nearly three decades, it might have been expected that the issue of partition would inevitably register itself in Irish fiction in a more immediate manner than had hitherto been the case. This seems not, however, to have happened. The Northern Irish conflict has certainly not lacked for narrative representation. For the most part, though, the various forms of cultural narrative that have come to dominate representations of the Troubles have focused obsessively on the violence of the region but in a manner that has largely stripped it of history and context. In most cases, that is, the situation has been perceived in terms of a desolate 'revenge tragedy' of communal reprisal and counter-reprisal in which violence has acquired its own demented tit-for-tat logic and is essentially devoid of meaningful historical origin or political content.

How are we to explain this curious occlusion of the border in the contemporary literature of the Troubles? Two answers will be proposed in this chapter, though they are really opposite sides of the same coin. Firstly, I argue, state borders have indeed been regularly occluded in contemporary fictional representations of the Troubles, but this occlusion must be seen not as incidental but as structural and constitutive. Secondly, the border is present in various ways in many narratives of the North, though usually only in displaced or sublimated modalities. In different contexts, different types of boundaries vary in permeability, and in some situations it may be easier to penetrate a fortified state border than to cross a communal boundary, as, for example, to cross from Jew to Arab in Palestine or from Catholic to Protestant in Northern Ireland. Once the issue is broadened out in this way, it soon becomes clear that if the inter-state border has not figured very prominently in Northern Irish writing, the same certainly cannot be said about sectarian or communal boundaries. While state borders are often only obliquely registered in narrative representations of the Northern conflict, the latter have featured very prominently indeed. For many writers, it would seem, the conflict in the North is generally not conceived as a story of state borders (of partition) at all, but as one of sectarianism and communal borders. It is, however, in the splitting off of these issues – in the severance of state from sectarian borders as though the two were entirely unconnected – that we can begin to discover the crucial ideological function served by some of the modes of writing that have dominated representations of the North until very recently at least.

The Northern Irish conflict is consistently narrated as a matter of intransigent communal sectarianism rather than as an issue of state-building because cultural narratives about Northern Ireland share much in common with dominant intellectual and academic discourses about that situation. As has been suggested earlier, these discourses have largely constituted that situation either in terms of a security crisis or in terms of an intransigent communal sectarianism that had much to do with the cultural pathology of the province and little to do with the wider state system in the British and Irish archipelago. The 'internal conflict' hermeneutic that dominated the political, academic and media establishments in the Republic of Ireland, Northern Ireland and the UK during the 1970s and 1980s did much to consolidate this perception. Cultural narrative, it might be argued, has helped to sustain a rather similar conception of things on a more popular level.

But while it is clear and incontestable that there is a sectarian as well as a state divide within Ireland, it cannot simply be inferred from this that partition is a mere epiphenomenon of a more primal sectarian divide. If the 1920–5 partition merely affirmed, as is so often alleged nowadays, a longstanding process of communal or regional-economic cleavage, then we might well ask why Northern Ireland includes the counties of Fermanagh and Tyrone as well as parts of South Armagh, the exclusion of which would have resulted in two states much more congruent with the putatively pre-existing regional/sectarian fissures. The answer, of course, is that the border is not simply a superficial phenomenon that passively 'reflects' some deeper, primal division, whether of an economic, ethnic or psychic kind. On the contrary, the border is a material political construct that emerged from a particular territorial and class conflict, and it is also a material condition by which that conflict continues to be shaped. Those who see sectarianism as the primary cause of either the 1920–5 partition or the later Troubles treat ethnic identities – and the rivalries they are presumed automatically to generate – as fixed and given. Viewed from an anti-essentialist perspective, however, ethnic identity is a historically changing social construct, recurrently reinvented in response to changing socio-political circumstances. Rather than regarding ethnic identity – and its supposedly reflex pathologies – as first cause and partition as mere secondary effect, or indeed vice versa, it would be better to ask how each has dialectically acted upon the other and to what effect. By relegating partition to the status of epiphenomenon, the dominant hermeneutic fails to ask how partition functioned, and still functions, in the continuous shaping of the sectarian identities that are alleged to be its root cause. A dialectical understanding of sectarianism and state politics would require acknowledging that the territorial shape of all the states involved, the character of their respective regimes, and the power positions of their incumbent élites are all closely interconnected factors.[16]

The literary and cinematic texts examined in this chapter belong to the period before the current 'peace process'. They are typical of a great deal of writing on the contemporary Troubles to the extent that they focus overwhelmingly on sectarianism while relegating state boundaries to the margins of the narrative, effectively preventing them from capturing the reader's interest. This consignment of state borders to the margins, and the corresponding magnification of sectarian boundaries, is not ideologically innocent. It expresses a specific ideological conception of the Northern conflict that is premised on the assumption that the problem of sectarianism can be detached from the question of the existing state order in the British Isles, an assumption that inevitably tends to underestimate the degree to which the sectarian conflict is rooted in conflicting national and state allegiances (themselves rooted in conflicting class and material interests) that cannot be settled without substantive overhaul of the current state order. In the end, however, questions of state cannot simply be made to disappear by narrative fiat. All of the fictional narratives to be discussed here disclose some dream or other of reconciling the divided communities they depict, and that dream inevitably resurrects, directly or otherwise, questions of state. That is, the dream of overcoming sectarian conflict requires as its inevitable corollary some conception, however vaguely delineated, of a state form that might accommodate such reconciliation. Hence questions of state and state borders return to haunt even those narratives in which they might seem to have been most determinedly repressed.

These issues are essentially registered at the level of form. As Marxist theorists such as Georg Lukács and Theodor Adorno insist, in literature what is truly social is form. Every form, argues Lukács, ultimately embodies an evaluation of life; hence form is always ideological. In a similar vein, Adorno states that 'what makes artworks socially significant is content that articulates itself in formal structures'.[17] What lends cultural forms their social significance is that when they take root in society they acquire the power to order and regulate perception in a manner made all the more effective by the fact that these forms appear not to be polemically or politically invested at all. In the case of Northern Ireland, many of the most popular and generically recurrent narratives about the conflict adopt the form of a romance that straddles the political divide. At first glance, works such as Joan Lingard's children's fiction, Bernard Mac Laverty's novel *Cal*, which was also made into a popular film, and Neil Jordan's hugely successful cinematic thriller *The Crying Game* appear to have little in common except their Northern Irish subject matter. Nevertheless, what they do share with each other (as well as with a lot of other narratives about Northern Ireland) – and what allows them to be read, therefore, not simply as wholly isolated projects but as constituents of a larger narrative paradigm – is that each represents a variation of the fundamental structure of the romance-across-the-divide. Secondly, and here too they are representative of the general body of literary fiction on Northern Ireland, all of these narratives tend to concentrate on militant republican violence, much more so than on the violence of Protestant paramilitaries or the British state security forces.

The reason why most narratives concentrate on republican violence perhaps is that Northern Irish republican nationalists call the established state order in the British Isles into question.[18] While Unionists have certainly been no less reluctant than nationalists to use political violence to attain their ends, their violence, like that of the security forces, is dedicated to upholding the existing state orders and state borders in the British Isles. In all of the fictions that I will examine, the nationalist figure will ultimately transpire to be the most problematical, the figure for whom it is most difficult to find some sort of satisfactory narrative resolution. This is not unconnected to the fact that in these narratives the drive to imagine reconciliation across the political divide seems always to be conditional on an acceptance of the already established state order, something which means that the militant nationalist will eventually either have to repent his opposition to the state or be eliminated or incarcerated by the state security forces. To put it another way, the republican nationalists at the centre of these texts constitute a 'problem' to which the texts attempt to find 'solutions.' In so doing, they are also implicitly resolving the issue of partition, even though for the most part they avoid explicit engagement with that topic.

## II

Addressing the St Andrew's Day Festival of the Royal Scottish Corporation in November 1925, British Prime Minister Stanley Baldwin remarked to his Scottish audience: 'Had there been a Walter Scott for Ireland there would be no Boundary Commission sitting today, and I would have been able to have devoted my weekend, as I intended, to preparing a speech worthy of the occasion.'[19] Baldwin's reference is to the Irish Boundary Commission established by the Anglo-Irish Treaty of 1921 to work out the final arrangements for the partitioning of Ireland. The withdrawal of the Irish Free State from the UK, which dissolved the Act of Union of 1801, could not fail to prompt individuals as preoccupied with the idea of Britain as Baldwin to ponder the state of the Union with Scotland. In this address at least, Baldwin seems confident that the Scottish Union appears to be more secure: thanks to writers such as Walter Scott, he contends, the Scottish Union has been raised from a merely legalistic to a solidly cultural bond between the two peoples.

As Baldwin was aware, there were many Anglo-Irish writers who had tried to do for the Irish Union what Scott did for its Scottish counterpart. Scott himself acknowledged that his *Waverley* novels were inspired by the work of the Anglo-Irish writer, Maria Edgeworth, whose novels, he remarked in 1829, 'may truly be said to have done more in *completing the Union* than perhaps all the legislative enactments by which it has been followed up'.[20] Wondering why in Scotland literature had helped to consolidate the political union whereas in Ireland it hadn't, Baldwin seems to conclude, somewhat limply, that historical accident may be sufficient explanation. 'How many people today read Maria Edgeworth?',[21] he asks, as though the weakness of the Irish

Union might be connected to the quality of the writers who championed its cause. A less culturalist approach would suggest that it was the material weaknesses of the Irish Union, as briefly sketched in the previous chapter, that prevented its Irish supporters from delivering the kind of triumphant celebrations that Scott's novels did.

In contemporary Northern Ireland one frequently gets the sense that the attempt to establish some sort of affective union between Catholic and Protestant, or between those who espouse Irish and British national allegiances, is operating under conditions of frustration not dissimilar to those that plagued Anglo-Irish literary unionism in the nineteenth century. Since the Troubles erupted, one of the most recurrent formal structures to appear in fictional narratives about the Northern situation is that of a relationship, or attempted relationship, between two characters from different sides of the political divide. In novels such as Maurice Leitch's *Poor Lazarus* or Glenn Patterson's *Burning Your Own* or in films such as Neil Jordan's *The Crying Game*, the relationship involves a male friendship, sometimes one with homoerotic overtones. More commonly, however, in novels such as Bernard Mac Laverty's *Cal*, Joan Lingard's *Across The Barricades* or Patrick Quigley's *Borderlands*, the relationship across the political divide takes the form of a Romeo-and-Juliet-type heterosexual romance between Catholic and Protestant lovers, a romance in which the lovers, who desire sexual union, must struggle against the centrifugal forces that pull their respective communities apart. Whether they be heterosexual or homoerotic, however, one of the most striking features about these romances is the frequency with which they come to nought. Again and again in these narratives, the romance across the political divide ends not in triumph but in frustration.

The interest and appeal of these romance narratives – which often flaunt an Oedipal idiom that invites a psychoanalytic reading – is their drive to imagine some kind of reconciliation between the two conflicting communities in Northern Ireland. A close analysis of some of these narratives reveals, however, that in the case of Northern Ireland the romance-across-the-divide is an anxious and contradictory literary mode. Before coming to an examination of the individual narratives, it is worth attending in more detail to the specific characteristics of the romance-across-the-divide as it has emerged in the Northern Irish context. In many respects, the form appears to function in terms of what Doris Sommer calls 'national romance'.[22] Her term refers to narratives in which the desire of lovers separated by inherited race or class divisions to be united with each other functions as a symbolic projection of a desire for national conciliation: in the erotic embrace of the lovers, antagonistic constituencies within the state come to recognise each other as allies. In *Foundational Fictions*, Sommer shows how romance novels contributed to various Latin American projects to consolidate the nation-state. In these novels, the obstacles that hinder the union of the lovers are also those that hinder the consolidation of the nation-state. The novels thus heighten the reader's desire not only for the removal of the obstacles to the romance, but also for the kind of state where its consummation could occur. Although they resolve the divisions confronting the lovers in various ways, what these foundational fictions have in common is that they meld erotic and patriotic desires in narratives that imagine the reconciliation and assimilation of different national constituencies cast as lovers destined to desire each other.[23]

While in some respects the Northern Irish romances-across-the-divide resemble the national romances described by Sommer, the crucial difference is that in Northern Ireland the conflict is not simply between antagonistic communities vying for power *within* the established frame of the state; rather, it is one in which the right of that state to exist, at least in its present form, is disputed. To put it another way, the struggle between nationalists and Unionists is not just about the distribution of power within the state; it is also about whether Northern Ireland can be the solely determining unit within which the two communities can imagine their future together. In the national romances examined by Sommer, the coming together of the lovers from traditionally antagonistic communities functions as a metaphor for the process of state consolidation as erstwhile enemies bond to form new national families. In Northern Ireland, however, the consolidation of the state is the goal of only one party to the conflict (the Unionists), while the goal of the other (the nationalists) is not to consolidate the state but to abolish or fundamentally restructure it so that their connections to the rest of Ireland can also be realised. In these circumstances, the romance-across-the-divide cannot emerge as a full-fledged national romance celebrating the consolidation of the Northern Irish state unless it takes the form of an explicitly Unionist wish-fantasy and ignores the hostility of northern nationalists to a resolution of this sort. This no doubt explains why, in so many of the Northern Irish romances, the relationship between the lovers so often either fails in the end, thus leading to closure of a tragic kind, or can only be realised in a private sphere where sexuality and politics are completely dissociated. They can almost never deliver the sense of confident consummation or triumphant closure that characterises the Latin American romances described by Sommer. In the national romances she describes, the sexual embrace of the lovers is concomitantly a political embrace since their union functions as a metaphor for political unification. In the case of the Northern Irish narratives, on the other hand, the sexual embrace of lovers from different communities can generally be realised only if sexuality and politics are determinedly held apart; that is, if the lovers detach themselves from their communities and politics altogether to escape into an anti-political privacy where sexuality becomes the sole domain of authentic existential fulfilment.

If Sommer's study offers a useful starting point for thinking about the romance-across-the-divide in fictional treatments of Northern Ireland, Nancy Armstrong's *Desire and Domestic Fiction* provides its essential counterpart and complement.[24] Here, Armstrong convincingly argues that from its inception the British novel endeavoured to detach the language of sexuality from that of politics, and thereby helped to usher in a whole new mode of middle-class power. In the novel, Armstrong argues, what mattered most about the individual was not his or her social identity but rather his, and especially her, sexuality. In other words, sexual subjectivity was detached from other forms of collective socio-political identity by being represented as an ontologically prior and more important form of identity. Accordingly, the novel did not so much reflect the rise of bourgeois individualism as prefigure and help to produce it by rewriting the relationship between sexuality and power. This dissociation of sexuality from power initially served to contest an aristocratic order founded on the principle of consanguinity, but the strategy was later directed against working-class forms of collective identity as well. Armstrong contends that by representing sexuality as anterior to and more important than other forms of subjectivity, the novel could individuate wherever there was collective identity and could ascribe psychosexual motives to what had been understood before as the transparently political behaviour of conflicting groups. In the nineteenth-century British novel, the world was organised by a fundamental gender division: the public political world, understood as an essentially 'masculine' domain, was represented as of lesser value or at least more alienated than the privatised world of domestic sexuality and personal realisation, which was now coded as an essentially 'feminine' realm.

What I want to suggest here is that the particular circumstances of the Northern Irish situation have stimulated a curious hybrid of the romance-across-the-divide, in which the drive to achieve a nationalising embrace on the one hand, and a contrary drive to dissociate sexual from political identity on the other, cut across each other, often in fundamentally contradictory ways. It is as if the allegorical romance mode (described by Sommer) has been called into being by the Northern Irish situation as an attempt to imagine resolutions to its communal dilemmas, but in the face of that conflict's intractability, stemming from the absence of any agreed-upon state order that might frame a political solution acceptable to both sides, the utopian impulse of the romance mode must give way to a 'realism' (of the kind described by Armstrong) shorn of any such transformative impetus. In other words, the Northern Irish romances cannot adequately be explained either in Sommer's or Armstrong's terms because these narratives represent a strange amalgam of allegorical romance and domestic realism in which a political tale of the national romance kind and an anti-political tale of escape into domestic privacy are often combined or overlapped – with the former usually being superseded, overwritten, or finally cancelled by the latter. In many of these narratives it is as if what promised to become a national romance founders on the uncomfortable realisation that, in the case of Northern Ireland, the consolidation of the state cannot be 'the solution' since it is precisely the determining unit of the state that is at issue in the first instance. Accordingly, the national romance swerves or modulates into a domestic novel where the sexual union of the lovers, rather than serving as a trope for some anticipated political union, can be achieved only by renouncing politics altogether.

Were these romances to adhere to the narrative impetus to imagine how Northern Ireland's communities might ultimately become reconciled, they would have to take seriously the relationship between sectarian conflict and the existing state order. But since they generally insist on seeing sectarianism as something altogether distinct from the question of the state, they usually stop well short of any such radical interrogation of the existing structures of power. The despairing flight from politics represented by the lovers' retreat into domestic privacy, then, must be read as a sign of imaginative failure: of an unwillingness or inability to imagine a transformed social order where the embrace of the lovers might be consummated. This imaginative failure is ultimately symptomatic of a corresponding faltering of political will: one that refuses to confront the fact that resolution to the sectarian conflict would require not just a modification of attitude on the part of the communities involved but substantive transformation of the existing structures of state power in the region as well.

In the case of Northern Ireland the texts that most nearly resemble the model described by Sommer are Joan Lingard's series of children's novels. The first two novels in the series, *The Twelfth Day of July* and *Across the Barricades*, tell the story of how Catholic Kevin McCoy and Protestant Sadie Jackson, both from segregated, working-class ghettos in Belfast, fall in love and defy their respective families and communities to be with each other. The narrative is built around recurrent sets of situations in which the reader is invited to share the couple's increasing frustration with the physical and psychological barriers that keep them apart. In these opening novels of the series, Lingard's narrative appears to be infused with the liberal optimism of the national romance, with Northern Ireland's two antagonistic communities represented by a pair of heroic lovers destined to overcome the unfortunate legacies that divide them. Kevin and Sadie are taken under the wing of the benign, elderly (Protestant) Mr Blake, Sadie's former geography teacher, and, in the protective shelter of his middle-class home in the suburbs, it appears that the young lovers have finally found a place where there are 'no barbed-wire barricades ... or burnt-out cars or words scrawled on the gable-ends of houses'.[25]

At the end of *Across the Barricades*, however, the plot takes a sudden swerve: Mr Blake is killed when his peaceful suburban home is petrol bombed – the work of some unidentified group that disapproves of mixed marriages – and the dismayed lovers set off for 'exile' and London. The nationalising embrace between Kevin and Sadie towards which the novel had appeared to be leading cannot take place within Northern Ireland, it would seem, and must be diverted elsewhere. Later, London too will be forsaken, and the couple will make a series of false starts in a variety of locales from the tenements of Liverpool to the farmlands of Cheshire, resisting at several points along the way the temptation (to which Kevin is especially vulnerable) to return to the County Tyrone borderlands in Northern Ireland, where the rest of the McCoys eventually settle. When Kevin and Sadie finally rid themselves of their residual Northern Irish entanglements, it is to move from Cheshire 'over the border into Wales', where they finally find a home for themselves in an isolated country cottage.[26] It is as if that final crossing of the less politicised Welsh border finally enables the nagging anxieties associated with its more bothersome Tyrone counterpart to be exorcised and laid to rest.

The most intriguing question raised by Lingard's series of novels is why the embrace of Catholic Kevin and Protestant Sadie cannot be realised in suburban, middle-class Northern Ireland, something the first two novels appear to anticipate. The answer to this question is surely related to the issue of state allegiance – to the fact that each community believes that Northern Ireland ought to belong to a different state. If Kevin's and Sadie's love were to be overtly represented as a nationalised embrace, Lingard's novels would sooner or later have to make it clear in which state that embrace was to be realised. In other words, if the romance between Catholic Kevin and Protestant Sadie were openly registered as an allegory of desire for their communities' reconciliation, then the question that would inevitably follow would be: in which state – a United Ireland or a Northern Ireland (independent or fully integrated into the United Kingdom?) – is that reconciling embrace to take place? The fact that the lovers' union cannot be realised within Northern Ireland amounts to a tacit admission that the issues of sectarianism and statehood are intrinsically connected, despite the narrative's determined attempt to hold them apart by focusing exclusively on the sectarian 'barricades'.

Lingard's novels are locked into the idea that Catholic and Protestant sectarianism is simply an unfortunate anachronism that can be understood without reference either to the material interests that subtend such attitudes or to the contested nature of the Northern state. Hence if the lovers are to be united, the impeding obstacle they must overcome is sectarian bigotry. The issue of divided state allegiance, on the other hand, is something the series appears more concerned to avoid than to confront – at least directly. In other words, the dilemma that Lingard's novels struggle to overcome is how to find an imaginary resolution to the problem of sectarianism without having to confront the attendant, and more complex, problem of reconciling conflicting national and state allegiances. The novels' critique of sectarianism, therefore, is never pressed beyond the point of reproving it as a distasteful 'prejudice'. Lingard's series always eschews any more fundamental interrogation of the structures of power that condition Catholic and Protestant relationship sin Northern Ireland and ignores the material class, national and state interests that animate sectarianism. In order to maintain its appearance of liberal even-handedness, which dictates that Catholic Kevin should not forcibly be compelled to surrender his nationalism and accept Protestant Sadie's state as his own, the series must find some way of resolving the thorny question of state allegiance without drastically compromising either party.

This delicate balancing act is achieved in the end, but only by moving the couple to the ostensibly 'neutral' ground of England and then Wales, exilic spaces purportedly extrinsic to the Northern Irish conflict. But since these countries are, like Northern Ireland, part of the UK, the lovers' move to the British 'mainland' is itself politically significant. That is, the nationalised embrace of Kevin and Sadie is finally realised within the UK, an apparently supra-national state, which is deemed not to compromise Catholic Kevin as exile in the Republic of Ireland would presumably compromise Protestant Sadie. It is Catholic Kevin's national loyalties that are finally surrendered, therefore, even if the novels' desire to circumvent the unpalatable logic of winners and losers in this struggle can only be accomplished by locating the nationalising embrace of the lovers in Wales – a place that, though culturally Celtic, has historically been the most fully integrated and least separatist of the countries in the UK. Wales, in other words, might be read here as a displaced 'solution' to the Northern Irish question: in this scenario, Wales, imagined as a place where a depoliticised cultural nationalism does not threaten the wider UK state system, becomes a model for what might yet be attained in Northern Ireland.

In this reading, then, Lingard's novels are informed by a liberal desire to imagine some kind of resolution between their Catholic and Protestant protagonists that would require neither the overt surrender of one party to the other nor yet any really substantive overhaul of existing state structures. Removing the lovers from Northern Ireland at the end of *Across the Barricades* can be read as an implicit acknowledgement that a nationalising embrace between the two communities the lovers represent is unlikely within that state. Their flight to England can be read as a despairing abandonment of politics for domestic privacy in the face of an intractable Northern Irish situation. This is partly the case, but since the question of affixing nationality to state allegiance is never quite forgotten in the three later novels things seem a little more complex. Indeed, it is only in the very last novel that the connections between nationality and state are finally brought into the open when Kevin and Sadie have a furious argument over precisely this subject. Kevin proposes at this point that they return to Ireland to live in the Republic, where he has found work. But when Sadie fiercely opposes this move, saying that since it was not *her* country, she would not feel at home', Kevin finally relents, admitting that in proposing the idea he 'must have been soft in the head'.[27] The connection between nationality and state allegiance at last becomes explicit in this exchange, but as soon as it does it is immediately and decisively foreclosed in Sadie's favour. Here, then, the narrative reveals what has been its fundamental dilemma all along: how to resolve the conflict between Catholics and Protestants within the existing state order but without appearing to favour one group over the other – 'Wales' represents the sublimated resolution to this dilemma.

It would be easy to dismiss Lingard's series as inconsequential 'children's fiction'. Nevertheless, these novels set up an elementary set of ideologemes in which we can observe, in skeletal outline as it were, a manner of reading Northern Ireland that would recur not only in literature but also in political and socio-scientific writings as well.[28] Lingard's narrative is organised in terms of both a temporal axis, which pits an atavistic Irish sectarianism against the supposedly post-nationalist modernity of the British 'mainland', and a spatial axis, which champions the space of private domesticity guaranteed by a well-functioning state as the alternative to the cyclical violence of competing communal factions. The crucial borderlines in this narrative structure are the barbed-wire barricades marking the dividing lines between Belfast's working-class ghettos. These are deemed the major clue to the violence of Northern Ireland, while the disputed border that partitions Ireland is relegated to the shadowy margins of the narrative. In this schema, both Southern and Northern Ireland are clearly value-loaded spaces associated with Catholicism and Protestantism respectively, but Britain is imagined as a secular value-free space without corresponding national or confessional attributes. The effect of this syntax of discursive spaces is to privilege sectarianism as the key to the conflict in a way that detaches it from the wider history and structure of the British and Irish state systems.

## III

Lingard's novels were first published in the early 1970s when it was still possible to imagine, perhaps, that some sort of reconciliation between the two communities might be worked out under the supposedly benign tutelage of the British state that had assumed direct control of the situation. As that conflict dragged on over subsequent decades, however, such optimism seems to have receded. Though the romance-across-the-divide has continued to be a recurring device in many fictions, the 'national romance' element is increasingly combined with, indeed subordinated to, another popular culture genre: namely, the political thriller. This generic modulation is suggestive. The thriller, as Michael Denning has shown, originates in the 1880s and 1890s with the exhaustion of the heroics of the classic imperial adventure novel (of the kind associated with Rider Haggard and Rudyard

Kipling). The 'thrillers' and 'shockers' that supplanted the old imperial adventure tale, Denning suggests, register a shift from an assertive, expansionist genre to a more paranoid world obsessed with vigilance and the defence of the realm. In the thriller, the action is displaced from the wild 'pre-modern' landscape of explorers and adventurers into a more opaque and sinister international underworld peopled by secret agents, securocrats and subversives. The thriller entered into the mainstream of British popular culture in the 1960s with the emergence of the cheap paperback and was dominated at the time by spy novels and the political climate of the Cold War.[29]

Later, events in the 1970s and 1980s, such as Palestinian hijackings and the Iranian hostage crisis, enabled the Anglo-American new right, then assuming power with the Reagan and Thatcher administrations, to construct 'terrorism' as the major threat to democracy and human rights in contemporary times. In these decades a corresponding preoccupation with terrorism is also registered in the thriller. As a genre, the thriller is obsessed with international politics and intrigue and is hence, as Denning remarks, ostensibly one of the most political of popular genres. But in the thriller 'politics' is associated neither with constitutional parliamentary activity nor with radical social movements. Instead, activity takes place primarily in a shadowy sub-world of subterfuge and intrigue that serves, Denning suggests, as a sublimated version of the world of late capitalism where social destinies seem increasingly shaped by an opaque tangle of global determinants that appear to defy legibility and conventional means of regulation and control.[30]

Tales about Irish violence and sinister Irish subversives were not new of course. Since at least the nineteenth century, the British popular press had displayed considerable interest in Irish agrarian secret societies and later in the Fenian brotherhood and the IRA.[31] Although it regularly draws on an existing reservoir of literary and cinematic narratives about such matters, in the contemporary 'Troubles thriller' older stereotypes and conventions are reworked in the contemporary climate of late Cold War moral panic. The emergence of the thriller genre as perhaps the major narrative model for representing the North needs to be situated, therefore, both in terms of the wider international scene and the domestic sense of deadlock and crisis management that obtained in Northern Ireland after the short-lived cross-community power-sharing Sunningdale Agreement collapsed in 1974. During the Thatcher period especially, the conception of Northern Ireland as essentially a 'security problem' was in the ascendant and the thriller might be read therefore as a literary analogue to the many other law-and-order discourses that dominated writing about the North in this period.

As noted earlier, in some of the thrillers at least the romance of reconciliation is not displaced. What happens instead is that the search for some sort of reconciliation between the two communities is now no longer imagined in non-violent terms but is deemed possible only if the militants who resist 'reconciliation' are eradicated from the text by the agents of the state. Two narratives that represent this curious hybrid of national romance and thriller genres are Bernard Mac Laverty's *Cal* and Neil Jordan's brilliantly reflexive twist on that structure, *The Crying Game*. *Cal*, a novel published in 1983, was later made into a successful film of the same title directed by Pat O'Connor and scripted by Mac Laverty.[32] *The Crying Game*, released in 1992, garnered rave reviews, and was an unexpected and massive commercial success as well. A crucial difference between romances such as the Lingard novels and these later narratives is the fact that in neither *Cal* nor *The Crying Game* is the love affair across the political divide successful. In Lingard's series, the love affair did finally triumph, even if only just and then only by substituting Wales for Northern Ireland. Mac Laverty's and Jordan's works proffer a different kind of resolution: one whereby the nationalist protagonist finally repents of his politics and learns to accept the state that he had hitherto opposed.

Mac Laverty's *Cal* is the story of an unlikely romance between a young, working-class Catholic, Cal McCluskey, and Marcella Morton, the widow of Robert Morton, an RUC reserve officer killed in an IRA assassination to which Cal was an accomplice. Although this killing takes place before the narrative proper begins, it overshadows all of the subsequent events in the novel. The narrative opens with a listless and unemployed Cal gripped by a sense of shame and abjection that stems from his part in the murder. That act also continues to haunt him through the unwanted attention of his former scholmate, Crilly, who had done the actual shooting, and Skeffington, a puritanical nationalist school teacher and IRA mentor to the two youths. On one of his periodic visits to the local library, Cal becomes attracted to the librarian, Marcella, whom he discovers to be the widow of Robert Morton, the murdered police officer. Impelled by a growing infatuation with Marcella, and by his anxiety to escape from Crilly and Skeffington who try to engage him in further violence, Cal eventually manages to get himself employed as a labourer on the Morton farm, some distance outside the town where he lives. When he and his father are burned out of their home because they are the only remaining Catholics on a Protestant housing estate, Cal takes up residence in a disused cottage beside the Morton farmhouse. While Robert's aged parents, with whom Marcella lives, are away from the farm, Cal and Marcella finally consummate their love, first in Cal's derelict cottage and later in the Morton house. But the sins of the past are not so easily left behind. When he returns to the town to visit his father for Christmas, Cal discovers that Crilly has planted a firebomb in the local library. Crilly and Skeffington are apprehended by the police, and Cal finally renounces his past political involvement by alerting the security forces to the bomb. Knowing that he too will soon be arrested, he returns to the Morton farm and waits passively for the police to arrive, glad finally to be able to atone for his misdeeds and, as the concluding line of the novel reads, 'grateful that at last someone was going to beat him within an inch of his life'.[33]

If *Across the Barricades* is a type of wish-fulfilment romance, *Cal* is a romance of a more tragic cast, the Oedipal idiom of which is obvious. The killing of Robert Morton, an RUC reserve officer and hence a representative of state law, functions as an originary act of symbolic parricide. Cal's subsequent seduction of Marcella, the dead man's widow, and a mother considerably older than he is, underlines the Oedipal overtones. Moreover, when Cal initially moves into the disused cottage on the Morton farmstead, Marcella provides him with some of Robert's clothes and when he later makes love to her in the Mortons' house he does so under the discomfiting gaze of Robert's photograph. The fact that Cal seduces Marcella while dressed in her dead husband's clothes links the earlier murder, in ostentatiously Freudian terms, to an unacknowledged desire to dispossess or displace Robert Morton, the only son of a family who have 'been Protestant farmers for centuries'.[34]

*Cal* operates in terms of an intricate braiding of sexual and territorial competitiveness imagined along confessional lines. When the Catholic McCluskeys, father and son, are burned out of their home, their eviction triggers a series of dispossessions that eventually culminates in Cal's making love to the widow of an assassinated Protestant policeman in the inner sanctum of a Protestant household. For all his doleful passivity, Cal steadily insinuates himself with the Mortons: first hired as a casual labourer, then as a full-time employee, later moving into their cottage, and finally into their daughter-in-law's bedroom. Dunlop, the Unionist foreman on the farm, is intuitively aware of Cal's stealthy progress; we are told that he 'was mad about the way [Cal] had managed to insinuate himself into the cottage'.[35]

Perhaps the most significant symbolic space in *Cal*, however, is the public library. It is here that Cal first encounters Marcella, and, when he takes an active stand against his former comrades, it is to prevent the library's destruction. Marcella's association with the library exemplifies Armstrong's view of the role played by both women and culture in the bourgeois imagination as 'feminising' influences that domesticate recalcitrant social forces. When Cal first visits the library we are told that he usually borrows popular music cassettes, but Marcella encourages him to borrow books, and she will later furnish his little cottage with books also. Marcella and the library both serve the process of domestication whereby Cal will come to reject the violently tribal world of sectarian working-class estates for the more humanising space of rural isolation, middle-class refinement and domestic sexuality. As in *Across the Barricades*, the Catholic working-class youth's initiation into sexual subjectivity is what alienates him from the less authentic world of communal political engagement. For Crilly, the irredeemable macho thug who proves impervious to such domestication, the library is simply 'Government property'.[36] That Crilly's violence is not merely anti-state but anti-middle-class is suggested by his secreting the incendiary device in a hollowed out copy of *Middlemarch*, the archetypal British novel of the 'middle way'. The 'feminised' library, then, is where Cal first begins to leave behind the restricted worlds of popular culture and brutal sectarianism, linked here mainly to the working-classes. Crilly's hypermasculine militant nationalist assault on the library, therefore, is tantamount to an assault on civilised value *per se*.

At first glance, *Cal* appears to be a narrative that unfolds in a hermetically sealed Northern Irish space. The interstate border does make one strange appearance, though, when after Mass one Sunday Cal drives across the border into the Irish Republic to see a football game in Monaghan. Although the intercounty sporting event can be linked to the ideologeme of Catholic nationalist territorialism, the actual border-crossing is innocuous and narratively unmotivated. Indeed, the only question it raises is why it happens at all, unless the crossing is somehow intended as a sign of the border's otherwise covert presence in the text. We are told that once over the border, Cal 'experienced the feeling of freedom he always got' on 'escaping the weight and darkness of Protestant Ulster' and being in 'the real Ireland'. Nevertheless, he soon discovers that he cannot really enjoy himself in the South any more because 'the thing he had done was now a background to his life, permanently there, like the hiss that echoed from the event which began the Universe'.[37] Cal's part in Robert Morton's murder has, it seems, exiled him forever from the innocently edenic Ireland of his earlier imagination. The function of the border-crossing is, therefore, an essentially negative one: its purpose is to seal off the border in narrative terms, to underscore the fact that the Republic can offer Cal no sanctuary.

As in *Across the Barricades*, where an otherwise undeveloped reference to Mr Blake as a (Protestant) geography teacher furnishes the sole hint that his tutelage of Sadie and Kevin (and, by extension, the text's tutelage of its readers) might have state-territorial implications, so too the seemingly innocuous presence of the border in *Cal* proves significant. After all, people familiar with Northern Ireland will recognise the murder of a man who was not only an RUC reserve officer but also the only son of Protestant farmers as one with quite specific resonance. Many Protestants in the border-adjoining counties are convinced that while professing to target members of the security forces, the IRA actually conducted a deliberate campaign against Protestant border families with only one son. The logic of this, they suggest, was that the deaths of their male heirs would compel Protestant families to sell their lands and move away, thus effectively pushing back the ethnic frontier and making it easier for the IRA to mount operations over the border. Though partition is never directly a theme in *Cal*, then, the similarity between such incidents and that on which Mac Laverty's plot turns certainly suggests that the border haunts this story in however displaced or subliminal a form. Indeed, one of Cal's recurrent nightmares is of a naked girl in an upstairs room who, upon his entry, jumps through the window and is 'skewered on some railings, screaming unceasingly'.[38] In this dream, Cal's desire to possess the girl sexually is always frustrated by her violent skewering on the railings, a suggestively gendered act of impalement on a boundary-marker that would seem to telescope the broader territorial obsessions of the text and the violence it associates with borders. It is only when we discover the finer nuances of Cal's relationship with Marcella, however, that the full import of this nightmarish scenario discloses itself.

The rather odd way in which the border insinuates itself without ever being overtly material to the plot has to be connected to several other, more remarkable, displacements in *Cal*. The transgressive union of lovers from hostile political communities that serves as an allegory of communal reconciliation in Sommer's national romances would lead us to expect the love affair between Catholic Cal McCluskey and Marcella Morton, widow of a Protestant landowner and policeman, to operate in precisely these terms. The crucial twist in this instance, however, is that *both* Marcella *and* Cal are Catholics. What appears at casual glance to be another romance-across-the-sectarian-divide turns out, on closer inspection, not to cross that divide at all. Marcella Morton, nee Marcella D'Agostino, is the daughter of Italian Catholic immigrants, and she has already married, despite some parental protest ('Why for in Catholic Ireland you want to marry a Protestant boy?'),[39] across the communal divide – a romance that occurs prior to *Cal*'s narrative proper. This union has in fact been severed (also prior to the narrative proper) by Robert's murder. The relationship between Cal and Marcella is transgressive, then, not because it crosses the traditional communal divide, but because it is actually conducted over the grave of exactly that kind of union, one it effectively cancels out by recovering Catholic Marcella from Protestant Robert and restoring her to the arms of Catholic Cal.

The essential displacement here, of course, is that Marcella is not just Catholic but Italian and therefore ostensibly extrinsic to the indigenous Irish divide altogether, belonging properly to neither one community nor the other. Yet given the cultural imaginary within which *Cal* is elaborated, Marcella's Italianness is hardly an innocuous signifier. Northern Unionists have consistently opposed a United Ireland on the grounds that they would be subject to papist tyranny, and Unionism's most famous political slogan is that Irish 'Home Rule is Rome Rule'. When Cal inquires of the Orangeman Cyril Dunlop, 'What's so terrible about a united Ireland anyway? one island, one country', Dunlop retorts 'And be ruled from Rome?'[40] The fact that Marcella returns to Rome to visit her Italian relatives immediately after Robert's murder, then, has more than a little symbolic significance. In fact, the web of associations linking Marcella to Rome and Rome to a United Ireland supports a reading of Cal's and Marcella's relationship as a veiled allegory or furtive fantasy of a nationalising embrace for which the state equivalent could only be a United Ireland.

Moreover, when Cal and Marcella become intimate, we learn that she is not exactly a loyally grieving widow. In fact, she voices strong resentment against both Robert Morton and his burdensome parents. Marcella and Robert had become sexually estranged long before his assassination, and, she tells Cal, 'I've never been to his grave since the day of the funeral.' She also complains about feeling tied to the elder Mortons by a nagging sense of duty towards them even though 'they're not related to me. Why should any of it be *my* responsibility?'[41] The point, then, is that the romance between Cal and Marcella unites two Catholics who both yearn guiltily, but with no little resentment, to escape from a Protestant mortmain. The complexity of *Cal*, therefore, stems from its appearing to promise a reconciliation between Catholics and Protestants while actually indulging in a furtive fantasy of illicit sex between a homeless, motherless Northern Irish Catholic boy and a displaced Roman madonna – a union suggestive of a likewise illicit United (Catholic) Ireland. It is only when the house of the *Mortons*, an heirless Ulster house of death, has been vacated by its Protestant owners that such an illicit (but correspondingly thrilling) embrace becomes possible.

If *Cal* does entertain this furtive fantasy, however, it is only to repudiate it later in the strongest of terms. Given that such a union is imagined here only in genocidal confessional terms (its consummation seems to require the absence of all of the Protestant characters from the scene), the narrative predictably recoils from the climax towards which it seemed to be arousing our desire all along. Cal is carted off to prison, where he anticipates, with masochistic gratitude, being beaten 'to within an inch of his life' by Robert Morton's colleagues in the RUC. The murder of the RUC man thus proves to be an Oedipal act which does not release Cal from the tyranny of the Father or of the Law, but rather confirms his castration, his abjection before the Name-of-the-Father as described by Freud in *Totem and Taboo*. In fact, Cal fears that, 'as far as Marcella was concerned, he had gelded himself that dark winter's night'. In addition, Robert's murder is cast not only in Oedipal terms but also in religious ones – an *original sin* ('like the hiss that echoed from the event which began the Universe') that damns Cal to an endless purgatory of guilt and self-recrimination, dooming him to be the bearer of 'a brand stamped in blood in the middle of his forehead which would take him the rest of his life to purge'. This mark of Cain makes legitimate sexual access to Marcella taboo since it 'seemed to throb whenever she was near'.[42] Paradoxically, then, the murder of Robert opens up the possibility of Cal's union with Marcella and simultaneously puts her forever beyond his reach.

The novel's sexual fantasy of two Catholics finding love in a Protestant bed must be paid for in the coin of a morality tale – with repentance and atonement. Cal's passive surrender to the flagellations of the state perfectly expresses this sense of an unwholesome onanistic desire, shamefully indulged, which must be exposed, punished and disowned. Ultimately, then, *Cal* must be read as a narrative of contrition whereby the repentant Catholic nationalist guiltily offers himself up as a sacrifice to the proper authority of the Northern Irish state against which he has offended.

After alerting the security forces to the bomb in the library, Cal does not even try to escape, but returns to Marcella's bed and awaits arrest. As his pursuers draw near, Marcella rejects him, unconsciously, as she 'grumble[s] in her sleep and jack-knife[s], closing him out'. This scene, in which Cal is finally barred from Marcella's body, recalls an earlier one when, repairing the fences on the Morton farm, he had smiled ruefully at the thought that he was literally 'fencing himself out'.[43] Both acts of exclusion are fatalistically accepted. From this perspective, the seemingly innocuous episode in which Cal crosses the border into Southern Ireland only to find no respite there proleptically anticipates what the narrative confirms through the relationship between Cal and Marcella. The border is figuratively crossed again in that relationship, but only to be permanently sealed with Marcella's final closing-off of herself to Cal. Neither on the farm of the Protestant Mortons (Northern Ireland) nor in the maternal sexual embrace of Catholic Marcella (a United Ireland) can Cal be accommodated. Given this impasse, the narrative can only be resolved, it seems, by his acceding to the existing state order.

In the Freudian version of the originary myth of the state, the sons kill their father to possess his wives. Afterward, suffering remorse, they renounce in the name of the dead father their claim to his women, thus averting (sexual) anarchy. The death of the actual father sets the scene for the consecration of the Law of the Father, with its interdiction against incest, which is constitutive of symbolic law and of the state. 'Murder,' then, is a name for the unthinkable condition of anarchy 'before' the rule of law. Since the establishment of the law requires a certain amount of repression, however, sacrifice functions within certain religious societies as a violent but regulatory act, which recognises repressed resentments and ritually vents them by re-enacting the founding death that ushered in the rule of law and the state.[44]

Read in these terms – a reading that its insistent association of violence and the sacred invites – *Cal* lends this Freudian myth of the state a specifically Northern Irish cadence. The act that precipitates the narrative, a murderous transgression against a representative of the state, functions less as a strike against state authority than a consecration of it since the whole narrative drive is towards Cal's recognition and repentance of his transgression. Cal finally submits to the authority of the state when he recognises that only the transcendental power of state law can break the cycle of reciprocal violence between the war-ring factions within its domain. Although the novel's tentativeness about the impartiality of the state to be thus recognised is telling, *Cal*'s final affirmation of the sanctity of state law is never really in doubt. The narrative insistently intertwines several different discourses – religious, psychoanalytic, humanist – to stress the enormity of Cal's transgression. The cumulative political implication is that Northern Irish republican nationalists harbour a genocidal desire for an inces-tuous act of reunification and that, given the horrific implications of their fantasy, they have no alternative but to renounce it and become reconciled with the state against whose law they have transgressed.

*Cal* is, therefore, formally at least, a complex and contradictory text. On one level, the novel is structured so as to invite us to identify with the Catholic couple's desire for sexual union, which can be read metonymically as the desire for a United Ireland. On another level, however, the novel strongly disavows the very desire it is inviting us to share. This complex logic of desire and disavowal draws on the paralysing ambivalence that characterises certain types of contempo-rary Irish nationalism. Many Irish nationalists, North and South, are considerably invested in the ideal of a United Ireland; most, however, also find IRA violence in the name of that ideal utterly repugnant. This ambivalence has led many to express a very complex sense of guilt about their own continued investment in the goal of reunifica-tion, and some to repudiate that goal altogether. This identification with the end and disassociation from the means, which probably de-scribes the typical mindset of most Irish nationalists, is not simply a psychological issue. In *The Historical Novel*, Georg Lukács argues that the ability to seize and channel 'fluctuating sympathies' is a decisive factor in any conflict. Commenting on Walter Scott's representation of British history, Lukács writes: 'Scott . . . recognizes that no civil war in history has been so violent as to turn the entire population with-out exception into fanatical partisans of one or other of the contending camps. Large sections of people have always stood between the camps with fluctuating sympathies now for this side, now for the other. And these fluctuating sympathies have often played a decisive role in the actual outcome of the crisis'.[45] It is in such contexts, where narrative can nudge ambivalent sympathies in one political direction or another, that literary and intellectual constructions of the conflict assume their importance.

Part of *Cal*'s fascination, then, lies in its narrative negotiation of the ambivalent desires and disavowals that condition contemporary Irish nationalism. The novel's political import is expressed most obviously in its resolution of this dilemma. In the end, the nationalist desire for union represented by the romance plot is reluctantly repressed and, through Cal, the novel fatalistically concedes the authority of a state for which it clearly has little enthusiasm. On a more important level, however, it is not so much its narrative resolution of the nationalist dilemma as its whole construction of it that discloses *Cal*'s political standpoint. Mac Laverty's novel is steeped in a religious idiom and the romance of reunion is conceived along exclusively religious lines: it takes the form of a Catholic embrace conducted over, and haunted by, a Protestant corpse. This is a reunion imagined, in other words, not in terms of the secular republicanism of the United Irishmen – in which Catholic, Protestant and Dissenter would be united by common Irish citizenship – but in terms of a sectarian nationalism that identifies Catholicism with Irishness and thereby excludes Protestants altogether. The causal logic at work here is that the desire for Irish re-unification inevitably breeds sectarian violence, and if that violence is to be repudiated then so too must be the desire for reunification that motivates it. The Northern Irish state must consequently be accepted as the lesser of two evils (as Cal submits to it) – a reading that overlaps with the revisionist interpretation of Irish politics. The questions that might well be addressed to *Cal*, and to the revisionist worldview, are whether reunification can only be imagined along such confessional lines, whether it must necessarily entail militarist violence, or, indeed, whether the only alternative to militant struggle must be masochistic surrender to the Northern state as currently constituted. The paralysing ambivalence that informs *Cal* is ultimately derived from its own confessional conceptualisation of the conflict in Northern Ireland as a zero-sum game of all-or-nothing territorial control, the only imaginable outcome of which is either a resigned acceptance of the Northern state (whatever one's reservations) or its violent overthrow in the name of a United Ireland. That the conflict might be susceptible to some more emancipatory political resolution is something the novel seems unable to imagine.

## IV

Neil Jordan's *The Crying Game* is probably the most widely consumed narrative about Northern Ireland in recent times.[46] It is a film repeatedly praised in an idiom that invokes the crossing of borders. Rebecca Bell-Metereau's analysis of the film, for example, refers enthusiastically to its 'constant transgression of boundaries'.[47] For Slavoj Zizek, its central love affair 'transgresses not only the barriers of class, religion, and race (in today's 'permissive' epoch, all these barriers are obsolete), but also the ultimate barrier of sexual orientation, of sexual identification.'[48] The title of Judie Wheelright's review, 'Opening the Borders', deploys the same idiom.[49] Although the conflict in Northern Ireland is intrinsic to the film's plot, and its protagonist is an IRA man, none of these critics mention one boundary which *The Crying Game* does not cross: namely, the border that partitions the Irish Republic and Northern Ireland. As in Mac Laverty's *Cal*, however, this border is not simply absent from Jordan's narrative; it haunts it, rather, as a spectral presence.

The film begins in a Northern Irish fairground with a Black British soldier, Jody, being lured into a trap by a young IRA woman, Jude. Jody is then held hostage, but strikes up a friendship with his guard, Fergus, a more humane individual than the rest of his IRA comrades. At one point Jody shows Fergus a photograph of his lover, Dil, and, when it becomes apparent that he is to be shot, asks Fergus to visit Dil in London someday and to take her out for a drink to their favourite bar, the Metro. When Fergus is ordered to shoot Jody and takes him into the woods, Jody makes a sudden dash for freedom, but is run over by a Saracen tank as the British Army moves in on the IRA. In the shoot-out that follows, Fergus manages to evade capture and eventually makes his way to London. There, he seeks out Dil, as Jody had asked, and becomes infatuated only to discover, in a pivotal scene, that 'she' is actually a male transvestite. The dilemmas of an increasingly bewildered Fergus are compounded when his old IRA comrades track him down and demand that he help them murder a British judge. The now very 'butch' and sexually jealous Jude, transformed from dowdy working-class Irish girl in Aran sweater into a stereotypically hard British career woman, threatens to harm 'the black chick' (Dil) if Fergus refuses. Determined to prevent this, Fergus cuts Dil's hair so that Jude will not recognise 'her.' Knowing that his former comrades are closing in on him, Fergus also confesses his part in Jody's death to Dil, thereby provoking a melodramatic denouement in which Dil shoots not Fergus but Jude, attacking the female body that had seduced 'her' Jody into IRA hands. In a compensatory act of recompense and self-sacrifice, Fergus takes the rap for Dil's act and the film concludes with an amorous scene in which a re-feminised Dil visits a rather contented-looking Fergus in a British prison.

On the surface, there would appear to be a world of difference between Mac Laverty's *Cal*, with its brooding religious symbolism and small-town atmosphere, and Jordan's coolly avant-garde *The Crying Game*, which moves suavely from its initial Northern Ireland setting to London's exotic cosmopolitanism. Nevertheless, the formal similarities of the two narratives are as striking as their differences. Both are structured in terms of a triangulated romance featuring a young, working-class nationalist who is an accomplice to the killing of a British law-enforcement figure. In both cases, this protagonist then becomes romantically involved with the dead man's sexual partner, which identifies him, if only as a 'reluctant accomplice', with the act of Oedipal parricide that triggers each plot. In both narratives, this reluctant accomplice wants out of the IRA after the initial act of violence, a desire that intensifies when he becomes sexually involved with the victim's lover. But in each case he continues to be hamstrung by his past, haunted by a guilty secret he is afraid to confess to his new lover and by the persistent intrusions of old IRA comrades. In both plots, the romance-across-the-divide ends with the hero's incarceration in a British prison. In each, the state security forces eliminate the IRA gang, while the protagonist is moved to expiate his initial transgression against the state by surrendering to those who enforce its laws.

What distinguishes *The Crying Game* from *Cal*, despite their uncannily similar morphologies, is that Jordan's film displays a far greater degree of tongue-in-cheek generic reflexivity by self-consciously subverting the genre-bound expectations it arouses. In other words, one way to understand *The Crying Game* might be to see it as *Cal*-as-masquerade or the 'national romance' in drag. The central irony that sets the two narratives apart is that the dead man's 'widow' in *The Crying Game* is exposed as a cross-dressing male. In Jordan's ludic version of the Oedipal scenario, then, the Irish Catholic son displaces the obstructing British rival only to discover that the nature of his desire is not what he thought. In many respects, this narrative functions as an exemplary enactment of Girardian mimetic rivalry with Fergus discovering that his desire is rooted neither in himself, as desiring subject, nor in Dil, as erotic object, but in a third party or model, Jody, whose anterior desire is merely imitated by Fergus. Dil is thus desired not for 'herself' but for 'her' desirability to Jody; one man's desire competitively replicates another's in an infinite mimetic series that will foment an endless cycle of sexual rivalry and violence if it is not controlled.[50]

If the relationship between Jody and Fergus can be read as a struggle for the phallus, which also represents the Law of the Father or the State, and the drive to possess the female as a desire to be restored to the pre-Oedipal Nation (conventionally figured as female in Irish nationalism), then the ironies of *The Crying Game* are indeed suggestive. Read politically, what Fergus discovers is the ruse of mimetic desire, whereby his militant nationalist drive to displace the British state (Jody) is revealed to be simply a desire to reconstitute state power under a new name. In other words, Fergus's Oedipal victory over Jody ultimately exposes the rebellious Irish son's desire to be the same as that of the murdered father whom he does not so much *displace* as *replace*. Fergus's shocked response to the sight of Dil's penis just when he is ready to enjoy heterosexual intercourse reinforces this Oedipal inversion by suggesting that, however unconsciously, what Fergus wanted all along was the phallus – or to be Jody. A traumatised Fergus then returns to his flat where he tosses about on his bed, tormented by visions of Jody smiling as if at a 'trick' he has played, enjoying post-mortem, as it were, a wryly vengeful joke on Fergus. The strict chastity that obtains between Dil and Fergus after the latter has discovered the real (nature of the) object of his desire represents Fergus's rueful response to this dilemma and, ultimately, its sublimation. The fact that this romance will never be consummated, since he is a 'straight' heterosexual and 'she' is a male transvestite, makes Jordan's film a 'baffled phantasy' of the sort that Stephen Tifft has described, in another context, as informing the very structure of an Irish nationalism vexed by a rebellious son's desire to displace the British father without having to insert himself into the position thus vacated.[51]

The apparently insurmountable impediment to the sexual union of Fergus and Dil represented by their different sexual orientations finds its objective correlative in the glass partition imposed between them by a British prison. This association of apparently immovable sexual impediment and carceral barrier seems to suggest the parallel impossibility of Fergus's sexual romance and his romantic nationalist politics. In other words, like *Cal*, *The Crying Game* situates the nationalist character in an utterly contradictory relation to his own desire. Just as Cal discovers that his part in the killing of Robert Morton makes Marcella available in one sense but simultaneously taboo, so too

Fergus will come to love Dil but the accidents of desire have forever stymied sexual consummation since he happens to be heterosexual and 'she' is not. In both cases, the nationalist protagonist's sexual desire seems, like his political desire, to be fated to remain baffled, beyond attainment.

For all its ironies and playful subversions, there are compelling reasons to resist interpretations of The Crying Game as a radical political narrative. Although it mobilises the figures of androgyny and transvestism, the ways in which the film both constructs and resolves the issues it raises prove remarkably conventional. The Crying Game uses the figure of the transvestite to interrogate the concept of gender as a natural category bound to a normative sexual identity, but it ultimately operates in terms of strategies that, like the domestic fictions analysed by Armstrong, structure events according to a moral economy in which politics becomes a dehumanising 'masculine' force and sexuality its civilising 'feminine' antithesis. In The Crying Game, no less than in the narratives by Lingard and Mac Laverty, the discovery by the naive Irish working-class male of his sexuality is synchronous with his disengagement from politics. Once Fergus becomes involved with Dil, his desire to untether himself from the IRA intensifies, and when the narrative dilemma becomes the threat that his past political life poses for his new sexualised one, these two commitments become irreconcilable. The audience's desire to see the romance between Fergus and Dil flourish necessarily entails a collateral desire for the elimination of all obstacles to that romance – in this case, Fergus's nationalist commitments, and his former IRA comrades who would hold him to those commitments. If his baffled sexual romance is to prosper, Fergus's unproductive political romance must be abandoned.[52]

To the extent that Fergus's amorous and political allegiances are orchestrated as conflicting loyalties, The Crying Game remains within the terms of a conventionally gendered narrative that posits politics and sexuality as antithetical domains. The whole thrust of the plot is to disentangle the one domain from the other by representing sexuality, in remarkably conventional terms, as a 'feminine' sphere of authentic value. Despite the fact that 'she' is a male transvestite of West Indian origin, Dil is made to serve all of the conventional functions of the domestic female. She is even more clueless politically than Fergus is sexually; she lacks, for example, even a rudimentary knowledge of or interest in the Northern Irish conflict that has cost her lover his life. Her subjectivity is defined in exclusively sexual terms, and she explicitly identifies herself with the nurturing role of the domestic female, at one point telling Fergus, 'I was always best looking after someone.' When Fergus becomes her gallant protector, first from the predatory gay male, Dave, and then from the 'butch' female, Jude, Dil plays the attentively nurturing 'little woman' bringing him vitamin pills in prison.[53] With no political beliefs or agency of her own, Dil's primary narrative function is to bring Fergus in from the political cold and to initiate him in the life-enhancing values of the 'feminine' domain she represents. The fact that Dil is male and homosexual complicates and ironises the kind of domestic retreat available to Fergus as an alternative to the cruel public/political sphere. Nevertheless, Dil's sex does not preclude the elaboration of this romance in the conventionally gendered terms that set off politics and sexuality as antithetical domains. The gendered distinction between politics and sexuality that structures this film is not subverted, and may indeed be consolidated in new pluralist idiom, by a male transvestite playing the part conventionally ascribed to women.

The scene from *The Crying Game* that has excited most comment is the one where Dil disrobes before Fergus and shocks him with the revelation of 'her' penis. The camera descends the apparently female body in exactly in the kind of scopophilic gaze that constructs woman, in Laura Mulvey's terms, as the passive erotic object of an active male vision.[54] The sudden exposure of Dil's penis abruptly and humorously disrupts this most conventional of cinematic constructions and the pleasure it usually invites. However, if *The Crying Game* seems inclined to celebrate the notion of a 'female' penis when it is Dil's, it exhibits a very conventional paranoia indeed when the 'woman-with-a-penis' takes the more threatening form of Jude-with-a-gun. When displaced by Dil as the object of Fergus's erotic interest, Jude suddenly reappears as the stereotypical female terrorist of cinematic convention: physically angular and unattractive, seething with sexual resentment, more deadly than her male colleagues. The viewer watches Jude first try to persuade Fergus to carry out an IRA assassination and then stick a gun in his face, clutch his crotch, and say, 'So I suppose a fuck is out of the question.'[55] Her political and sexual motives are so laminated to each other in these scenes that the audience cannot help but view her politics as a psychotic displacement of a frustrated sexual drive.

These two different representations of the woman-with-a-penis seem connected by a shared logic: the 'female' phallus can be celebrated here only on condition that a demarcation between female political and sexual power is maintained. The political nationalist Jude is thus a nightmarish inversion of the sexual but apolitical Dil. There is something both profoundly logical and highly disturbing about the feminine Dil executing the macho Jude, savagely pumping bullets into that female body while ranting misogynistically against its 'misuse' for political rather than properly sexual purposes. So negative is the film's representation of Jude throughout, in fact, that when Dil finally rises up to riddle her with bullets the audience automatically exults in the spectacle of her death.[56] The terminus towards which the film moves, then, is the vanquishing of Jude, a butch female and Irish political subversive engaged in a suicidal mission to assassinate a British judge.

One of the more intriguing and potentially radical things about *The Crying Game* is that it manages to weave several UK minority subject positions into a single narrative. This is innovative because the established construction of Northern Ireland as an anomalous 'place apart,' belonging to the UK but still the site of a foreign 'Irish problem', effectively partitions Northern Irish minority issues from British minority discourse on the 'mainland'. If *The Crying Game* flirts with the possibility of connecting minority discourses that have historically been held apart, however, it does so in largely cynical ways. When Judie Wheelwright noted approvingly that the film 'works hard to confound audience expectations' since 'the British squaddie is black, the ruthless IRA volunteer is soft-hearted, and the female lead is played by a man', she was celebrating what most critics lauded *The Crying Game* for: its anti-essentialist subversion of stereotyped identities.[57]

What this overlooks, however, is that the different minority subject positions in the film are orchestrated so that each effectively neutralises the other. The growing sympathy between Fergus and Jody during the latter's captivity is helped along by their common working-class and colonial backgrounds. Yet since Jody is the only personalised British soldier in the film this effectively identifies British Blacks with the British state (or, more precisely, portrays the British Army in black-face). It suggests, therefore, not that the Black British and Northern Ireland's working-class nationalists have anything in common in terms of their subaltern relationships to the British state, but that they can meet only in a relationship of murderous antagonism. As if to underline this, Jody at one point refers to Northern Ireland as 'the only place in the world they call you nigger to your face'.[58] It as though Tottenham, where Jody comes from, or indeed the British Army in which he works, have somehow evolved beyond racist vulgarities of this sort. Neither Jody, as the humane male agent of British military power, nor Dil, the sexy feminine agent of its domestic values, function as signifiers of dissident minorities within the British state; instead, they serve a co-ordinated function as the twin arms of its repressive and ideological authority. Northern Irish republicans, on the other hand, are depicted as agents of both racial and homophobic persecution, first as Jody's would-be executioners and later as threats to Dil. The different minority groups – Northern nationalists, Blacks, homosexuals and transvestites – encounter each other in Jordan's film only as each other's deadly enemy. *The Crying Game*, then, can be considered a progressive narrative only if the interrogation of essentialist identities is considered a sufficient political end in itself. But since the film is indifferent to the structures of power that constitute the various minorities it features, it must be considered superficial by any conception of the political measured in terms of commitment to social change.

The morphology of both *Cal* and *The Crying Game*, then, is hostile to Northern Irish nationalism, identifying it as a force to be purged. The original act of violence that impels each narrative is the killing of a representative of British state law by Northern Irish nationalists, and the protagonist of each narrative must acknowledge and expiate this act by disowning his nationalism and surrendering to the state in a spirit of resigned penitence. This acknowledgement of state authority by the nationalist rebel is crucial because it transforms the state from an interested party in the conflict into a neutral arbiter of it.[59] It would be a fundamental error, then, to (mis)take sympathetic figures such as Cal or Fergus as evidence of ideological sympathy for Northern Irish republicanism. On the contrary, these protagonists are sympathetic only to the degree that they must be if they are to function as efficient conductors in the transfer of emotional identification from Northern Irish nationalism, where it is initially positioned, to the British/Northern Irish state, where it is finally affixed.

It could be objected, of course, that such a reading mistakes an understandable hostility to murderous IRA violence for an antagonism to Northern Irish nationalism more generally. Yet when Catholic Kevin or Cal or Fergus renounces militant nationalism it is always to repudiate politics completely. Once they have embraced the values of domestic sexuality, these protagonists are ready to put aside the delusions of political commitment altogether. They never abandon militant nationalism for other alternatives such as working-class politics or constitutional nationalism or non-violent socialist republicanism or whatever. The conservative thrust of these narratives is confirmed by the fact that everything is reduced to a manichean choice between militant republicanism or a repudiation of politics altogether in a spirit of fatalism or strong resignation. Their plots trace a linear trajectory that runs from murderous political activism to self-sacrificial resignation and no contrapuntal plot lines disrupt this trajectory. Constitutional nationalism, to cite only the most obvious alternative, is never suggested as even a remote possibility for Kevin, Cal or Fergus when they abandon violence. Its curious absence from these narratives is not difficult to explain: in Northern Ireland, constitutional nationalism is also, in its aspirations, an anti-state nationalism. Its inclusion, therefore, would only re-open in a different modality the morally and politically vexed question of the legitimacy of the Northern Irish state and the circumstances of the nationalist minority there. Accordingly, a narrative that posits a manichean conflict between state law and paramilitary chaos makes it much easier to legitimate the state and to reduce the Northern Irish situation to apparently simple moral choices. Focusing on militant nationalism to the exclusion of all alternative modes of nationalist resistance would appear to be a 'bait-and-switch' stratagem for eliding what these narratives construe as the real problem: not simply nationalist excesses but 'excess' Northern nationalists whose awkward loyalties cannot be accommodated by the current state order.

This is why the figure of the 'reluctant accomplice' is pivotal to *Cal, The Crying Game* and many other narratives of this kind. Such a character is always guiltily complicit in, rather than fully responsible for, an original act of transgression against the state. Never a zealously militant nationalist, he is rather the militant-with-a-troubled-conscience. If he temporarily comes under the spell of militant nationalism, it is not because of any coherent critique of the Northern state or reasoned advocacy of a united Ireland, but rather because of an inchoate resentment against the existing order. Figures such as Cal or Fergus are invariably politically inarticulate in these narratives: the device serves, in a manner analogous to media censorship, to silence and occult the militants. The reluctant accomplice, therefore, is the perfect vehicle through which to express and to purge the ambivalent sentiments of Irish and British audiences who may not themselves be at all disposed to support militant nationalism, but who may harbour serious doubts about the legitimacy of the Northern state or the received wisdom on the conflict there or the UK's role in it. The reluctant accomplice serves as an uncomprehending scapegoat who initially registers such doubts only to repudiate them all the more convincingly and to offer himself up as a propitiating sacrifice to the sacred order of the state he has questioned. Identifying with this character thus allows the audience to work through its own doubts and misgivings.

That the protagonists of *Cal* and *The Crying Game* end up with nowhere else to go but the state prison, however, is surely symptomatic of a nagging dissatisfaction in these narratives about the limited resolutions they proffer. Good fences may make good neighbours, but something there is that doesn't like a wall, and the state-as-penal-institution is a less than reassuring image on which to end, especially given Northern Ireland's terrible history where prisons are concerned. The combination of noble fortitude and doleful passivity with which the former militant condemns himself to the penitentiary seems to signify not so much a firm conviction that the nationalist cause is inherently unjust as a reluctant acceptance that the cost of achieving Irish reunification is unthinkable. In other words, these narratives repudiate Northern Irish nationalism in sorrow as well as in anger because the cost of dismantling the state border seems too high to contemplate. At the end of *The Crying Game*, as he and Dil gaze at each other wistfully through the bullet-proof glass partition, Fergus exudes a sense of rueful regret and virtuous self-sacrifice. The structure of feeling his demeanour epitomises is a defeatist one, which holds that because they would be too difficult to change, some things must simply be accepted.

The critics cited earlier are not wrong, then, when they sense that *The Crying Game* is preoccupied with borders; it is just that they conceive the issue in metaphorical terms only. Camera shots that telegraph the issue of borders to the audience frame *The Crying Game*. The film opens with a tracking shot from which a carnival fairground on the far side of a river is viewed through the arches of a bridge. The bridge here is a conventional image of separation and connection, while the carnival suggests a utopian image of community yet to be attained. The narrative closes with a sequence in which the two protagonists converse through a glass partition in a British prison. Far from suggesting the 'opening' of 'borders' implied by the title of Judie Wheelwright's review, therefore, the narrative trajectory of *The Crying Game* would seem to suggest the idea of community impeded and the final irrevocability of some sexual and political barriers.

## V

Some would argue that the fact that Sinn Féin has signed up to the Good Friday Agreement signals the exhaustion of the republican campaign to end partition and acquiescence to the Northern state of a kind quite consonant with the resolutions imagined in the literary and cinematic narratives examined above. From this perspective, the cross-border dimensions of the Agreement are essentially a palliative designed to reconcile Northern nationalists to the Union by according them nominal institutional links to the Irish Republic. In return for this concession, and for some state recognition of a depoliticised Northern Irish cultural nationalism, republicans have been compelled, it is suggested, to accept the legitimacy of the Northern state as a democratic unit of self-determination. In a state in which Catholics remain disproportionately concentrated among the poor and educationally disadvantaged – Catholic working-class areas in Belfast have unemployment rates double those of the city's average – the cross-border links, it is argued, serve essentially to spruce up what remains a deeply sectarian state.

Interpretations of this kind, which assume republican exhaustion and acquiescence, have issued from several quarters. Some of the more confident or triumphal strands in Unionism have interpreted matters in this way, but the most virulent accusations of 'sellout' stem from hardline republican militants determined to pursue another phase of military struggle. The latter have not explained why militarism should be any more successful in the future than it has been in the past, especially since the anti-Agreement militants have neither the levels of communal support nor the political organisation Sinn Féin republicanism has. Some left-wing republican dissidents and anti-partitionist socialists have developed a more complex critique, which construes the shift in Sinn Féin strategy not in terms of 'sellout' but in terms of the consistent limitations of the republican analysis. From this perspective, the weakness of republicanism is that it always put more effort into vanguardist guerrilla struggle than into the development of mass working-class activity. Where they once placed unwarranted faith in armed struggle to deliver their goals, republicans now, it is suggested, place equally unwarranted confidence in the ability of alliances with bourgeois nationalists, North and South, and in US investment, to overcome the sectarian structures inherent in Northern society. Now as in the past, they contend, republicans demonstrate too little confidence in the working-class nationalists that constitute their core constituency, and hence have courted other social agents to help secure their goals when they really need to work to create both cross-communal and cross-border working-class alliances.[60]

In a shrewd analysis of the circumstances that led to the current 'peace process', Joseph Ruane has suggested that, during the twenty-five years of struggle in Northern Ireland, 'all parties overestimated their capacity to achieve their particular goals – republicans to force a British withdrawal, the British and Irish governments to defeat republicans, the British government to impose a power-sharing agreement on loyalists and unionists, and the latter to achieve a new internal settlement. The possibility of peace came not from an abandonment of these goals, but from a more realistic appraisal of each of each participant's ability to achieve them.'[61] If Ruane is right what this suggests is that in the present conjuncture all the parties to the Northern conflict remain wedded to much the same goals as before but have revised the means to attain them. Both nationalists and Unionists are invested in the Agreement, therefore, for antithetical reasons and have wildly different expectations of the economic dividends expected to flow from the new arrangements. Unionists expect the cessation of violence to lead to an economic upswing that will allow Northern Ireland to demonstrate that it is after all a viable society, and increased prosperity will, they hope, gradually diminish nationalist alienation from the state. In such circumstances, they wager, nationalists will content themselves, despite republican rhetoric, with nominal links to the South. Nationalists, on the other hand, anticipate that the logic of current economic development on the island is towards greater co-operation and eventual convergence between North and South, and that the cross-border institutions will help create the conditions that will see the border eventually become defunct. The Agreement, therefore, represents no seismic shift in attitudes, no sudden capitulation, on either side where 'the border bit' is concerned; instead, it attempts to channel the contest over the ultimate sovereignty of the region into a political structure where both sides can pursue their different ends without recourse to arms.

The tentative climate of the current conjuncture in the North finds expression in new narrative developments. In the texts discussed earlier the conflict is narrowly imagined in terms of zero-sum struggles between state security forces and paramilitary subversives in which all other social agents are sidelined. Plot endings remain stalled in an unredeemed now: visions of collective social transformation are entirely absent. The 1990s have witnessed the debilitation of some of these narrative structures and the tentative emergence of new alternatives. Variants of the thriller format continue to thrive. Already, though, *The Crying Game* seems a transitional text in this respect, part of a wider reworking of the genre in the direction of political satire and caricature. Colin Bateman's *Divorcing Jack* (1995) and Robert MacLiam Wilson's *Eureka Street* (1996) exemplify this trend. The narratives discussed earlier tend to be limited by perspectives that are at once too presentist and too narrowly local. The cycle of communal violence; the bitterly divided and segregated communities; the fact that most violence is concentrated in working-class ghettos: these are consistently taken as unexamined givens, as the circumstances that make Northern Ireland what it is; they constitute the conditions that the humane characters seek to transcend. All too often, there is little attempt imaginatively to explore why the communities should be so divided in the first instance, why the cycle of violence should be so sustained, or why so concentrated in working-class districts. One of the more positive developments in recent fictions, therefore, is the attempt historically to deepen and geographically to widen this social frame. Novels such as Seamus Deane's *Reading in the Dark* (1996) and Maurice Leitch's *The Smoke King* (1998) explore periods before the present Troubles, opening up a longer historical perspective against which the present must be assessed. Glenn Patterson's ambitious *Fat Lad* (1992), which moves between England, Northern Ireland and the Irish Republic, and reaches back over several generations to incorporate a historical span that extends from partition into the present, conceives the North not only in terms of local determinants but also those of late capitalism more generally. This is not uncritically to endorse these more recent narratives; in some the stress on individual redemption endures, and in others the North is now to be redeemed not by the British security forces but by the energies and excitements of global capital. Nevertheless, in these narratives the future at least remains open to transformation; a sense of the North simply as an atlas of atrocity gives way to a sense that new social forces are on the move.

## Chapter 4

# Agonies of the potentates: journeys to the frontier in the novels of Amos Oz

## I

The decisive Jewish victory in 1948 left Israel in control of some 73 per cent of the land of Palestine (54 per cent was originally awarded in the United Nations Partition proposal). When Egypt and Jordan annexed Gaza and the West Bank respectively, Palestine was effectively expunged from the map, the entire territory absorbed into other states by way of a trilateral partition. Just twenty years later, however, the State of Israel secured control over the remaining Palestinian territories in the 1967 War. This effectively reunited, militarily at least, the sundered territory. For Israelis, the consequences of the 1967 victory were manifold and complex. The capture of Jerusalem and the seizure of the 'lost' Biblical territories of Judea and Samaria (the West Bank) revived the prospect that a 'Greater Israel', that would include all of historic Palestine, might now be realised. In the decade before 1948, the Zionist leadership had conceded that this maximalist goal was unattainable, but partition was reluctantly accepted, and the ambition that a 'Greater Israel' might one day be attained was never entirely abandoned. Even after its victories in 1948, Israel never committed itself to the boundaries agreed in the 1947 UN Partition Plan or to the borders agreed in the 1948–9 armistice agreements with the Arab states.[1] The major difficulty attaching to a full annexation of the Palestinian territories captured in 1967, and to the immediate declaration of a 'Greater Israel,' however, was that this would have incorporated an additional 1.3 million Palestinian Arabs within what was defined as a Jewish state. This would effectively have transformed Israel into a binational society and in so doing would have challenged its specifically Jewish character. The Israeli establishment's response to this dilemma was neither to annex the territories nor to surrender them, but to revert to incremental settlement tactics that resembled those in the pre-state period. Its strategy, that is, was to develop creeping Jewish settlements in the newly captured Palestinian areas, incrementally pushing forward the Jewish frontier, and finally establishing *de jure* title over these settled areas when conditions permitted.

This strategy has been remarkably successful in territorial terms, but it has not been without its problems. The harsh daily realities of military occupation, settlement activity, dispossession and land confiscation in the West Bank cast Israel's pre-state settlement period, until then regarded as an heroic era of nation-building, in rather a different and less glamorous light. At the same time, the availability of a cheap Palestinian labour supply, increased military and financial dependency on the US, and the development of a consumerist society all hastened the decline of classical 'socialist' Zionism and paved the way for the emergence of the Zionist right, which now represented itself as the most vigorous champion of the new wave of Jewish settlement and expansion.[2] Moreover, the ongoing Palestinian resistance to the occupation restored Palestinians to the centre of Israeli consciousness. Israel continued to see itself as a vulnerable society besieged by a hostile Arab world, but its own brutal repression of the Palestinians in the territories challenged its self-image as the innocent victim of unwarranted Arab aggression.

In Israel, as in Ireland, the political crisis in which that state has been immersed since the late 1960s also manifests itself as an intellectual crisis that has found its most overt expression in the field of national historiography. Since the late 1980s, when books by 'New Historians' such as Simha Flapan, Tom Segev, Benny Morris, Avi Shlaim and Ilan Pappé appeared in quick succession, Israeli historiography has witnessed the emergence of its own distinctive version of 'revisionism'. Clearly prompted by the contemporary Israeli–Palestinian conflict, all of these New Historians returned in their works to the birth of the nation-state and suggested that the conventional state-sanctioned version of its foundation in 1948 involved a drastic sanitisation of events, especially with respect to the Palestinians.[3] The domestic challenge to official Israeli versions of events was not, however, confined to the New Historians. Prompted by the ongoing settlements in the West Bank, Israeli sociologists such as Baruch Kimmerling, Gershon Shafir and Uri Ram developed new theoretical perspectives that identified Zionism as a colonialist enterprise that could instructively be compared to other colonial settler societies in the US, South Africa and elsewhere.[4] This colonialist perspective is usually dismissed by both the left and right wings of the Zionist establishment, and still remains marginalised in the mainstream Israeli academy because it flouts the conventional insistence that Jewish settlement in Palestine is exceptional. In the area of cultural studies, too, scholars emerged who adopted a colonialist methodology, and who argued that this offered valuable insight not only into Zionism's treatment of the Palestinians but of Oriental Jews as well. Ella Shohat's work on Israeli cinema and Ammiel Alcalay's attempt to re-situate the Oriental Jews in terms of the wider political and cultural history of the Levant are important examples of this new scholarship.[5] So too are the works of Israeli-based cultural critics and social scientists associated with the 'post-Zionist' journal, *Theory and Criticism*.[6]

This chapter will be concerned not with this new scholarship, however, but with the kind of domestic Israeli dissent associated with Amos Oz, one of Israel's most distinguished contemporary writers. While the dissident academic scholarship described above offers quite a trenchant critique of Zionism, I shall want to suggest that Oz's ostensibly critical stance is of a much more recuperative cast. Debates about historiography by their very nature reach small, usually specialised academic audiences. In contrast, the works of leading contemporary Israeli writers such as Amos Oz, A. B. Yehoshua, Yoram Kaniuk, David Grossman and others reach a much wider and less specialised readership in Israel and especially in the West.

Of the major contemporary Israeli writers, Oz is the one who reaches the widest non-Israeli audience (his works have been translated into thirty languages, and he is the Israeli writer whose works are most often translated into English). He is also a prominent public intellectual associated with the Peace Now movement and in that capacity he has published several non-fiction books – *In the Land of Israel, On the Slopes of Lebanon* and *Israel, Palestine and Peace* – on the Israeli–Palestinian conflict. Leading newspapers and magazines in the Anglophone world such as *The Guardian, The Observer* and *The New York Times* regularly carry his articles on the conflict. Once described by *Newsweek* as 'a kind of Zionist Orwell',[7] Oz's international image is that of an anguished dissident leftist who champions a reasonable compromise between Israelis and Palestinians, an apparently moderate stance valiantly held between right-wing Israeli expansionists on one side and belligerent Palestinian extremists on the other. Within Israel, there are many public intellectuals more radical than Oz, but for many outside Israel it is he who represents the contemporary voice of 'dissident Israel'. Like Conor Cruise O'Brien, Edward Said or Nadine Gordimer, Oz's ability to combine the roles of distinguished cultural intellectual and outspoken political dissident lends his voice an authority that commands international attention. It is this that makes his position important to investigate.

Oz is also of particular interest for this study, however, because he has long supported the idea that partition represents the only viable solution to the Israeli–Palestinian conflict. Although he opposed an outright Israeli annexation of the West Bank and Gaza after 1967, Oz argued that the occupation of these territories could be defended on tactical grounds until the Palestinians recognised the legitimacy of the State of Israel. In an article published in the *New York Times Magazine* in 1982, he suggested that once that objective had been achieved, however, the two peoples would ultimately have to agree to partition the land between them. '[W]e must in the end come back to what has been socialist Zionism's standing offer to the Palestinian Arabs – reasonable partition of the country in accordance with demographic realities; recognition for recognition; security for security; self-determination for self-determination.'[8]

For all its appearance of moderation, there is a great deal in Oz's pro-partitionist position that is open to question. The construction of events in the passage cited above suggests that socialist Zionism had always held out a 'reasonable partition of the country in accordance with demographic realities' as a standing offer to the Palestinians. The historical record attests that in reality no such 'standing offer' was ever available from any of the leading Zionist parties.[9] On the contrary, by their constant expansion of Jewish settlements in the territories, the Zionist left and right were both working since 1967 to establish 'facts on the ground' that would dictate that should any two-state solution eventually emerge it could work only to the advantage of Israel. Moreover, while Oz advocates a just compromise based on 'reasonable partition', he has never indicated what kind of territorial division this would require or where the partitioning borders should be. In an article published in *The Guardian* some days before the signing of the Oslo Agreement, he wrote: 'We and they [Israelis and Palestinians] – along with most of the Arab world – are ready now to consider a partition of the land between its peoples.' 'What partition and under what conditions', he argued, 'this question still involves a complex process of bargaining ... All this must be clarified around the negotiating table, and calls for wisdom, patience, and vision.'[10] Again, this ostensibly seems quite reasonable: it is after all the work of statesmen and not novelists to delineate borders and the ethical decision to compromise, Oz suggests, is ultimately more important than the details of how land will be divided. Yet the suggestion that the details can be worked out later allows Oz, like the Oslo Accord he champions, to skirt the objections of its Palestinian critics: namely, that the envisaged settlement allows Israel to retain most of the gains it illegally accrued since 1967, and asks Palestinians to legitimate the surrender of what they have already lost. For its critics, far from being an even-handed compromise, the Agreement resurrects the partition 'solution' in a context in which Israelis have already secured possession of the lion's share of historic Palestine and can thus dictate how much land shall be returned to the Palestinians and under what conditions. Far from reversing an illegal conquest, they suggest, the Agreement effectively postponed crucial issues such as the fate of Jerusalem, the refugees, settlers and Palestinian statehood to 'final status' negotiations. Instead of guaranteeing a just and principled settlement on such matters, therefore, these were all reduced to technical issues to be worked out in negotiation, giving the Israelis, by far the stronger of the two sides involved, the opportunity to concede as little as possible on all of them. Oz's post-Oslo writings never seriously engage such criticisms.

In Oz's literary writings the issue of borders is also an observable preoccupation, but an elusiveness of kinds may be noted there too. Despite his high profile as a public intellectual, Oz's novels almost never present themselves as directly political works at all in the way, for example, Conrad's *Nostromo* or Tolstoy's *War and Peace* or Nadine Gordimer's South African novels take national politics as their manifest theme. Written in the mode of psychological realism, Oz's plots are usually centred on Oedipal family romances: his central protagonists usually suffer some form of chronic neurosis, which frequently expresses itself in the form of crises concerning sexuality and procreation. In Oz's fiction, that is to say, the contemporary political stresses of Israeli society are converted into narratives of psychological distress.

In these novels mention of Israel's borders recurs like an insistent yet curiously muted refrain. Characteristically, the border impinges on the consciousness of Oz's fictional protagonists, as on the attention of his readers, only in a casual, almost perfunctory, manner: a radio news bulletin, only half attended to, refers to troop movements along the border; a visitor to a kibbutz catches a glimpse of an Arab village just beyond the frontier; an evening newspaper mentions a minor incursion across one or other of Israel's boundaries. A constant, nagging, even ominous presence, the border nonetheless generally makes itself felt only at the peripheries of consciousness in Oz's novels; it is something that momentarily attracts attention but does not detain it. His novels, that is, do not present themselves as being about borders; we cannot understand their function in his creative work at the thematic level. Nevertheless, this studied casualness is also deceptive and can deflect attention from the fact that the border in these instances usually functions as something more than just the incidental motif it appears. Several of Oz's novels, for instance, are set in kibbutz communities on Israel's frontiers and narrative resolutions frequently involve taking the protagonists on a journey to the actual site of the border. *Elsewhere, Perhaps*, for example, reaches its climax with a military engagement between Israeli and Syrian forces over a disputed strip of frontier territory. *My Michael* draws to a close with a journey by its central protagonist, Hannah, to the Lebanese border. In *A Perfect Peace* Yonatan journeys to the border and crosses it momentarily into Jordan only to turn back in terror. In one register, then, the border appears in these novels as one casual leitmotif among others. In another, it consistently returns, however, as a crucial site of narrative complication, the place where crises long in the making finally come to a head.

Oz's preoccupation with borders must be situated in terms of a wider Israeli border crisis that ultimately goes back to Israel's version of the 'myth of the frontier'.[11] In the pre-state *Yishuv*, when Jewish settlement in Palestine was still expanding, the outer borders of the Jewish community were largely conceived as they were in other colonial-settler societies: physically, as an open frontier that one had a civilisational duty to push back; culturally, as a line marking the division between civilisation and primitivism. As in other colonial-settler societies, a whole complex of ideas affixed themselves to the frontier: the concept of pioneering as a national mission; the concept of a Zionist duty to redeem the entirety of the Biblical land of Palestine; visions of the frontier as a place of escape from metropolitan discontent. The establishment of the State of Israel in 1948 could at once be celebrated as the heroic culmination of this pioneering process and also as Israel's particular version of 'the closing of the frontier', the termination of the epic stage of expansionist nation-building. In the late nineteenth and early twentieth centuries, analogous closings of the frontier had triggered cultural crises in America especially but also in Britain.[12] For settler societies whose self-conceptions were defined in terms of immigration and territorial expansion, the closing of the border meant that the state had finally fulfilled its programme, something that might also imply, however, that it had lost its original sense of missionary purpose. In Israel's case, this crisis was complicated because less than two decades after the frontier had seemed closed the Six Days War opened it up again. This new opening of the frontier represented the return of the repressed in Israeli culture, dragging to the surface once again a whole cluster of issues to do with pioneering, settlement, national destiny, and the fate of the Palestinians that had agitated Zionist cultural and intellectual debate during the pre-state period.[13]

Oz's novels, I will argue, represent an imaginative response to this societal crisis that may usefully be understood as a distinctively Israeli variant of what John McClure has called 'late imperial romance'.[14] The classical nineteenth-century Western imperial romances, McClure argues, were designed to satisfy Westerners' collective longings for adventure and the exotic. These romances did not manufacture their dreams out of thin air; they depended for their (re)production on regions rich in the 'raw materials' of adventure, magic, mystery and Otherness – on regions and populations untouched by the disenchanting forces of Western rationalisation and secularisation. 'For much of the nineteenth century', McClure argues, 'the relation between romance and imperialism was a symbiotic one'. 'Imperial expansion created new heroic professions (explorer, colonial soldier and administrator, missionary), and new sites for the playing out of old stories: quests for wisdom or treasure, struggles with demons or magicians, tests of strength against monstrous enemies.'[15] But since imperialism represented the extension of the modernising and rationalising processes that eradicated magic, mystery and Otherness, its new global reach towards the end of the nineteenth century now threatened to abolish the 'raw materials' of exoticism, adventure and mystery on which romance thrived. What emerges at this point, McClure argues, is a new kind of romance – 'late imperial romance' – which offers a critique of imperialism but still remains complicit in its ideology. In works such as Joseph Conrad's *Heart of Darkness* (which McClure considers a foundational text in this development), the classical nineteenth-century imperialist romance is debunked as a sham. But even as such works struggle to 'disenchant' the conventional equation of overseas expansion with chivalric or sacred struggle, they nonetheless remain tied to imperialist ideology because they can conceive of this disenchantment only by positing some impermeable boundary between 'civilisation' and its 'savage other'. In this way, the sense of an exotic Other world is preserved, but only at the cost of creating a fatalistic vision of a bifurcated world stalled in permanent division between a dull and uninspiring 'modern' zone and an adventurous but chaotic and disordered 'non-modern' one, the latter now deemed totally beyond either Western intervention or any kind of positive social transformation or rescue.

In this chapter I will undertake close readings of two of Oz's novels – *Elsewhere, Perhaps* and *A Perfect Peace* – that can be seen to operate in these terms. In these novels, the central protagonists are obsessed by Zionist dreams of adventure and the exotic, but Oz's actual narratives work to disenchant these dreams, to suggest that Israeli dreams of adventure in Arab lands are no longer tenable and dangerously out of place. This disenchantment of expansionist Israeli fantasies is achieved, however, not by means of some sort of radical or utopian imagination that can envisage a transformed world in which Israeli and Palestinian might recognise each other or co-exist alongside each other on new terms. Instead, what Oz's novels suggest is that his Israeli protagonists must cease to venture into Arab lands because to do so is to invite destruction on themselves. Expansionist dreams of adventure in exotic lands are shown to be dangerous, therefore, but this is achieved by positing a world of Israelis and Arabs permanently stalled in division, separated by an immutable boundary, which becomes an index of absolute distinction between the two peoples. This narrative strategy, which subtends several of Oz's novels, can be interpreted, I will suggest, as the literary objective correlative of the partitionist stance that Oz publicly endorses as a Peace Now activist.

## II

Oz's first novel, *Elsewhere, Perhaps*, tells the story of the kibbutz community of Metsudat Ram by the Syrian border. It is a densely populated novel and the distribution of narrative consciousness across numerous members of the kibbutz creates the effect of a communal narrative rather than that of any single individual. At the centre of this dispersed narrative, however, is the story of the Harish family. Reuven Harish, schoolteacher and poet, belongs to the founding generation of kibbutz settlers. He is a dedicated and idealistic Zionist, but his life has been soured by the fact that his wife, Eva, abandoned him to return to Germany. Eva, we are told, 'left her husband and children and married a tourist'.[16] The tourist in question, Isaac Hamburger, is also her cousin, and a rich businessman and night-club owner in

Munich. Eva's marital infidelity constitutes a rejection of Israel for the Diaspora and of the collectivist principles of the kibbutz for the capitalist comforts of Germany. Her departure takes place well before the novel opens, and Reuven Harish's daughter, Noga, is already a young teenager growing into sexual awareness when the narrative proper begins. The girl regularly daydreams of her absent mother and the fairytale-like Europe where she imagines her to live. Subconsciously aggrieved by Eva's desertion, and by her father's zestless sexual affair with another schoolteacher, Bronka Berger, Noga becomes involved with Bronka's husband, Ezra, and becomes pregnant by him. The main plot of *Elsewhere, Perhaps* centres on whether or not the pregnant Noga will abandon the kibbutz to join her mother in Europe or remain with her increasingly enfeebled father in Israel.

The second part of the novel opens with the arrival of the sinister Diasporic Jew Zechariah-Siegfried Berger, perhaps the most powerfully drawn character in the narrative. Brother of Ezra Berger, by whom Noga has become impregnated, Zechariah-Siegfried had, like Eva, come to live on the kibbutz for a short time when it was first established but had then returned to Europe where he is now partner to Eva Harish's second husband in Munich. Travelling to Israel to recruit acts for his partner's night-club, Zechariah-Siegfried Berger visits his brother's family at the kibbutz where he takes an inordinate interest in the pregnant Noga and makes a determined bid to seduce her into returning to Europe with him. His purpose in doing so is never entirely clear, but Siegfried's sinuous manner, his seediness and the suspicions of the kibbutz community indicate that he means no good. Many in the kibbutz believe that he wants to seduce Noga himself, or to pimp her (the Munich 'night-club' seems a euphemism for brothel), or simply to take her away with him out of a malicious desire to frustrate her idealistic father and the kibbutz community. This latter part of the narrative is self-consciously constructed to convey something of the quality of fairytale or morality tale. Zechariah-Siegfried, the wandering Diasporic Jew, and Herbert Segal, the kibbutz secretary, engage in a subtly waged but determined contest for Noga's allegiance. Siegfried himself describes this contest as one between 'two fairies clashing over an innocent soul'[17] with himself cast as the wicked fairy and Herbert Segal as his benevolent antagonist.

The first chapter of *Elsewhere, Perhaps* consists of a meticulously delineated geography of the kibbutz of Metsudat Ram. The kibbutz, we are told, is located at one end of a green valley overshadowed by a towering mountain range which rises just beyond the state border and which 'completely blocks the view to the east'. On the one side there is the kibbutz with its 'strict symmetry' and 'severe lines', the archetypal gridded space of settlement, civilisation, and disciplined order; on the other, the rugged and barren mountains – 'bare and rocky, cut by zigzagging ravines' – whose violent disorder contrasts with the geometric regularity of the kibbutz. Moreover, the narrator remarks: 'There is a kind of enmity between the valley, with its neat, geometrical patchwork of fields and the savage bleakness of the mountains. Even the symmetrical architecture of Kibbutz Metsudat Ram is no more than a negation of the grim natural chaos that looks down on it from above.'[18]

The spatial field delineated here recalls the imaginative geography of classical Zionism, which conceived of Israel as a closed utopia of Western civilisation within an otherwise chaotic and desert-like Asiatic landscape. In one of the foundational texts of Zionism, Theodor Herzl tried to win imperial support for a Jewish state in Palestine on the grounds that '[w]e should there form a portion of a rampart of Europe against Asia, an outpost of civilization as opposed to barbarism'.[19] Decades later, Chaim Weizmann invoked a similarly manichean cartography when he described the Jewish settlement in Palestine in terms of an elemental conflict between civilisation and chaos: 'On the one side, the forces of destruction, the forces of the desert, have arisen, and on the other side stand firm the forces of civilization and building. It is the old war of the desert against civilization, but we will not be stopped.'[20]

The spatial division that structures this Zionist cartography has its roots in the imaginative geography of nineteenth-century imperialism and may be observed in the Western imperial adventure novel especially, which, as John McClure writes, 'translates the basic imperial division of the world (metropolis and colonies or potential colonies) into a familiar romance division, with the West represented as a zone of relative order, security, and secularity, the non-Western world as a zone of magic, mystery, and disorder'. In the imperial romance, the relationship between these two spaces is inherently ambivalent. This cartography seems to confer an inherent privilege on the West, which is conceived as the zone of civilisation, but the safety and security of the West's ordered space offer no real outlet for adventure; this can easily become rigidly routinised and stultifying space – what McClure describes as a 'banal, quotidian world of calculation and compromise from which the heroes of romance are always in flight'. Hence it is to the spaces of disorder that the imperial romance is really drawn: 'Without unordered spaces, or spaces distorted by war, it is impossible to stage the wanderings and disorientations, the quests and conquests and conversions, the ordeals and sacrifices and triumphs that are the stuff of romance.'[21]

In *Elsewhere, Perhaps* this imaginative cartography becomes the object of the novel's troubled reflection. The spatial field delineated in the opening chapters is divided into zones of order and disorder, but the border between the two turns out to be worryingly obscure and elusive. The kibbutz of Metsudat Ram, we are told, is situated inside the state border, but:

> This border, prominently marked on the maps with a thick green line, is not visible to the observer, since it does not correspond to the natural boundary between the lush green valley and the bleak, bare mountains. The soil of Israel overflows the limits of the valley and spreads up the lower slopes toward the barren heights. So the eye and the mind – or, more precisely, geology and politics – come to be at odds with one another. The kibbutz itself stands some two miles from the international frontier. We cannot define the distance more precisely without entering into the bloodstained controversy over the exact location of this line.[22]

The lack of a clearly defined border between the apparently distinct fields of order and chaotic disorder is represented here as a destabilising element that threatens to undo the whole manichean construction on which the kibbutz's sense of its place in the world depends. Although the state border 'prominently marked on maps with a thick green line' is perfectly clear and unambiguous on paper, its reassuring 'thickness' there is undermined by the fact that it has no analogue on the ground. The map and the territory, then, are not the same; in fact, the lie of the land gives the lie to the ostensible clarity of the map and opens up a seemingly 'unnatural' disjunction between the two. In other words, the discourse of 'natural frontiers' threatens to undo the authority of the state map by suggesting that the 'soil of Israel overflows the limits of the valley and spreads up the lower slopes toward the barren heights'. This disputed patch is called, significantly, 'the Camel's Field',[23] and is tilled by shadowy Arab *fellahin*, associatively linked in the text with the glowering mountain range that overshadows the kibbutz and that impedes its view to the east. The low-level skirmishing between these Arab peasants and the kibbutz farmers remains constantly in the background to the main action of the novel, and the narrative finally comes to a climax when matters escalate into open confrontation and 'the Camel's Field' is seized by the Israeli Army.

*Elsewhere, Perhaps* begins, then, with two apparently discrete spaces to which the different values of 'order' and 'chaos' can confidently be ascribed. In Oz's treatment, the crude distinction that subtends this imaginative cartography becomes the object of the novel's troubled reflection, and is worried over and ironised to the point where the governing binary threatens to dissolve, though it is never entirely dismantled. At the end of the novel, the anxieties that trouble the opening chapter seem to be allayed when the state map and 'natural frontiers' are forcibly made to fit. The troubling discrepancy between the paper and actual landscape now seems to be closed since the state map and the natural terrain are brought into some apparently more satisfying alignment. But there is little in the novel to suggest that this forced fit, however decisive it appears, can really secure some definitive closure to the cartographic anxieties, the competing realities, that bedevil the kibbutz.

If the conflict between Israel and its vaguely defined Arab Other is constructed in spatial or geographical terms, the differences within the kibbutz community are structured primarily along generational lines, with each generation associated with conflicting sets of values. The older generation that founded the kibbutz is comprised of pre-state settlers of European origin. Mostly German, Russian and Polish born, this immigrant generation still has memories of European pogroms and the Holocaust and of the early days of frontier settlement in Palestine. As Oz depicts it, this generation, though still doggedly faithful to the values of Zionism and the collectivist ethos of the kibbutz, displays the fatigue and decline that inevitably accompanies old age. The memory of a more 'heroic' pioneering era is present in the novel, but only in the form of this generation's somewhat hazy and slightly suspect recollections of that time.

While the older generation displays a sense of fatigue, the younger is characterised by a sort of sluggish torpor and a constant yearning for excitement that manifests itself either in restless dreams of wars of conquest or longings for escape to distant climes. One of the ways in which generational differences are signalled in the novel is in terms of their different attitudes to borders. The older socialistic pioneers like to cite internationalist slogans such as 'The concept of social justice does not recognize national boundaries,'[24] but their own tense lives on the borderline between Israel and the Arab world disclose the tremendous disjunction between lofty ideals and lived reality. In fact, one of the ironies of their situation is that in one sense these settlers seem only to have exchanged one set of frontiers, one set of ghettos, for another. Thus, Aaron Ramigolski, the kibbutz's first martyr, 'left his family and his home in Kovel, on the Polish–Russian border' only to be killed on the Palestinian frontier.[25] Young Rami remembers that his father used to say: 'Israel must be the opposite of the ghetto. If we're going to live in a ghetto here, we might as well have stayed in Europe. At least there we didn't have the *hamsin*.'[26] The novel seems to imply, however, that for the kibbutz elders living constantly under the shadow of war, the besieged mentality of the ghetto remains the abiding reality of their lives. Their native-born Sabra children, in contrast, disdain their elder's worthy humanist platitudes and are compulsively drawn to the excitement of border wars. Young Rami, for example, goes off to join the army hoping that 'things on our border don't get too hot before I get there, because I want to be in on the action'.[27]

As Oz constructs things, then, the lived experience of the older generation fails to tally with its socialistic Zionist slogans, and an element of routinised repression attaches to the overly disciplined regime of the kibbutz. The younger generation displays repressed yearnings that express a negative, and potentially disastrous, attempt to find some form of cathartic release from this tensed-up situation. As in late imperial fiction generally, the excessively ordered, overly timetabled, secular world of the kibbutz proves inimical to desire and adventure. The younger generation rebels against this enclosed world, craving a war of conquest that would take it across the frontier into exciting zones of mystery and adventure.

The novel is haunted not only by the menacing Arab world across the contested state border, but also by a second space: that of the Jewish Diaspora. The structuring device that articulates this relationship is that of the family divided between Israel and Europe. When the novel opens, the Harish family is split between the small Israeli kibbutz where Reuven and his children live, and the Germany to which Eva has returned. This trope of the split family is clearly a figure for the divide between those Zionist Jews who have committed themselves to the hard life of the Israeli frontier and the seemingly more prosperous and comfortable Diasporic Jews in Europe. Because they turned their backs on the Zionist dream and returned to Europe, Eva and Siegfried are essentially apostates to Zionism and as such represent a challenge to the morale of the kibbutz community. Eva's return especially is marked as a form of 'betrayal'; it has shattered her husband's self-esteem and now threatens to lure her pregnant daughter away as well. What we have in the novel, then, are two kinds of desire, each rooted in a certain dissatisfaction with Israeli space, and expressed as yearnings to stray beyond its borders: Rami's 'masculine' desire for military adventures, which he hopes will find outlet in the impending war with the Arabs, and Noga's more 'feminine' desire to be with her mother in Europe, which may ultimately be no less destructive.

The Europe of *Elsewhere, Perhaps* is a remarkably ambivalent space. For the older generation, it is a remembered place of dread and degradation: the land of ghetto life, forced flight, and the Holocaust. But it is also the scene of its earliest childhood memories and hence, paradoxically, a space of troubling attraction and uncanny desire: a remembered land of green woods, blue lakes and bell-towers. Despite its Zionist ideals, Europe possesses for this generation a quality of nostalgic and romantic appeal that the harsher Asiatic landscape of the Middle East lacks. In the early part of the novel especially, this immigrant *nostalgie d'Europe* is rendered with considerable empathy, expressed by way of the triangulation of the divided Harish family. Europe is associatively linked with Reuven Harish's melancholy desire for his lost wife, and with Noga's dreamy longing to be with her absent mother. As such, Eva and the landscape of Europe merge to become the object of a wistful desire cathected with sexual and feminine, even maternal, attributes.

There is a second triangulation at work in the novel, however, that ultimately acts to disenchant this sense of Europe as a viable alternative to Israel. This triangle is activated mostly in the second half of the novel when the contest between Israel and Europe is reconfigured as a struggle between kindly Herbert Segal and Zechariah-Siegfried Berger over the destiny of the now pregnant Noga. This contest is really one for the soul and the reproductive future of Israel, which Noga represents. It is essentially a struggle for succession, one to determine whether Zionism or the Diaspora will ultimately win the younger generation's allegiance. The tug of war in Noga's interior consciousness between the two sites is initially figured as a contest between paternal duty to her ailing father, Reuven, and a maternal desire to join her mysterious mother, Eva. Configured in this way, the tug of love between Israel and Europe has an anxious but essentially benign character registered in terms of the child's conflicting loyalties to both parents. But when the relationship between Zionism and Diaspora is reconfigured, now in a mode exterior to Noga's consciousness, as a struggle between Herbert Segal and Zechariah-Siegfried *over*

*Noga*, its whole tenor is altered and it acquires a much more ominous character.

The Europe of Zechariah-Siegfried is a place at once both sinister and seedy. Zechariah-Siegfried is an Iago-type figure smothering with *ressentiment*, and in his attitude towards the kibbutz community, and towards Reuven especially, he exudes a kind of oily malignancy that is conveyed with considerable power. He works as a pander to the Germans whom he despises. By his own account, he has come to recruit Israeli acts for the 'night-club' in Munich that will pique his German clients' debased taste for the perversely exotic: 'The Germans were eager to taste the choice fruits of the land, the piquant flavour of the new Israel. They were excited by men with breasts, singing fish, white Negroes, and Israeli Jews – non Jewish Jews.'[28] Whatever its ultimate purpose, Siegfried's attempt to lure Noga away to Europe is tainted by the fact that as one of the elder members of the kibbutz, Hasia Ramigolski, remarks: 'he's the type that's fond of dirt'. Hasia links his degenerate character to the Diaspora in general: 'They're all the same, those Jews who went back to Germany after the war. They're up to no good. All kinds of underworld figures.'[29] Hasia's crude prejudice is ironised in the novel, but nevertheless the whole construction of the contest for Noga and her unborn baby waged between the benevolent kibbutz secretary and the debauched Diaspora Jew serves to confirm Hasia's basic thesis. To return to Germany, land of the Holocaust, is to be complicit with the abject and self-hating perversity that Zechariah-Siegfried personifies.

The construction of Zechariah-Siegfried in *Elsewhere, Perhaps*, which represents the Diaspora Jew as a combination of cosmopolitan capitalist fat-cat and degenerate pimp, has its source in anti-Semitic constructions of Jews generally. Although it is incomprehensible except as an attempt to combat European anti-Semitism, the Zionist movement also incorporated a great deal of anti-Semitic conceptions of the Jewish Diaspora into its own ideology. Zionism, that is to say, accepted anti-Semitic conceptions of the Diaspora Jew as effeminate, parasitic and degenerate, but argued that the Zionist project in Palestine would create new 'manly' Jews who would be in every way the antithesis to the demoralised ghetto Jews of the Diaspora. In order to disenchant the idea that the Diaspora might constitute a viable alternative to Israel, *Elsewhere, Perhaps* draws on this classical Zionist discourse of racial and sexual degeneration. In Oz's novel, then, since the lure of the Diaspora is identified with the degenerate Zechariah-Siegfried, only

Zionist space – whatever its discontents – seems to carry redemptive promise.

Siegfried is one of the most striking figures in this novel because he is not merely a stereotype, however, but a complex composite character. He represents a menace to Israeli space in the form of the dangerous, somewhat sinister, lures of the Diaspora, but he is also associated with the forces of consumer capitalism and as such constitutes another kind of threat to the ascetic and rather spartan lifestyle of the socialistic kibbutz. His arrival is linked to an inflow of consumer goods: he brings with him a suitcase packed with tape recorders, electric shavers, expensive dress materials and so forth. To buy the goodwill of the generally sceptical kibbutz community, he plies almost everyone there with gifts. He suggests to Reuven Harish that he might be able have an edition of his poetry published in Germany. To the children he gives gifts suggestive of travel – a model railway set and a shiny new bicycle.

The Diaspora and consumer capitalism, both associated with Siegfried, are each identified, therefore, with modes of circulation that threaten the integrity of the nation-state and the national ideals exemplified by the kibbutz. As a 'deserter' who damaged communal morale when he left the kibbutz after 1948 to return to Germany, and as a figure for capitalist consumerism who tempts the kibbutz to abandon its ascetic values for gifts connotative of luxury and wanderlust, Siegfried is an overdetermined figure in whom a number of threats are combined. The degeneracy with which he is associated turns out to be not simply 'outside' of Israel in the Diaspora, but 'inside' it as well in the form of a transition from its old collectivist and socialistic ethos to a modern capitalist one.[30] In the late 1960s, when *Elsewhere, Perhaps* was written, this transition was already well advanced. During the pre-state period, the Zionist leadership in Palestine had generally favoured co-operative forms of community (the best known being the kibbutz) as the most efficient way to advance Jewish colonisation there. By the 1950s, the new Israeli state had developed a capitalist class structure, however, and in the 1960s Israel was increasingly integrated into the international capitalist system. Even in the pre-state period, the economy of the *Yishuv* was extremely dependent on outside support, and in the first two decades of statehood this dependency increased, with billions of dollars flowing into the Israeli economy in the form of grants from West Germany and donations from Jewish communities in Europe and in North America.[31] Siegfried is the compelling figure he is, then, because through him is registered one of the most fundamental sources of tension in the novel: that between the actual 'openness' of the Israeli economy – its chronic dependence on 'outside' support from the rejected worlds of Europe and the Jewish Diaspora – and the Zionist attempt to construct Israel as a self-enclosed, self-reliant utopia.

What *Elsewhere, Perhaps* presents us with, then, are two equally troubling spaces, each the source of dangerous temptations for its Israeli protagonists: on one side, the vaguely defined Arab space and the disputed 'Camel's Field' across Israel's eastern border; on the other, the Diaspora, which threatens both in its capacity as an alternative to Israel and as source of capitalist corruption. The dangers associated with each place are developed alongside each other in the text in the form of parallel plots that never really meet until the problems represented by each are 'resolved' simultaneously in the novel's closing chapters. In the penultimate chapter, the contest between the kibbutz members and the stubborn Arab *fellahin* who persist in tilling the 'Camel's Field' comes to a head and the Israeli army is summoned, the Syrian army is outgunned, and Israel's borders are extended to enclose the disputed stretch. During this skirmish Reuven Harish dies, and, intuitively associating Siegfried with his death, Noga finally rouses herself from her long trance of indecision, shakes off Siegfried's spell, and demands that the kibbutz have him expelled. Noga's decision to remain with the kibbutz, the final exorcism of the sinister Diaspora Jew, and the seizure of the 'Camel's Field', all coincide, therefore, in this denouement. The anxieties of succession associated with Noga's indecision about leaving are dispelled, the disputed border is set to rights, and the distinction between kibbutz settler and shifty Diaspora tourist clearly reasserted.

One might be tempted to conclude from this conjunction of events that *Elsewhere, Perhaps* endorses a fantasy of Israeli expansion that would see the troubling disjunction, with which the novel opens, between that state's actual borders and its 'natural frontiers' finally resolved. When the novel was published in 1966, the Biblical provinces of Judea and Samaria still remained outside of Israel, and for many Israelis the 1967 victory offered a glorious opportunity to 'reclaim' those lands, and to bring state borders and what were often referred to as Israel's 'borders of destiny' into greater alignment.[32] There is little warrant for this reading, however, since several things in the novel controvert it. Firstly, there is the fact that the text itself does not positively approve the Israeli seizure of 'the Camel's Field'. That annexation is described in a deliberately clichéd and mechanical prose which parodies the military jargon of army reports and which inhibits any interpretation of the event as a glorious or heroic episode of national assertion. Secondly, several of the most sympathetic characters in the text voice their opposition to the seizure. Noga, for example, describes the whole affair as 'pointless' and the development of Rami from disturbed adolescent into mature manhood is marked by his renunciation of his earlier jejune enthusiasm for border wars when he declares: 'Those twenty-three dunams aren't worth all the fuss.'[33] One of the kibbutz members who *does* support the seizure of the disputed territory is Reuven Harish who contends: 'The issue may be no more than symbolic. But only fools refuse to recognize that life is made up of symbols.'[34] When the shelling begins, Reuven experiences 'a powerful surge of excitement' but soon begins to retch and vomit. His excitement is represented, negatively, as the 'powerful feverish flush that grips weak men when they suddenly have a ringside view of violent fighting'. The only two Israelis to die in the skirmish are Reuven and the driver of the Israeli armoured tractor that first crosses 'the invisible line'.[35] We are told, somewhat cryptically: 'There was a symbolic link between the two deaths, as anyone with any sensitivity would appreciate.'[36] The implied 'link' is evidently that between nationalistic poets like Reuven – who celebrate war but who do not themselves have the stomach for battle – and the unfortunate foot-soldiers who lose their lives carrying out the deadly deeds poets extol.

In all sorts of ways, then, *Elsewhere, Perhaps* seems to repudiate rather than to endorse Israeli expansionism. The novel ultimately works to disenchant the desire for escape or adventure 'outside' Israel associated with either the Arab world or the European Diaspora. For Noga to go to Europe would be to fall into the clutches of Siegfried and the sinister future he seems to have planned for her there. For Rami to chase after the thrill of conquests across the Arab border would be to court the risk that he too might die, like Reuven, in the mess of his own vomit. At the end of the novel, the two younger protagonists grow out of their earlier romantic enchantments with border-crossings and exchange their adolescent yearnings for some more exciting life elsewhere for the mature responsibilities of marriage and domestic life in the kibbutz.

In a sense, the whole point of *Elsewhere, Perhaps* is to assert the importance of 'staying put' in Israel despite an acknowledged sense of alienation and a consequent urge to transgress its national boundaries. In this respect, the novel displays many of the typical features of colonial-settler writing in its various manifestations from South

Africa to the US to Australia or New Zealand. Imaginative literature in these locations displays an enduring preoccupation with questions about national indigenousness or lack of it in countries made up of immigrants from diverse national backgrounds whose relationship to the new lands they claim is usually filtered through aesthetic vocabularies imported from their ex-homeland. In such writing, the settlers typically feel themselves to be transients, overburdened with memories and attitudes belonging to an older world. This besetting sense of dislocation leaves the settlers suspended between new and old worlds and feeling that they belong properly to neither. There is a recurrent tension in such literature between the imperative to stake national title to the new land and the imported European aesthetics through which the settlers attempt to come to imaginative terms with their new surrounds.[37]

Thus, Reuvan Harish, poet of the kibbutz, driving through the plain of Sharon, observes the beauties of the surrounding countryside:

> Neatly tended fields, new villages with their red roofs, fenced pasture lands, avenues of trees shading the road, water towers on the hilltops. Well-kept orchards, white-carpet flowerbeds with their network of gleaming metal pipes. It should have been a soothing sight. But the harsh sun, the glass-blue sky, the fierce early-afternoon light, the straight road like a gash in the flesh of the green fields, for once all these depressed Reuven Harish. A man born in the gentle light of northern climes can never resign himself to the to the stark bright glare of this country. Even patriotic poems merely betray the poet's continual longing to come to terms with this cruel light.[38]

In this, as in several other passages dispersed across the novel, the older generation of Zionist settlers display a characteristically colonial-settler sense of being aliens even in the very midst of the land that they have 'made to bloom'. Overburdened with the cultural baggage of an older world, they lack an indigenous frame of reference that would allow them ever to be truly at home with a landscape that consequently defies symbolic inhabitation. Some of the Sabra children claim that the reason why their elders don't deal with the Arabs severely enough is because 'they're still Europeans even here in Asia'.[39] Elsewhere, however, the narrator comments: 'Even the younger people, who are born here, feel a sad longing for far-off places, unknown, unnamed places that are far, far away and full of sadness.'[40] The older generation's nostalgia for Europe lives on in its children, then, as a kind of surrogate nostalgia for imagined worlds they have never known.

The European-born Jewish settlers in *Elsewhere, Perhaps* display ambivalent feelings, combining sentiments of nostalgia and hostility, towards Europe that have much in common with those that other colonial settler communities display towards their metropolitan 'mother-countries'. But there is also a crucial difference since in this instance the ex-homeland is associated with genocidal anti-Semitism. Noga dreams of a European landscape that is the stuff of fairytale and pastoral, but when Reuven returns in his dreams to the world of his childhood the bells that have so much charm for his daughter take on the quality of sinister nightmare: 'Bells. As if everything were dead, and only the bells were alive and singing, singing and alive, ding-dong sleep, ding-dong die, done ding-dong, die down dong.'[41] Noga's nostalgia (or pseudo-nostalgia) is for a postcard pastoral Europe of bells and steeples; but the same landscape can take on in Reuven's memory the quality of a gothic nightmare. The novel seems to suggest that the existential insecurity generated by the Israeli condition of being suspended between the European and the Arab worlds triggers a desire to flee into one or the other world: to try to be wholly at home in one or the other place. *Elsewhere, Perhaps* implies, however, that this is a temptation that Israeli Jews must resist since venturing into the Arab world across the border or returning to Europe are both associated with threats to their very survival.

But it is precisely in this *double disenchantment* that we discover one of the serious ideological cruxes of the novel. By rendering the Israeli conquest at the end of the novel in an anti-heroic register, the novel intimates its opposition to any messianic desire for Israeli expansion. Its whole drive is to challenge the equation of such expansion with the glories of heroic national or sacred struggle ('Those twenty-three dunams aren't worth all the fuss'). Nonetheless, since it simultaneously works to disenchant the European Diaspora as a viable alternative to Israel – by associating it, via the figure of Zechariah-Siegfried, with corruption, seediness and death – the novel seems implicitly to endorse the classical Zionist assumption that only in Israel can Jews fully realise themselves. It is this assumption that has always underpinned the Israeli state's commitment to the 'ingathering' of the Diasporic Jews, and this in turn underpins its laws that grant automatic citizenship to any Jews who do 'return' there – whereas no such rights are extended to the Palestinians dispossessed in 1948 and after. The question that might be asked is whether it is really possible simultaneously to oppose Israeli expansion and yet to uphold the Zionist ideal of the 'ingathering' of the Jewish Diaspora? Surely these 'ingatherings' create pressure for expansionism, lending weight and urgency to the aspirations of those who would lay claim to Israel's un-reclaimed 'Camel's Fields' in order to create space for a new influx of immigrants? *Elsewhere, Perhaps* disapproves of Israeli expansion, then, but it also expresses considerable hostility towards the idea that Jewish existence in the Diaspora could constitute a viable alternative to life in Israel: in this way, the novel discloses a tension symptomatic of Zionist ideology more generally

Like many Zionists, Oz would probably contend that there is no necessary connection between these two issues. Historical practice, however, would tend to suggest otherwise. In the period before the establishment of the Israeli state, Jewish immigration was essential to the Zionist enterprise since only in this way could Jews ever become a demographic majority in Palestine. In the period of the mass immigration after 1948, many of the new Oriental Jewish immigrants were sent to settle in neighbourhoods and villages 'abandoned' by the Palestinians during the war, thus allowing Israel to stake claim to these villages and to make sure that the dispossessed inhabitants could not return to live there. As Ammiel Alcalay has remarked, by scattering immigrants along the borders, two birds were killed with one stone: these immigrants acted as a buffer against continuing acts of resistance by exiled Palestinians, and since they therefore bore the brunt of that resistance they 'were also initiated into the state's rites of power, suspicion, and fear regarding the Arabs'.[42] After the seizure of the West Bank and Gaza in 1967, right-wing settler organisations, such as that led by Meir Kahane, argued that a growing wave of anti-Semitism in America and the Soviet Union would provide the basis for a massive new wave of Jewish immigration that would require a new territorial outlet. In addition, some supporters of the increasingly powerful radical right called openly for a 'transfer' of the West Bank Palestinians out of the territory in order to create space for settlement and to ensure the security and ethnic homogeneity of the extended Jewish state.[43] In Israel, Jewish immigration, whether used as means to exclude Palestinians from the labour force or to provide human material to settle the frontiers, has always been connected – as it was in other settler societies – to the struggle against the indigenous population. Oz's vocal opposition to right-wing expansionists such as Kahane, and to their messianic dreams, is well documented.[44] Nowhere in *Elsewhere, Perhaps*, however, are the connections between Zionist attitudes to the Jewish Diaspora and Israeli expansionism openly engaged, and this inevitably limits the force of the novel's anti-expansionist stance.

Though *Elsewhere, Perhaps* can be read as a novel which expresses an anxious opposition to Israeli expansionist sentiment, it is ultimately the limits of that critique that require comment. Expansionist sentiment may well be registered negatively in this novel, but it is so exclusively on the basis that it is potentially hazardous for Israelis only. The suggestion is that to succumb to the thrill of border wars, as Rami does in his immature adolescence, is for Israelis to capitulate to self-destructive or suicidal temptation. Nowhere, however, is there any serious imaginative engagement with what Israeli expansionism would mean not for Israelis but for the Arabs who will be its immediate victims. At the end of the novel, the Arab peasants who had tilled 'the Camel's Field' are displaced, but since these are never more than shadowy spectres, their perspective never comes within the moral compass or existential horizons of the novel. Indeed, the chain of associations that links these anonymous, depersonalised peasants with the harshness and hostility of the natural environment, and with the mountains that tower menacingly over the kibbutz, creates a structure of feeling in which the Arabs are consigned to the realm of nature in a manner conventional to some of the most regressive strands in Zionism.

That said, there are passages where Oz does seem to imply that the classical Zionist narrative has always deluded itself about the Arabs. In an early chapter, for example, there is a section that briefly recounts the origins of the kibbutz of Metsudat Ram:

> For a thousand years the place was a total wilderness, until our first settlers set up their tents and made the desert bloom by the latest agricultural methods. True, a few Arab fellahin dwelt or wandered here before our arrival, but they were poor and primitive, in their dark robes, and easy prey for the hazards of the climate and natural disasters, floods, drought, and malaria. No trace remains of them except some scattered ruins, whose remains are gradually fading away and merging, winter by winter, with the dust from which they came. Their inhabitants have fled to the mountains, from where they hurl their baseless, senseless hatred down at us. We did nothing to them. We came with plowshares, and they greeted us with swords. But their swords rebounded against them.[45]

This passage rehearses the official Zionist version of history. The standard tropes of that narrative include: the idea that Palestine was an empty and uncultivated land that the Jewish settlers wrestled from a primal state of nature; that it was only thinly inhabited and that the original natives had no serious title to the land in any case since they were merely wandering nomads; that even if the natives were dispossessed, they themselves were principally to blame since it was they who greeted the well-intentioned settlers with swords that then 'rebounded against them'. The passage is delivered, however, in a *faux naïve* register that undercuts the official narrative, and which intimates an ironic awareness of its inadequacies, evasions and tergiversations. It is intimated that the hostility displayed by the Arabs across the border towards the kibbutz is not at all 'baseless and senseless', as the official version would like to suggest, but has its origins in a history of dispossession, a history again repeated when 'the Camel's Field' is seized.

The curious thing about *Elsewhere, Perhaps*, however, is that while the limitations of the official version of classical Zionism are knowingly intimated in passages such as this, at no stage is the official Zionist narrative ever seriously challenged in some more direct way by any of the characters. The more moderate and sympathetic members of the kibbutz, such as Noga or Rami or Herbert Segal, may not approve Israel's seizure of the land beyond its borders, yet they never seriously protest the annexation either. Nor do they ever make connections between the 'illegitimate' act of dispossession that ends the novel and the apparently 'legitimate' earlier phase of settlement that brought their own kibbutz into existence. Instead, the strategy here is to trivialise the annexation of 'the Camel's Field' as something 'not worth all the fuss'. But if this suggests that the deed is not exactly the stuff of epic nation-building its supporters think it, it also effectively diminishes the moral significance of the act as well. Oz, in other words, is prepared to ironise the dominant Zionist narrative, but only within narrow and well-contained limits. By silencing Zionism's principal victim, the Palestinians, who never appear in the novel, his text mutes and neutralises its own ironies, and pre-empts any traffic with a radically alternative version of history to the dominant discourse.

## III

*A Perfect Peace* was first published in Hebrew in 1982, but the narrative opens in the winter of 1965 and closes two years later with the Six Days War in 1967.[46] Yonatan, the novel's central protagonist, lives with a constant sense of being summoned to a more exciting life, somewhere away from the kibbutz on the Syrian border in northern Israel where his life with his wife Rimona is listless and unhappy. When Rimona had first become pregnant some years earlier Yonatan had felt unready for the responsibilities of parenthood and she had therefore had an abortion. Her second pregnancy ended in a stillbirth due to gynaecological problems related to the earlier abortion, and her doctor advised her to have no more children. Burdened by this unhappy past, she and Yonatan have become sexually withdrawn and remote from each other. Their muted unhappiness finds expression in a mutual yearning for far away places: Yonatan daydreams about escaping to Shanghai or Rio de Janeiro or the US where he would be without family ties and completely free to remake himself; Rimona is obsessed with anthropological books about the religious and fertility rites of tribal Africa, and listens constantly, in a sort of lethargy, to an album of African music called *The Magic of Chad*.

To his father, Yolek Lifshitz, kibbutz secretary, Labor Party dignitary and former Knesset member, Yonatan's moody behaviour typifies the self-indulgence and nihilism of his generation. The tension between father and son is compounded by the fact that Yonatan's longing for escape frequently takes the form of a fantasy in which he is summoned to America to join Benya Trotsky, wealthy owner of a Florida hotel chain. Earlier in life, Trotsky had been an immigrant to Israel from Russia, and had become involved in an unhappy infatuation with Hava, Yolek's wife and Yonatan's mother. Because Hava has always refused to confirm whether Yonatan is Yolek's or Benya Trotsky's child, Yonatan's fantasy of life in America has the character of a family romance in which he dreams of discovering 'his other father'[47] whom he has never known. The contest over Yonatan between Yolek, the cantankerous old Zionist pioneer and statesman, and Trotsky, one-time international socialist and now a wealthy American capitalist, is – as in the earlier dispute over Noga in *Elsewhere, Perhaps* – essentially an allegorical struggle for legitimate succession between Israel and the Diaspora.

The wintry routine of the kibbutz is punctuated by the sudden arrival of an eccentric young Russian-born Jewish immigrant, Azariah Gitlin, a Spinoza enthusiast, musician and skilled mechanic who becomes friendly with both Yonatan and Rimona. Eventually Azariah moves in with the young couple to form a sort of tacitly accepted albeit tense *ménage à trois*. After a night of feverish 'free-for-all' sex, Yonatan arises and, in a mood of revulsion against the 'whorehouse' activities they have indulged in, decides that the time has finally come for him to answer the call to flight that has long tormented him.[48] It has become clear to him that the place to which he is being summoned to meet his destiny is the ruined city of Petra, the ancient Nabotean capital south of the Dead Sea, which lies to the south of Israel inside the Jordanian border. Armed, and dressed in his army fatigues, he leaves the kibbutz without a word to anyone and hitches south and across the Negev Desert until he finally arrives at Ein-Husub, a small outpost 'half army camp, half tumbledown frontier settlement'.[49] From there, he hopes to make his way to Petra where he will at last, he hopes, find perfect peace.

The emotional climate evoked in the novel is that of a severely traumatised and nervy society living in a condition of constant military crisis and national alert. The relentless vigilance, recurrent mobilisations for war, constant radio reports of low-intensity border skirmishing, and the dread of impending catastrophe exert an enormous mental toll on all the characters. Yonatan, whose very psyche appears to have been invaded by the war, most vividly exemplifies this state of existential dread. During an earlier period of military service, he had once carried a screaming Jewish colleague on his back from the battlefield only to discover when he reached the Israeli lines that the blood in which he is saturated is his own and not that of the rescued comrade, who had not been wounded at all but was simply in a state of shock. In his nightmares, Yonatan repeatedly relives this ghastly scenario as well as a collateral one in which his father is brought back during the 1948 war to the kibbutz on an army stretcher, his body 'butchered with biblical cruelty' by the Arabs from a nearby village. Looking down at the paternal corpse in frozen dread, Yonatan is aghast when his father rises to rebuke him for his apathy and orders him to counterattack the village because '[i]f we lose, not only you but the entire Jewish people will die like dogs'.[50]

The narrative structure at work here is quite a conventional one in which the trauma of war is registered as a crisis of impaired masculinity.[51] Yonatan's yearning to flee Israel for some strange anonymous city is clearly a symptom of his desire to escape the crushing burden of national responsibility placed on his young shoulders. The dead weight of the Jewish colleague, which had almost overwhelmed Yonatan, represents the heavy weight of historical responsibility that the Israeli soldier must carry to defend his Jewish co-nationals. But this enormous burden threatens to crush its bearers, leaving them morally desensitised and emotionally exhausted, and unable to reintegrate into civilian society or to conduct conventional relationships. The historical trauma of war, in other words, threatens to undermine normative masculine subjectivity, creating a kind of castration crisis in which the male finds himself unable or unwilling to assume the paternal legacy. This is expressed in the novel by that sense of irritated resentment that Yonatan feels towards his father and by his own unwillingness to assume the role of father. Hence the transfer of male succession from one generation to the next is jeopardised.

*A Perfect Peace* begins, then, with a condition of national trauma registered as a masculine crisis in which the hero finds himself alienated from the demands of the dominant Zionist narrative. As will be seen, the whole thrust of the plot that follows is not to subject that dominant narrative to radical critical investigation, however, but to compel the alienated masculine protagonist to recognise its importance and consent to its ideological address. This is engineered by sending Yonatan on a Conradian-like voyage into the heart of darkness in Arab Jordan. At the end of the novel, he will eventually return, chastened and renewed, from this dangerous but ultimately regenerative voyage into the wilderness, now ready to accept the life in Israel he had earlier refused.

One of the most notable episodes in the earlier part of the narrative describes an excursion by some younger kibbutz members to picnic among the ruins of the nearby Arab village of Sheikh Dahr. The Israelis, we are told, destroyed this village in the 1948 war and its surrounds are still scarred by the struggles of that time. This deserted village is, therefore, clearly a potent memory-site. It recalls actual historical atrocities such as the massacre by the Irgun in April 1948 of perhaps as many as 250 Palestinians in the village of Deir Yassin, events that triggered the mass terror that led to or accelerated the Palestinian exodus in 1948.[52] The visit to Sheikh Dahr in Oz's novel, then, involves a highly charged encounter with what might be called the primal scene of the establishment of the Israeli state.

From the outset, the village exudes an eerie and *unheimlich* quality that makes the visitors uneasy. Although it appears entirely uninhabited, the young Israelis feel themselves the object of a threatening and unseen gaze. A radio bulletin that morning had reported the escape of a murderer from an Israeli prison, and the visitors worry that this escapee, or perhaps an Arab infiltrator from across the border, may be hiding somewhere in the ruins. Yonatan and Udi, who can remember visits by the village sheikh to the kibbutz in the days before 1948, recall that as children they would lie awake at night in the dark 'too scared to admit how scared we were of that smoky wind' that carried the smells of the Arab village across the kibbutz. When Azariah wonders whether someone is hiding there, Udi remarks laconically '[i]t's only a scalping party of Red Indians'.[53]

*Literature, Partition and the Nation-State*

One of Udi's hobbies is to collect relics of the Biblical past, and he voices the opinion that there is an ancient Jewish village underneath the Arab one. He remarks to Yonatan:

> Take a look at that landscape over there, Yoni. All the Arab terraces have been washed away, but that bottom course of stone still left down there must be from Second or First Temple times. Whatever Jews built, lasts. No flood can touch it.[54]

Mention of the flood triggers Yonatan's memory about how someone in the kibbutz had once proposed that the site of the devastated village be turned into a dam. Yonatan's father, Yolek, had at first ridiculed the idea, snorting contemptuously that 'this wasn't Switzerland and there wasn't any money to spend on fantasies of paddling swans serenaded by fräuleins with mandolins' of the kind to be seen on European chocolate boxes.[55] Later, his father had become obsessed with the idea, however, and insisted that it was indeed technically possible to build the dam, and he still corresponds with experts in the Hebrew University and the Weizmann Institute about the matter.

For the different members of the picnic party, the ruined village provokes different sentiments. The aggressively militant and racist Udi thinks of 'digging up the skeleton of some greaseball from the village cemetery, wiring it together, and standing it up in his garden to serve as a scarecrow and shock the entire kibbutz.'[56] Yonatan is more rueful and ponders the eerie silence of the place: '[F]rom the ruins of Sheikh Dahr came not a sound of protest, not even the bark of a dog. Nothing but the silence of the earth and another, more subtle silence that seemed to blow down from the mountains, the silence of deeds that cannot be undone and of wrongs that no one can right.' Throughout the visit, Azariah's memories return to the ordeals he himself had experienced in his flight from Russia and he also remembers his 'twin aunts believed to have been murdered by the Nazis in the Poner Forest'.[57] Standing somewhat apart from the rest of the group as usual, Yonatan falls into a reverie and looks longingly to 'the easternmost mountains, which seemed in this, flowing, honeyed light to be within shouting distance'. The mountains, we are told, 'loomed like steep breakers that seemed so imminently about to tumble westward that Yonatan felt an urge to run to them at once and plunge in head first'. In an attempt to dispel his reverie, he challenges Azariah to a race. Azariah demurs, protesting 'I have run quite enough in my life' and 'I came here to stop running.' Only in the kibbutz, he tells Yonatan, have wandering, constantly running Jews like himself 'begun to learn the art of relaxing and the secret of sending down roots'.[58]

This episode clearly constitutes an extended reflection on Israeli practices of memory and forgetting with regard to the Palestinian-Arab past in general and to 1948 in particular. Udi's preoccupation with ancient Jewish sites alludes to the ways in which Israeli archaeology has always been one of the key disciplines deployed to establish evidence of ancient Jewish settlement in Palestine and thereby to assert the primacy of Jewish over Arab title to that land.[59] His remark that what Jews build endures whereas Arab construction is ephemeral reiterates a dominant theme in conventional Zionist discourse: namely, that Arab connections to Palestine were relatively transient and superficial and Jewish connections older and stronger. The allegedly voluntary 'flight' of the Palestinians in 1948 was often taken as confirmation that they lacked the authentic emotional bond to the land that Jews had.[60]

In several respects, Oz's novel seems to acknowledge the underlying tensions and anxieties, and indeed the colonialist assumptions, that subtend this dominant discourse. The Jewish insistence on rootedness in the land is shown to be haunted throughout by a concomitant anxiety about a lack of connection and misgivings about rootlessness, dislocation and wanderlust, conveyed here by way of Yonatan's yearning for the distant mountains and Azariah's immigrant memories. References to the 'Red Indians' suggest, moreover, uneasy parallels between Israel's treatment of the Palestinians and the genocidal treatment meted out to the native populations in North America. Udi's reference to his 'fantastic plan to finish off the greaseballs'[61] across the border idiomatically recalls racist Anglo-American attitudes towards Mexicans and suggests a parallel attitude on the part of Israelis to the Arabs across their borders. His demented desire to nuke the Arabs, in order to end the unbearable sense of siege once and for all, is in turn associatively linked to Yolek's desire to build a dam on the site of the ruined Arab village. In their own way, both projects represent a desire to erase all trace of Arabs from the landscape and in so doing to eradicate the threat to Israeli repose that they pose both as material enemies and as guilty and distressing memory. Yolek's obsession with building a dam over the Arab village alludes to the many means employed by the Israeli state – ranging from the planting of forests to conceal the marks of Palestinian habitation to the construction of new Jewish towns on the sites of destroyed Arab ones – to obliterate discomfiting traces of the Palestinian past.[62] Since Yolek's dam is

associated, moreover, with kitschy European pastoral – Swiss swans
serenaded by damsels with mandolins – the erasure of the Palestinian
past is linked to the ways in which Israelis have attempted to remake
the 'Oriental' landscape into a surrogate 'Europe.'

But while this return to the primal scene of the establishment of the
Israeli state, and to the haunted memory-site of the 1948 Palestinian
expulsion, unsettles the dominant Zionist narrative, it is never allowed in Oz's treatment seriously to challenge it. Contemplating the
ruined village, Yonatan cannot help but think that Israel's treatment
of the Palestinians constitutes a kind of primal sin of dispossession
that can never be escaped:

> And now there's not a dog left in Sheikh Dahr and all of the
> fields, those that we quarreled about and those that we didn't,
> and all their sorghum and barley and alfalfa, are ours. Nothing
> is left now but those blackened walls on the hill and maybe their
> curse hanging over us.[63]

These rueful reminiscences register a philosophic sense of guilt, yet
in the episode as a whole Palestinian suffering is always measured
in the scales with Jewish suffering in the Diaspora. The visit to the
village is structured in terms of a contrast between Yonatan, with his
desire to run, and Azariah, who wants to learn 'the secret of sending down roots'. Thus while the Israeli-born Sabra contemplates the
terrible human cost of establishing the State of Israel, the child of the
Diaspora recalls the terrors he experienced in Eastern Europe and the
death of family and relatives at the hands of the Nazis. The memory
of the Diaspora, therefore, counterbalances Yonatan's sense of guilt by
suggesting that for the persecuted Jews of Europe the establishment
of the Israeli state was an absolute imperative, a desperate act of sheer
survival.

It is undisputedly the case, of course, that there can be no adequate assessment of the establishment of Israel that does not take
serious account of the extraordinary suffering endured by Jews as
a consequence of European anti-Semitism generally and the Holocaust especially. That established, it must also be acknowledged,
however, that the relationship between Jewish suffering in Europe
and the suffering caused to Palestinians as a result of Jewish settlement in the Middle East can morally be computed in quite distinct
ways. From one perspective, the barbarous treatment meted out to
European Jews, whether as victims of pogroms or when they were
shipped like sub-humans to concentration camps, ought to serve as

an ironclad reminder that no people should ever again be treated with such brutality. Unfortunately, however, the memory of Jewish genocide in Europe has more commonly been used by the Israeli establishment and others to mitigate what Jews did to Palestinians in 1948. The dominant strands in Zionist discourse, as Yerach Gover has put it, have usually assumed that in the final analysis Palestinian and Israeli suffering count in the scales against each other not as 'pain compared with pain, but rather "pain" with "real" pain'.[64] That is to say, while Israelis rightly insist that the world must never forget the Holocaust of the Jews in Europe, many Israelis have no less insistently sought to minimise the sufferings their state-building enterprise has inflicted on Palestinians. Instead, the memory of the Jewish ordeals suffered in Europe has been used to immunise Israel against moral judgement on the atrocities committed in 1948 or indeed during its later occupation of the remaining Palestinian lands.

In *A Perfect Peace* the relationship between Jewish and Palestinian suffering is, on the whole, it seems, conjugated in the latter of these two ways. The destroyed Arab village does clearly serve as a topos of troubled conscience in the novel and the episode in question tacitly acknowledges that Israeli society is built atop the ruins of Palestinian society. Nevertheless, the episode also seems to suggest, in conventional Zionist manner, that Palestinian suffering should be weighed against Jewish suffering, and not that the ethical principle that makes the latter intolerable should also make the other inexcusable. One of the more curious aspects of the episode is that the only one who actually wants to dig up the past is Udi. His plan to unearth the buried Arab skeletons of 1948 and to wire one up in his garden is constructed as part of the same pathological disorder as his genocidal obsession with discovering a 'fantastic plan to finish off the greaseballs' in one definitive blow.[65] Udi's desire to excavate the past is depicted, that is, as a sort of a morbid and sensationalist delight in shocking the humanist sentiments of the kibbutz elders. In actual historical fact, however, it has not been hawkish xenophobes like Udi but rather Palestinian and dissident Israeli critics of Zionism who have insisted that it is imperative that Israel should come to political and moral terms with its actions in 1948. However by linking the desire to rake up the buried 'skeletons' of 1948 with the unattractively racist Udi, the episode seems to pathologise such desire, to suggest that there is something macabre and grotesque about exhuming these buried memories, that they might be better left unearthed.

Ultimately, it seems, where the dialectic between memory and forgetting is concerned, the novel remains trapped in a liberal Zionist impasse. To obliterate the memory of 1948, as Yolek would do by submerging the Arab village under the waters of the dam, is represented as a colonialist attempt to erase embarrassing traces of past violence and dispossession. But to excavate the Arab skeletons of 1948 is associatively linked to a gratuitous attempt to offend the kibbutz elders. Hence the desire to forget the violent past and the determination to remember it are both negatively marked in this passage, and there is no imaginative provision in the text for some positive and progressive retrieval of that past. Nowhere does the text provide for some kind of alternative radical memory in which Israeli violence against the Palestinians might be recalled to serve as reminder of the need to make just reparation. The haunted memory-site of 1948 is witnessed through Jewish eyes only; because there are no Palestinians in the novel, there are no subjugated knowledges, no outlawed memories, to infuse that site with alternative significance.

Yonatan's romantic yearnings are constructed in ways that recall imperial romance and adventure fiction. For him, the kibbutz is an unbearably regulated place where he feels spiritually numb and sexually sterile. The journey across the Negev to visit Petra, then, is a desperate bid for self-renewal, but it also conceals a suicidal desire for self-annihilation that would put an end to all the unbearable tensions of his existence. In the 1950s and 1960s, treks to Petra had assumed some considerable symbolic importance in Israel. Driven by a thirst for adventure, and uneasy with the idea that with the establishment of the Israeli state the old days of pioneering into the wilderness were now at an end, several small bands of Israelis had set out in the 1950s to reach Petra. In one of these expeditions in 1953, the five who stole across the border on this quest were killed on the return journey. Within Israeli society, then, the quest for Petra had come to stand for an exotic longing for a world beyond Israel's borders: an ambivalent longing that expressed at once a sense of dissatisfaction with the narrow confines of contemporary Israel, and a desire to rediscover the more adventurous climate of the pre-state settlement period.

Yonatan's desire for the wide-open and ungridded space of the Jordanian desert is marked in Oz's novel by the ambivalent tension that John Noyes has identified with the representation of wide-open spaces in colonialist discourses generally. Noyes argues that the desire for vast expanses of borderless space is ascribed a positive value in colonialist writing only if it acts as the prerequisite to eventual appropriation and mastery, which will put the landscape to socially productive use for the colonist. But, Noyes remarks, the desire for vast open spaces can also take the form of a destructively narcissistic longing for oneness with the landscape, something that threatens the dissolution of subjectivity and the abandonment of a commitment to the social altogether. Since desire of this kind represents a threat to the project of mastery, it is ascribed a negative value. The problem, Noyes contends, is that when the settler initially apprehends the vast and boundless landscape it is never entirely clear which of these two responses will ultimately predominate and consequently this moment is always fraught with tension.[66]

In *A Perfect Peace* that tension takes some time to resolve itself. At Ein-Husub, Yonatan has to decide whether to continue on his journey over the Israeli border to Petra or to disown that desire and put his sojourn in the desert to socially productive use by serving an apprenticeship with Tllalim as a desert surveyor. The redemptive possibilities offered by Ein-Husub, 'half army camp, half tumbledown frontier settlement', are soon made evident. Yonatan spends his first night there making love with Michal as he 'had never before made love'.[67] This sex, his first satisfying intercourse in years, is represented in terms that overlay the female body and the desert terrain – 'Step by silent step he caressed her body, as if trying to find his way across unfamiliar territory in darkness'[68] – thereby melding a masculine sexual and territorial mastery. The following morning Tllalim – a harlequinesque composite of male virility and spatial mastery who describes himself as '[c]ertified surveyor, desert rat, devil of a fellow, geologist, lover, and lush'[69] – advises Yonatan to stay on at Ein-Husub where he can work with him as his deputy surveyor and continue to enjoy sexual relations with Michal or some of the other young women of the place. At this point, Yonatan is still so in thrall to his romantic fantasy of crossing the border into Jordan, however, that he refuses Tllalim's offer.

Irritated by what he sees as Yonatan's sickly death drive, Tllalim vividly describes what is in store for him should he persist on his journey to Petra. He will scarcely be across the border, he tells him, when the Atallah Bedouin will fall on him in darkness and first gang-rape and then dismember him. Oz's narrative is patently working at this point to distinguish between a productive mastery of space and a romantic longing for open spaces that cannot be made productive and onto which the death drive is therefore projected. Either Yonatan can stay with Tllalim and 'be [his] deputy surveyor'[70] or he can stubbornly persist with his excursion to Petra and become a hapless victim of the Atallah Bedouin. In other words: to remain in Israel is associated with masculine sexual mastery over the land and the women of the frontier settlement; to cross into Jordan is associated with a terrifying fantasy of occupying an abjectly subordinate sexual position as the hapless victim of an Arab gang-rape.

As in Oz's earlier novels, different responses to the landscape are elaborated in terms of distinctions between different aesthetics or modes of writing it. The travelogue that Yonatan carries with him describes Petra in an exotic idiom that draws on nineteenth-century Orientalist fantasy:

> At the beginning of the last century, John Lewis Burckhardt, an intrepid Swiss traveler, reached the ghost city disguised as an Arab. Looking down from a precipitous height, he caught sight all at once of the red shrines that time forgot and was staggered by their awesome majesty. For a full hour he stood there, a man turned to stone. Later he described in detail the enormous columns carved with mysterious glyphs, the stone galleries climbing one above the other in the torrid air like catwalks, the Greco-Roman auditorium built by the Emperor Hadrian, the palaces, the fortifications, the arcades, the temples, the tombs, and all of them rose-red.
> ... Half-awake, Yonatan sought to picture the magically moribund world that awaited him. The steep steps cut into the mountainside, the great staircase ascending almost two hundred meters above the city to the sanctuary of ed-Deir, its walls surrounded by Medusa heads. And still others leading up to the Mount of Sacrifice, with its pool for collecting the blood of the victims, on either side of which, lifting skyward, were two colossal monoliths carved in the shape of human phalluses, the remnants of a vanished orgiastic cult. An unearthly dread, so the booklet reported, overcame all those who dared to climb the mount and look down on the nightmarish ruins below. Here and there among the mounds of debris the visitor to Petra might encounter human skulls and thighbones, even whole skeletons, bleached by the sun and preserved by the dryness and heat in a state of polished perfection.[71]

The astonished or petrified gaze of the observer of Petra here suggests an ominous loss of distinction between the observer and the scene observed, a deathly dissolution of the self into the 'magically moribund' landscape rather than an assertive assumption of control over it. Tllalim, who has already been to Petra, assures Yonatan that it is 'just another ruin. A pile of stones. Like all ruins.'[72] His remarks work to demystify Burckhardt's. Tllalim's transformation of the Negev

landscape into the rational script of the state survey map is offered in
Oz's novel as a socially productive alternative to Burckhardt's sterile
poetics of enchantment. Burckhardt's Oriental sublime has an awe-
some and opulent splendour, but its glamour is the despotic glamour
of orgiastic sensual indulgence, barbaric passion, and sadistic blood-
lust. The aesthetic register deployed here is that of the violent, quasi-
pornographic Orientalism of nineteenth-century Europe as exemplified by novels such as Flaubert's *Salammbo*.

The danger that *A Perfect Peace* associates with imperial travel writing and exotic Orientalist fantasy of this sort is that its concepts of adventure and heroism are deemed wildly inappropriate to Yonatan's
time and circumstances. One of the things that Yonatan must learn
from Tllalim, it seems, is that he must relinquish the classical imperial fantasy of being able to travel at will through the land of the
Other. He must learn to accept that he cannot hope, in the manner of
famous nineteenth-century travellers such as Burckhardt or Richard
Burton or T. E. Lawrence, to pass himself off as the Other. Imperial
masquerade may have been available to Burckhardt, who travels to
Petra 'disguised as an Arab,' but Tllalim tells Yonatan:

> If those [Bedouin] demons get hold of a *krasavits* like you, of a
> real peaches-and-cream kibbutz sweetheart, they'll fall on you
> like darkness. Before you can reach for your gun, they'll be ass-
> fucking away like mad. Ten, twenty, thirty Atallah, all with their
> pricks up your ass. And when they've fucked you fair and square,
> they'll kill you. But not all at once. They'll kill you piece by
> piece . . .[73]

This passage starkly underscores the terrible cost of blithely trespass-
ing Israel's borders. The danger of straying into the domain of the Arab
Other is conveyed in a gothic register that conjoins racial aggression
and sexual humiliation.

Yet if the imperative to respect state borders is indubitably established here, it is accomplished in a manner that remains completely
mortgaged to the same racist stereotypes of Arabs purveyed by the
Zionist expansionists Oz's work attempts to oppose. If the border between Israel and the Arabs must be respected and maintained, it is
because the place beyond it is a terrifying habitat of demons, a space of
absolute evil populated by savage homosexual Asiatic nomads who
inflict grotesque tortures on straying Western innocents. As the distinction between Yonatan's 'peaches-and-cream' whiteness and Arab
'darkness' makes clear, the state border is reinforced here by transforming it into an impermeable racial boundary between Israel and a

realm of absolute Otherness associated with a perverted eros that is in turn linked to the death drive. The distinction between these two worlds is deemed so absolute that no amount of disguise will enable one to cross between them. Even as *A Perfect Peace* works to disenchant classical imperial romance at one level, it still re-maps the space between Israel and its Arab Outside in a rigidly manichean manner that, to borrow John McClure's terms, 'initiates a new type of imperial romance, one in which the discovery that imperial power is limited, and the prospect of an endless struggle with Otherness, become paradoxically redemptive'.[74]

Having Yonatan ignore Tllalim's warning and persist with his desire to cross into Arab territory enables Oz to drive home this message. In the American myth of the frontier, Richard Slotkin writes, the narrative requires an action in which the border between civilisation and the wilderness is crossed, and '[t]hrough this transgression of the borders, through combat with the dark elements on the other side, the heroes reveal the meaning of the frontier line (that is, the distinctions of value it symbolizes) even as they break it down. In the process they evoke the elements in themselves (or in their society) that correspond to the 'dark'; and by destroying the dark elements and colonizing the border, they purge the darkness from themselves and from the world.'[75] In *A Perfect Peace*, the crossing of the Israeli–Jordanian border functions in rather similar terms, though in Oz's case there is no actual confrontation with the 'dark elements' on the other side, only a symbolic one when Yonatan discharges his rifle at the empty sky. Once he does so, he literally vomits all over himself and turns back immediately to take up the position of deputy surveyor inside Israel that Tlallim had offered him. The narrative function of the crossing, then, is to confirm the border's existence, to affirm its necessity. The meaning of the frontier line established by its crossing, then, is that there is an absolute distinction between the two fields it separates: Israel is equated with life and mastery; the Arab world outside of Israel with abjection and death.

The sickness that Yonatan purges in the act of crossing the Israeli–Jordanian border is his unwillingness to accept his properly masculine duty to reproduce the nation. When Yonatan crosses into Jordan he scrambles along Wadi Araba and as he does so, he thinks to himself 'how scary, that word "father"' and recalls that the 'gynaecological tragedy' that has caused Rimona's second child, Efrat, to be stillborn had originated in his refusal to accept the earlier child. He recognises, in short, that it is his unwillingness to shoulder the responsibilities of fatherhood that has caused these reproductive tragedies. When he discharges his gun at the moon and then retches, the scene suggests a purgative discharge of guilt and grief and a cathartic overcoming of a sexual blockage, something that prepares him to return to Israel and later to take up the obligations of paternity and patriotism he had earlier evaded. The chief aim of the narrative, then, is to reconcile Yonatan (and the reader) to a central tenet of Zionist ideology by proving that there is no fulfilling life outside of the boundaries of Israel and by showing that the desire for escape is therefore nothing more than a displaced desire for self-extinction.

As soon as Yonatan re-crosses the border and takes up the task of surveying Israeli space, a whole cluster of crises that earlier bedevilled the novel is resolved with magical rapidity. Soon afterwards we learn that the fugitive who had been hiding out in Sheikh Dahr is apprehended and five gazelles are spotted standing outlined against the village skyline. When this happens, the earlier *unheimlich* quality of the village, and all that it stands for, is finally exorcised. The appearance of the gazelles suggests a sign of grace, it acts as a signifier for a re-enchantment of Israeli space. At the same time, Benya Trotsky's offer to fly Yonatan and Hava to America is decisively refused by Yolek, and Azariah's application to join the kibbutz community is accepted. Rimona gives birth to a baby girl. Where before there had been a stressed and irritable atmosphere, reflecting a sense of individual and communal frustration in the kibbutz, a more relaxed spirit of compromise suddenly prevails towards the end of the novel as individual destinies are sorted out. For example, although Trotsky's plan to bring Yonatan and Hava to America is decisively rejected, the new kibbutz secretary, Srulik, takes the sting from this refusal when he accepts Trotsky's offer of a donation to build a music hall or library at the kibbutz. The fact that Trotsky's donation is accepted in this instance contrasts with *Elsewhere, Perhaps* where a similar offer by Siegfried was contemptuously refused. This seems to imply that some sort of *modus vivendi* can be reached not only with foreign capital but also between the competing claims of Israel and the Jewish Diaspora (which is relocated from Germany in the earlier novel to the less ominous America in this later one). The sense that pragmatic new solutions can be found to old problems is also implied by the fact that although the exact paternity of Rimona's baby is unknown, no one is particularly bothered. Even the threat of emigration that haunts this novel, as it does nearly all of Oz's work, is to be resolved by a pragmatic compromise: one of the new secretary's innovations is 'to approve funds for vacations abroad', which will eventually allow each kibbutz member 'three weeks to see the world'.[76] Some limited travel beyond Israel's boundaries is sanctioned, then, but of a regulated and recuperative kind that does not recklessly endanger the state by deflecting vital energies from the home front.

This denouement involves a meticulous sorting out of spatial fields. Internal Israeli space is to be pragmatically shared by native-born Sabra and new European immigrant (as Yonatan and Azariah share paternity of the new baby). Relations with the spaces outside Israel's borders are also orchestrated in various ways: a *modus vivendi* can be reached with the American Diaspora, but Arab space beyond Israeli boundaries is a place of death with which there can be no productive traffic. Only when these 'outside' spaces have been allotted distinct qualities can approved passages begin to be negotiated between them. It is important, however, to note that the imagined community envisioned here is styled in ways that privilege Israel's Ashkenazi élite. For instance, when Rimona becomes pregnant she begins to overcome her earlier depression and this emotional recharge in turn is linked to her abandonment of her anthropological and musical obsessions with primitive Africa. Once she becomes pregnant, we are told, '[S]he no longer copied out African charms on little index cards'. The narrator speculates that as she sits sleeping the music that issues from the record spinning on the turntable may be 'not *The Magic of Chad*, not the Mississippi blues given her by Hava, but a Bach violin concerto'.[77] Rimona's fascination with things African (and African-American), then, is associatively linked with her depression and her convalescence with classical European music, the epitome of Israeli Ashkenazi 'high culture'. Yonatan's recovery commences when he abandons his destructive desire to voyage into Arab lands, Rimona's when she forgets her morbid fascination with Africa. These gestures might be seen as the novel turning its face away from the Middle East and Africa; as its insistence, in other words, in concord with classical Zionism's imaginative cartography, that Israel is a Western society with little or nothing in common with its surrounding hinterlands.

Even as the destinies of individual characters are sorted out in *A Perfect Peace*, with an almost fairytale-like distribution of prizes and rewards, in the background the political tensions between Israel and the Arab states continue to mount, and the novel culminates with a brief account of the 1967 war. 'On the northern border hardly a day went by without firing. One night the kibbutz was hit by border raiders, who sabotaged the water pumps, blew up an empty tin shack in the citrus groves, and crossed back into Jordan before dawn.'[78] Day by day this skirmishing escalates until eventually, we are told, 'the situation on the borders had worsened and crack units were almost continually in a state of full alert'. When the war breaks out Yonatan, now reintegrated into the kibbutz, and Azariah are called to service. The war itself is allotted only a few short sentences, all delivered in the same deliberately low-key, non-committal monotone that was used to describe the annexation of 'the Camel's Field' in *Elsewhere, Perhaps*. Yonatan's reconnaissance unit fights in the Sinai and when his unit commander is killed on 'the sixth and last day of combat, [Yonatan] took over its command'. The Israeli victory is recorded in a single clipped sentence: 'Israel won and pushed forward its front lines.'[79]

The fact that Oz's novel moves, on the one hand, towards quite an upbeat conclusion, which sees his main characters mature and grow into their social roles with some assurance, but nevertheless ends with a clipped, deliberately low-key account of yet another Arab–Israeli war initially seems somewhat odd. The individual redemptions seem to have an aura of wish-fulfilment that is somehow out of kilter with the wider historical narrative in the background where, it seems, no such fairytale transformations are to be expected. As already seen in the case of *Elsewhere, Perhaps*, however, splits between redemptive individual transformations and downbeat socio-historical 'diminuendos of resignation'[80] of this kind are characteristic of Oz's work. This is because, for Oz, individual maturity, the adult capacity to assume the burden of one's destiny, seems always to require the abandonment of the desire for some transfigured social order and its dangerous promises of release. Oz's characters, that is, must always learn to live with an uneasy tension between Israel and its Arab neighbours; de-cisive transformations with happy endings on this front are not to be expected. The desire for some sort of millenarian or utopian transfig-uration of the Middle East world that would bring the terrible tension of living in a state of siege to some decisive end is always associated in his novels with a lack of emotional and personal maturity. For Oz, indeed, it is precisely the desire for a decisively transfigured order that contains the seeds of historical catastrophe because such utopian longing conceals a desire for a perfect peace that is ultimately the antithesis of real life with its inevitable constraints and frustrations. The whole point of *A Perfect Peace*, then, and it is this that makes the downbeat low-key endings inevitable, is that this side of death 'there is no perfect peace'.[81]

Paradoxically, then, the symbolic enclosure of Israeli national space towards which *A Perfect Peace* works requires, even demands, a lack of closure on the narrative level. Only by maintaining a sense of a permanently, even ontologically, aggressive Other to serve as national adversary can the necessity for a continued commitment to the Zionist project be upheld. In his capacity as a public intellectual, too, Oz has also maintained that between Arab and Jew there can be 'no perfect peace'. The anti-utopian aesthetic of the novels, in other words, has its political corollary. The best to be hoped for in the Middle East, Oz suggests, is a slow, decidedly non-utopian compromise between the two sides, something that will leave neither entirely happy. When awarded the International Peace Prize of the German Publishers' Association in Frankfurt in 1992, he commented in his acceptance speech:

> I do not believe in the possibility of a perfect peace – remember the 'crooked timber of humanity'. Rather, I work for a sad, sober, imperfect compromise between individuals and between communities, who are bound always to remain divided and different but who are nevertheless capable of working out an imperfect coexistence. The Psalmist says, 'Mercy and truth are met together; justice and peace have touched' (Psalm 85, 10–11). Yet the Talmud points out an inherent tension between justice and peace, and offers a more pragmatic concept: 'But where justice prevails, there is no peace, and where peace prevails, there is no justice. So where is the justice that contains peace? Indeed it is in partition' (Sanhedrin 6, p. 2).
> ... All I can add to this is just the notion that only death is perfect. Peace, like life itself, is not a burst of love or mystical communion but precisely a fair and sensible compromise between opposites.[82]

In this passage, a 'peace process' (uncannily similar to that which would emerge after Oslo) is defended in the same anti-utopian spirit in which Oz's novels habitually conclude. Isaiah Berlin's 'crooked timber of humanity' is invoked to suggest the impracticality of utopian dreaming. Because such utopian endings are ruled out in advance, both individuals and communities 'are bound always to remain divided and different' but, happily, 'imperfect compromises' can still be reached. But these 'imperfect compromises' can be attained only so long as expectations are not too high, because where there is too strict an insistence on justice 'there is no peace'. In the circumstances, the reasonable thing to do is to split the differences and thus 'partition' emerges as the key term that will resolve 'the inherent tension' that, on Talmudic authority, must always exist 'between justice and peace'. The philosophical meditation here modulates into the thesis that political partition represents the only 'fair and sensible compromise' to the Israeli–Palestinian question.

Nevertheless, Oz's audience is also counselled not to expect anything too perfect, not to demand too radical a transformation, since utopian desires for the perfect are allied with a death drive. Nor should they press too much whether the kind of partition settlement that might emerge is really just because 'where justice prevails there is no peace'. Oz does not inquire whether a partitionist solution is still feasible after thirty years of Jewish settlement in the West Bank. He does not ask whether, even if it were feasible, partition would be the most emancipatory outcome or whether it would really allow for any meaningful self-determination for Palestinians. It is difficult not to conclude that this anti-utopian insistence that Israelis and Palestinians are always destined to remain different, and that both sides must accept an unsatisfactory compromise in the interest of imperfect peace, is little more than an apologia designed to fend off the suggestion that what a partition of historic Palestine at this stage would essentially do is to ratify the unequal gains won by Israel as a result of its past acts of eviction and its repeated overstepping of its own borders.

## IV

The external border, as Franco Moretti argues, conventionally functions in the novel as 'the site of *adventure*, one crosses the line, and is face to face with the unknown, often the enemy; the story enters a space of danger, surprises, suspense'.[83] In some instances at least, border excursions of this kind can require the reader to travel outside of the self; they can imaginatively challenge the reader to encounter the national Other – to meet, reckon with, or recognise the national 'enemy' on his or her own ground. In Oz's fiction, however, the treks to the frontier involve no such encounter. His Ashkenazi protagonists are never required to travel out of themselves in this way; they never really engage with the Palestinian or Arab 'enemy' on the latter's own ground, and there is no meaningful exchange with alterity.

This is because, despite the obsession with state borders and national frontiers in Oz's fiction, his novels exclude any fully realised representations of Palestinian or Arab characters. Palestinians and Arabs clearly haunt his Jewish-Israeli characters like a burden of dread or as a source of bad conscience, but what is missing from Oz's fiction are fully realised Palestinian or Arab characters with their own interior lives and consciences, with their own voices, with their own capacity to express their predicament, to explain their hostility to Israel, or to evaluate their Israeli counterparts. Oz's novels, therefore, exemplify a certain kind of Israeli writing in which the Israeli–Palestinian situation is registered not so much as an historical and ethical conflict as an existential condition. In such literature, as Ehud Ben Ezer remarks, 'the Arab no longer constitutes a moral question for the Israeli. He becomes the Israeli's nightmare'. In works of this kind, only Jewish characters have inner worlds that are extensively portrayed. The Arabs, in contrast, as Ben Ezer observes, are depicted less as individuals than as 'a symbol of the existential dread that engulfs the Israeli protagonist and prevents him from living his life as he would have wished to have lived it. The image of the Arab is a projection of the inner anxieties of the Israeli characters.'[84] The whole thematic orientation of such fiction, as Gilead Morahg notes, is consistently unilateral because the emphasis is not on the conditions that generate conflict between Arabs and Jews but on the ways in which Jews cope with the consequences of such conflict.[85]

Despite the fact that Oz's novels consistently work to reject fantasies of imperial adventure (by identifying them with the death drive), the Arab Other in his works is nonetheless invariably consigned to an alterity so radical as to preclude dialogic exchange or inter-subjective recognition. It is true that in situations where a colonial history has created societies segregated into racial and sectarian enclaves it is quite difficult to give imaginative representation to the lifeworlds of others. For this reason, it is instructive to compare Oz's work to that of other leading novelists in comparable situations such as South Africa or Northern Ireland. Some of the works of the South African novelist J. M. Coetzee might appear to resemble Oz's since in Coetzee's fiction too the chasm between the worlds of the white and the non-white characters is sometimes so wide as to inhibit full human exchange. In Coetzee's *Foe*, for instance, the tongueless Friday is an inscrutable figure whose silent presence unsettles the authority of the two white narrators, Susan Barton and Foe, but since Friday is dumb direct dialogue between black and white characters remains impossible. Yet in novels such as *Age of Iron*, Coetzee's white narrator, Mrs Curran, does make several excursions that bring her into contact with fully realised Black South African characters and the novel recounts several situations in which she is compelled to evaluate herself through their eyes. Other contemporary Jewish novelists, such as A. B. Yehosua, Sammy Michael, Yoram Kaniuk and David Grossman, have tried to give imaginative life to Palestinian characters in their works and to construct narratives in which the reader's empathy is not wholly monopolised by Jewish protagonists. This is not to suggest that the imaginative engagement with alterity in the examples cited here is always artistically sustained or politically radical. But that imaginative effort, whatever its degrees of success or failure, is at least attempted whereas in Oz's case it is never risked.

In many respects, however, the similarities between Oz's novels and the Northern Irish narratives examined in the previous chapter are quite striking. In both cases, the plots typically centre on a protagonist who is initially involved in some sort of Oedipal rebellion against the authority of the state, but who is eventually brought to recognise the self-destructive nature of that revolt. In the Northern Irish case, the plots are typically structured in terms of an act of violence in which a Catholic protagonist murders a representative of the state, but eventually sees the horror of that crime and surrenders to the authority of the state he had sought to overthrow. In Oz's case, the initial sense of alienation takes a different form: the desire to flee Israel to live in the Diaspora or to seek dangerous adventures across the Arab border. But these protagonists will eventually come to understand, as do Noga and Rami in *Elsewhere, Perhaps* or Yonatan in *A Perfect Peace*, that they have been guilty of overvaluing the world beyond Israel's borders, and this then leads to a renewed commitment to the state. In both situations, the plots function in terms of a rather similar strategy: they engineer a crisis that will cause the protagonist eventually to affirm the state order that he or she had initially thought to reject. The essential plot sequence is also largely the same. The protagonist's dissent against the state is channelled into what are coded as destructive or irrational courses of action; he or she begins to recognise this; this recognition of error leads to a fatalistic ending in which the current state order, even if viewed as oppressive in ways, is nonetheless accepted since the contemplated alternatives have emerged as unthinkable.

It is easy to miss just how narrow and loaded this range of options really is. In both Northern Ireland and Israel all sorts of progressive dissent to oppressive state orders, dissent of a kind which does not fall into these limited categories, can be conceived. But the search for a more emancipatory kind of dissent is precisely what is missing in the fictions examined here. The Oz novels discussed in this chapter and the Northern Irish novels examined earlier share in common down-beat, entropic endings because in both cases opposition to the state is conceived only in destructive terms; no constructive opposition emerges in either instance. Since the only kinds of dissent represented are coded as negative and destructive, the possibility of another trans-figured social order different to the present unhappy one is foreclosed from the outset.

These similarities are neither fortuitous nor merely formal and aes-thetic. In Ireland and in Israel especially, the danger that an irredentist drive to reunify partitioned territories might drag the communities in-volved into a situation of total communal warfare has always been a possibility. This is the doomsday scenario recurrently rehearsed by Oz in his role as a Peace Now activist struggling against the Israeli right. Conor Cruise O'Brien has also consistently invoked apocalyptic sce-narios of this sort, initially in his campaign against the IRA and, later, in his bids to oppose any agreement that would entail Southern Irish involvement in the North since this too, he contends, will inevitably be interpreted by Unionists as creeping reunification. For both individ-uals, the bedrock argument for partition is always that since the only available alternatives are catastrophic, then partition is by default a positive good, a defence against disaster. It is this apparently narrow choice between 'partition' and 'disaster' that is ultimately false and restrictive. Opposition to partition need not always be reactionary; these state divisions can be contested in ways that are emancipatory and progressive and that advance democracy. Partition may be de-fended on the basis that to dismantle it might lead to even worse catastrophes. But this invocation of apocalypse around the bend can all too easily obscure the fact that for some groups – Northern Irish nationalists, Palestinians most of all – partition was never a check against future catastrophe: it was the political catastrophe they have since been trying, in the interests of self-determination, to overcome. Where Oz and Cruise O'Brien are concerned, however, it is the down-side to partition that is always occluded. Their concern is not with the underdogs who have suffered most by partition; that concern is, to borrow a phrase, always limited to 'the agonies of the potentates'.[86]

For some, both Oz and Cruise O'Brien will be regarded as coura-geous defenders of partition against chauvinistic irredentist nation-alisms dedicated to recovering 'lost' territories. But labelling the Israeli and the Irish situations simply as 'irredentist' does more to distort than to illuminate history. The partition of Ireland created a sit-uation in which a substantial section of Irish nationalists was coerced into an adjacent sub-unit of the UK as second-class citizens. Since then, this minority has insisted on its membership of 'the Irish nation' to combat the oppressions to which it was subjected, and it is this more than anything else that puts nation and state system at odds in Ireland. The Israeli situation is quite different in this respect. Since 1967, the State of Israel has, by settling a quarter of a million Jews beyond its borders, deliberately gone about manufacturing a national-minority-across-the-border type situation similar to that which the southern Irish state inherited against its will in 1921. Unlike the Northern Irish nationalists, moreover, the Israeli national minority 'outside' the state in the West Bank is not an oppressed community; it is a privileged settler minority, arrogantly exploiting the spoils of military conquest. In sponsoring these settlements beyond its borders, the State of Israel has effectively put nation and state at odds with each other in ways that remain as yet unresolved.

Chapter 5

# The meaning of disaster: the novel and the stateless nation in Ghassan Kanafani's *Men in the Sun*

'Mold your sword into a ploughshare.'
'You've left no land.'
Samih al-Qasim

## I

The 1948 disaster led to the destruction of Palestinian society and to the dispersal of the Palestinian people across the Middle East and beyond. Today there are almost a million Palestinians within Israel while close to three million others live in the West Bank and Gaza. It is estimated that approximately another four million live in the Diaspora, most as proximate exiles in Jordan, Syria and Lebanon, just across the border from what was once their home. In some of the Arab states the conditions of the displaced Palestinians are much better than others, but, as the fate meted out to them in Kuwait after the Gulf War attested, the treatment accorded to the Palestinians can alter rapidly according to circumstances. Whether they live in refugee camps in Lebanon, as prosperous citizens in Jordan, as guest workers in Kuwait, in the squalor of Gaza, or as second-class citizens in Israel, the relationship between Palestinians and the established state order in the Middle East continues to be deeply vexed.

The crux of the problem for Palestinians, however, is that the oppressive conditions that generate a distinctive sense of Palestinian national consciousness among these scattered communities are not necessarily those that allow for the translation of that consciousness into a collective project of state formation. Where a subject people live in a contiguous national territory controlled by a foreign occupier, national consciousness can be directed towards expelling the occupier and building an independent state on that territory. But where the land that would constitute the national territory is already controlled by other local states, and the national community is divided up into 'minorities' spread across several states, the obstacles to nation-state formation are patently more complex. To put it simply, the difficulty for the Palestinian people is that while their stateless condition induces nationalism, their dispersal across so many states thwarts the construction of a common nation-state. To this extent, the Palestinian predicament resembles that of the Kurds. But for the Palestinians, the logistical difficulties are compounded by the fact that the people who have taken over most of their national territory were themselves the victims of the most appalling genocide in Europe. Hence the Palestinians have always had to wrestle with the fact that they are the victims of victims. As such, they have always found it difficult to get a considered hearing in the West – all too often their resistance to Israeli oppression is represented not as a struggle for self-determination, but simply as the latest malign episode in the age-old persecution of the Jews.

The obstacles that stand in the way of Palestinian national self-determination, therefore, are multiple and daunting. Perhaps it is not surprising in the circumstances that the Palestinian national struggle has sometimes seemed poorly co-ordinated, with the national leadership continually revising its territorial goals and state ambitions as well as the means to secure them. Since the partition of Palestine, the Palestinian national struggle has been persistently hampered by its inability to resolve two basic problems: firstly, that of defining commonly acceptable politico-territorial goals; secondly, that of discovering the modality of resistance appropriate to the attainment of such goals. Instead, the Palestinian national leadership has worked its way through a whole variety of different politico-territorial 'options': pan-Arab nationalism, the bi-national state, the two-state solution, and, more recently, an interim Palestinian National Authority in parts of the West Bank and Gaza. The rapidity with which different goals have been taken up and discarded since 1948 is testimony to the difficulty of finding the means necessary to realise any of them. As the problems inherent in a particular goal or strategy became apparent, the Palestinian political leadership has generally simply re-defined its goals and moved on to search for some new methods to attain them.

Though means and ends have developed unevenly over time, it is possible to trace, in a schematic way at least, successive phases in the Palestinian struggle when different goals and strategies gained ascendancy. In the period between 1948 and 1967, Palestinian nationalism remained largely subsumed under a wider pan-Arab nationalism that held that the liberation of Palestine first required the achievement of a comprehensive pan-Arab unity between the existing Arab states in the region. In these years, the stated objective of Palestinian nationalism was the destruction of 'the Zionist entity', a slogan usually cited as confirmation of Palestinian fanaticism, but one which needs to be contextualised in terms of the actual destruction of Palestinian society after 1948. After the disastrous Arab defeats in 1967, Palestinian support for pan-Arabist solutions waned and gradually gave way to the goal of establishing a 'secular democratic state' within the historic boundaries of Palestine. The object in this instance was the creation of a binational state that would give equal recognition to the national identities of both Jews and Palestinians. The idea represented a radical departure from the more vengeful versions of Palestinian nationalism; its ambition was visionary since its object was a sharing of land and citizenship between two peoples, one of whom had only recently inflicted a disastrous defeat on the other. The prime difficulty with the strategy was that in order to work it needed Israeli support and co-operation. But in the absence of such support, the dilemma was whether a binational consociational arrangement could be imposed by force on a people that wanted no part of such arrangement.

The period between 1974 and the Algiers Conference of 1988 was one marked by the gradual abandonment of the goal of a binational state in favour of establishing a separate Palestinian state in the West Bank and Gaza. At the Algiers Conference, the ascendancy of the 'two-state' strategy was confirmed when the Palestinian Liberation Organisation (PLO) explicitly and unambiguously recognised the legitimacy of all of the existing states in the region, including Israel. The Palestinian National Council adopted two documents – The Palestinian Declaration of Independence and the Political Programme – that clearly spelled out Palestinian goals and the means necessary to achieve them. These documents endorsed the UN Partition Resolution of 1947 – which had been categorically rejected until then – as the source of legitimacy of the proposed Palestinian state. Moreover, diplomacy and peaceful negotiation with Israel, to be conducted through the framework of an international conference, were identified as the preferred means to achieve this goal, thus effectively completing the displacement of military by political strategy towards which events had been directing the PLO in any event.[1]

This development is usually hailed nowadays on all sides, including by many Palestinians, as a conceptual breakthrough of great moment, and as the emergence of an overdue sense of 'realism' on the part of the Palestinians. What is often forgotten is that the ascendancy of the 'two-state' solution was essentially a symptom of Palestinian weakness – this goal was adopted not because it was the one that best answered Palestinian needs, but because it was the only one which (in the absence of their ability to attain the binational state and given the constant extension of Israeli settlements in the remaining Palestinian lands) the PLO now felt had any chance of success. What the Palestinians have discovered since the Algiers Conference, however, is that once they started to lower their sights in this way, they might well be commended for their 'realism', but they would also continually be pressed to lower expectations even further, the dictates of the imbalance of power between themselves and the Israelis impelling them towards ever more drastic compromises.

The problem, it should be noted, has never been resistance itself. Ever since the Arab Revolt in the 1930s, Palestinians have resisted the attempts to annihilate them as a society with remarkable resilience and resourcefulness. But territorial division and geographical dispersal have inevitably exerted a huge toll. At different moments the burden of the revolt against Israel has been taken up by different sections of the Palestinian people. In the 1970s and 1980s, it was mainly the refugee communities in the Diaspora that waged guerrilla wars against Israel. In the 1990s, the burden shifted to the *intifada* in the Occupied Territories. The Palestinians inside Israel have tried for decades to combat state discrimination, but this has mostly been conceived as a civil-rights issue only tangentially related to the wider nation-building project pursued by the other sectors of Palestinian society. While the burden of struggle has been transferred from one section of the community to another at different historic moments, it is the task of combining and co-ordinating these struggles that has consistently eluded Palestinians.

## II

It is in the context of this exceptionally difficult national struggle that the development of the modern Palestinian novel needs to be assessed. The novel does not, of course, take absolute precedence over other arts in the struggle for Palestinian self-determination, yet it does seem clear nevertheless that when the Palestinian intelligentsia dream of giving expression to the national longing for form, it is to the novel that they look. One finds this sense that the novel can perform a special role in the national struggle, for example, in Yasser Arafat's remark in an interview with Mu'in Bsisu that 'our Palestinian, Lebanese, and Arab poets and writers have composed odes and articles which have become part of the siege . . . but I am waiting for more; I am waiting *for the novel* which will penetrate Arab public opinion and not just break the windows of the house'.[2] Curiously, even the poets themselves seem to concur with this privileging of the novel over poetry, traditionally the major genre of classical and modern Arabic literary expression. Mahmud Darwish, usually considered Palestine's national poet, remarked in 1982 that 'the poet was once everything to Arabic culture: journalist, professor, leader'. Still, he continued, '[t]he form to which I most aspire to fulfil now is in the novel. There is no one in this age that I envy more than the novelists because the novel can expand to include everything . . . In the novel you can sing, and speak poetry, prose, ideas, and practically everything.'[3] Similarly, in an interview in 1989 with Salma Jayyusi, Fadwa Tuqan, Palestine's most famous woman poet, suggested that the demands of giving expression to the Palestinian struggle called for a literary form more capacious in its scope than poetry. 'I find,' she remarked, 'that the poem is no longer capable of accommodating the riches of the *intifada* experience in all its aspects. Poetry alludes, but oblique reference does not seem to be enough at the moment. I dream of a bigger work, a work that can accommodate my vision of those great happenings more than the poem can, and I have become haunted with the idea of writing a novel that embraces all aspects of the *intifada*.'[4]

It is as if in these yearnings for the more expansive, synoptic scope of the novel that would give expression to the epic sweep and geographical diversity of their struggle, Palestinians dream of recovering some sense of the totality of their experience shattered in 1948. When they dream of the 'big' novel that 'can expand to include everything', it is as if these leading intellectuals look to the novel imaginatively to prefigure a restored national collectivity that has still to be realised politically. Contemporary literary critics frequently point to the similarity between the modern nation, which attempts to compass all the people of a territory in a single historical process, and the technique of the great nineteenth-century realist novels, whose emplotment meshes multiple characters and sub-plots into an overarching narrative trajectory.[5] While the Palestinian intellectuals cited above seem to intuit this connection between novel and nation, the obverse side of their dream of the 'big' novel however, is a nagging sense that the Palestinian novel has not, perhaps cannot, meet this enormous burden of expectation. In *Arabesques*, a novel written in Hebrew by Israeli–Palestinian author Anton Shammas, Paco, a West Bank Palestinian novelist, and his Egyptian counterpart, Billy, discuss their work. When Paco tells Billy about the novel he is writing, the Egyptian asks him 'How many words have you got in it?' Paco blushes and replies that he has not counted. When Billy insists that Paco give him some idea of its length, the Egyptian laughs and tells the abashed Palestinian, 'It's not a novel that you're writing, my dear boy, but a novella!'[6]

In a richly suggestive essay on the modern Arabic novel, Edward Said develops an argument that recalls Shammas's fictional conversation. Comparing the Egyptian realist novel with its Palestinian and Lebanese counterparts, Said remarks that for the novelists of the latter countries the stately and encyclopaedic fullness of Egyptian Naguib Mahfouz's great realist novels has proved 'maddeningly, frustratingly *not* possible'.[7] The weighty solidity, thick description and textual density of Mahfouz's realism, Said suggests, depend on the sense of a territorially stable and well-integrated national society. On the other hand, he muses, for the Lebanese, whose nation-state collapsed in the 1980s and for the Palestinians, whose country disappeared from the map in 1948, the novel is inevitably 'a risky and highly problematic form'. In the de-centred, centrifugal and openly insurrectionary conditions of Palestinian and Lebanese existence, he argues, the well-sculpted solidity of Mahfouz's classical realist novels cannot be replicated. In Lebanon, Said remarks in a brilliant phrase that clearly extends to include the Palestinian experience as well, 'the novel exists largely as a form recording its own impossibility'.[8]

Some of the dilemmas of the modern Palestinian novel are not, of course, unique to the Palestinian situation but are shared by its counterparts in other colonised, underdeveloped and semi-peripheral societies generally. The nineteenth-century Irish novel, for instance, has long been perceived as a poor relation to its Western European and British counterparts, and the absence of a strong Irish realist novel tradition in particular has long troubled critical inquiry. In Latin America, the situation is often described in similar terms. Jean Franco comments, for example: 'All too often the nineteenth-century Spanish-American novel is clumsy and inept, with a plot derived at second hand from the contemporary European Romantic novel.'[9] Indeed, as Franco Moretti has observed, it is recurrently argued in critical commentaries on the development of the novel in most parts of the world, that the novel is essentially a Western European import that can be adapted only with considerable difficulty to local exigencies. Hence, he argues, the sustained classical realist traditions of France and Britain really constitute not the rule but the exception where the historical 'rise of the novel' is concerned.[10]

Many reasons might be adduced to explain why the attempt to develop the social realist novel outside Western Europe should prove difficult. In colonised and semi-peripheral regions, as Antonio Candido has remarked, the cosmopolitanism of the literati was always offset against the illiteracy (at least in the dominant literary culture) of the great majority. Hence not only were the values of the literati usually rooted in Europe, but many wrote 'as if their ideal public was in Europe and thus often dissociated themselves from their own land'.[11] Difficulties stemming from peripherality to the literary system dominated by Western Europe were exacerbated, moreover, by exceptionally sharp domestic class divisions in these regions, divisions over-determined by cultural distance where a colonising culture was forcibly imposed on local indigenous ones. The Irish writer and critic Seán O'Faoláin, for example, attributed the weakness of Irish realist narrative in the nineteenth-century to the fact that conventional realist technique 'was inconceivable in a population cloven in two as irreconcilably as the white landowners and black slaves of the American South before 1865'.[12] In short, where the literati attempted to marry local materials to imported European models, and where several different cultures characterised by their own temporalities disjunctively coexisted, the linear narration, thick description and organicism that characterised classical Western European realism were often difficult to reproduce.

Many of the dilemmas of the Palestinian novel, as well as many of the cultural 'tasks' that confront the Palestinian literary and scholarly intelligentsia, can be conceived, therefore, in terms of their wider macrosocial structural determinants in the colonial and underdeveloped world generally. In the Palestinian context specifically, three fundamental 'tasks' in particular may be identified. Firstly, a basic aim of Palestinian writing is to offer a Palestinian counter-narrative to the more established Israeli version. The Israelis were the victors in 1948 and they have retained the upper hand ever since. Israel enjoys, moreover, an extremely close relationship with the US, which in turn enjoys huge power over the international media. Hence, outside of the Arab world at least, the authoritative version of Israeli–Palestinian relations is largely defined in Israeli and US terms. One of the abiding objectives of Palestinian narrative, therefore, is to challenge the suppression of the Palestinian version of events and to insert the Palestinians back into history.

Secondly, because so much Palestinian land has been confiscated by the Israelis – by settlement, obviously, but also by re-naming it in the Jewish language – much Palestinian writing is engaged in what James Clifford calls 'textual rescue' or what Edward Said describes as a process 'to reclaim, rename, and reinhabit' the alienated landscape through the imagination.[13] The recitations of litanies of lost villages and towns in Palestinian poetry or in novels, such as Emile Habiby's *The Secret Life of Saeed, The Ill-Fated Pessoptimist*, or in memorial books, such as Walid Khalidi's massive encyclopaedia of destroyed villages, *All that Remains: the Palestinian Villages Destroyed in 1948*, are some of the more striking examples of a much wider enterprise.

Thirdly, given the catastrophic nature of recent Palestinian history, a great deal of Palestinian writing struggles to come to terms with the trauma involved, to nurse into narrative what Fredric Jameson has called the 'hurt' of history.[14] Political calamity of the magnitude suffered by the Palestinians inevitably exerts an enormous human toll; it induces a sense of individual and collective humiliation, frustration, recrimination, rage, anomie and despair. One of the functions of writing in such situations is to perform the work of mourning (*trauerarbeit*) – a necessary and inevitable part of any longer-term process of historical recovery. In addition, as Edward Said has remarked, 1948 represented more than simply a political catastrophe for the Palestinians. It also meant that 'Arabs everywhere were forced additionally to confront as their own problem, and taking an especially provocative form, one of the greatest and still unsolved problems of Western civilization, the Jewish question'. The Zionist success in 1948, he continues, posed unprecedented challenges to the whole notion of a collective Arab identity and to the whole project of Arab modernisation, thus generating problems that not only Palestinians but Arabs everywhere were compelled to address. Hence, Said observes, the disaster of 1948 needs to be grasped not alone as a human tragedy but as a shattering crisis in narrative within the entire Arab world as well. For the Palestinian writer, he remarks, 'nothing in his (*sic*) history, that is, in the repertory or vocabulary provided to him by his historical experience, gave him an adequate method for representing the Palestinian drama to himself'.[15] One of the tasks that has devolved to literature and the novel, as well as to other modes of writing, then, is that of making sense of the 1948 catastrophe, not only of registering the human misery it entailed, but of divining its meaning and significance for the Arab world.

For the novelist at least, in circumstances of extremity such as these the pressure to employ the codes and devices of social realist narrative is enormous. Firstly, in a situation where the Palestinians are faced with the prospect of their disappearance as a nation, social realism, with its propensity for thick description and vigilant social observation, seems to have the testimonial or documentary capacity, the ability to promise a full and faithful account, that no other narrative mode can readily match. Secondly, the social realist novel has long been championed in radical circles where the novel tends to be viewed as a 'weapon' of struggle. In situations of revolutionary struggle, progressives usually expect the novelist to express his or her message with as much transparency as possible so that it can reach the widest possible audience. In the heat of the South African anti-apartheid struggle, for example, novelists tended largely to adopt, in Elleke Boehmer's words, 'an upfront, hard-hitting, mimetic aesthetic, and therefore to pay less attention to form as such, to experiment, nuance, and the play of ambiguity for its own sake'.[16] In short, in situations of extreme repression and revolutionary struggle, social realism seems to answer more directly to the exigencies of political commitment and protest writing than more experimental or modernist literary modes can do.

The paradox that this suggests perhaps is that it may well be the case that the felt need for the 'big' social realist novel is often strongest precisely in those colonised and peripheral regions of the world where social conditions, for reasons noted earlier, make it most difficult to realise. To put it another way, the same social conditions that create the pressure towards social realism can also frustrate its realisation. This gap between felt imperative and inhibiting conditions would go some way to explaining why the Palestinian novel more particularly should largely remain 'a form recording its own impossibility'. In the case of the Palestinians, for example, it is precisely because they are a scattered and stateless people, segregated into different communities by the current state order in the Middle East, that the demand for the 'big' or synoptic all-encompassing novel should seem so pressing. But it is also this geographical dispersal, compounded by the sharply different social conditions in which the scattered communities live, that makes it exceptionally difficult to produce the 'big' novel that would bind these scattered communities into the coherence of a single narrative. The Palestinians scattered across the Arab world may all share a common sense of national consciousness and solidarity, but can these diverse locales – with their different textures, sharply diverse social conditions, distinct temporalities – be collectively contained within the linear narration of the traditional social realist novel? In the standard accounts of the connection between novel and nation-state, the territorial compass of the nation-state is assumed as a given. In such situations, the function of the novel is to act, in Franco Moretti's words, 'as a sort of literary railway, to weave the network covering a country in all its extension'[17] – in other words, to make that territory available for imaginative occupation. In the Palestinian situation, the difficulty is that this connective function is always problematic since the national community is never simply here and now within a shared and geographically contiguous national landscape – it is always somewhere else as well.

If conditions of geographical dispersal create problems of one kind, the demands of political commitment can generate difficulties of another order. That progressive Palestinian writers, including novelists, are called on to align themselves with the national-popular struggle may be accepted as a given; what remains open to question is which causes or strategies the writer should endorse and what constitutes effective 'resistance literature'. For some, the mere intention to oppositionality, expressed in the rhetoric of protest and militancy, will constitute a revolutionary literature. Others have rightly pointed out, however, that the fact that the writer wills or intends a work to be oppositional is no guarantee that it will actually be so. As Benita Parry observes, the Zhadnovist demand that Russian literature should serve the Soviet modernisation project engendered only 'an official literature', which saw literature surrender its critical function and offer up 'vapid fabrications of an heroic and optimistic populace'[18] at a time when the dilemmas of the communist venture needed seriously to be engaged. The manifest difference between the Russian and the Palestinian situation is that between the tyranny of an oppressive bureaucratic state and the very different kind of tyranny that goes with a condition of statelessness. But in situations of extremity of whatever kind, an obvious difficulty for the writer is that the pressure to maintain solidarity with an oppressed people can exercise its own kind of tyranny and can serve to smother dissent or critique because some will always dismiss anything that refuses the current consensus among the oppressed as an unaffordable luxury. The whole concept of literature as a weapon of 'resistance' also lends itself to the idea that literature should be affirmative: that its duty is to endorse the value of struggle, to celebrate those who do struggle, to will the people on to victory. But the sheer determination to struggle is not always enough since, as noted earlier, the real difficulty for the Palestinians has never been resistance per se but, rather, how best to articulate and co-ordinate that resistance. A literature that simply celebrates the will to resist, and that fails to ask whether the goals or strategies employed are sufficient, runs the risk of simply becoming 'an official literature', of reifying the very idea of resistance itself and of commodifying the sacrifices expended in its name. In so doing, the writer not only runs the risk of betraying art's critical function, but of sanctioning the reckless squander of the people's most precious resource.

The suggestion developed here is that in the Palestinian context (as in other colonised and peripheral regions) there are powerful pressures that compel the writer towards realist narrative, but that the social and historical conditions that would allow the realist novel to flourish do not always exist in such situations. It might be tempting to conclude, therefore, that the Palestinian writer should simply abandon the clumsy machinery of social realism for more flexible modernist or postmodernist techniques. Nevertheless, the thesis which I want to develop in this chapter is that what distinguishes the most ambitious Palestinian novels is that the drive for narrative realism, for fidelity of detail, for the synoptic view, is not surrendered but that due to the exigencies of the situation that social realist drive is in fact shot through with what, following Theodor Adorno, we can call an essentially modernist sensibility. For Adorno, modernism's essential gesture is negative. By this he means, as Neil Lazarus has written, that modernist works 'alluded to the existence of domination and violence through their own internal ruptures and contradictions – ruptures that were unavoidable because they traced the scars and contours of social antagonisms and constraints'.[19] In its ruthless refusal to affirm the world, in its relentless fidelity to the suffering of modern man, modernism's negativity disclosed itself, for Adorno, as essentially critical. Modernism's cardinal virtue, that is, was to register without compromise 'the ways in which the administered world thwarted the realization of utopia'.[20] Hence, for Adorno, even in the most opaque, elusive and ostensibly apolitical of modernist works, an aesthetic of emancipation could be discovered. Indeed, the works he championed most were those that were most determinedly resistant to self-conscious ideological appropriation – and hence neutralisation. This was because it was these works that most strenuously attempted to evade the reduction of everything to the logic of commodification that Adorno identified as a cardinal feature of the modern world system.

Three of the most artistically accomplished and politically compelling Palestinian novels to emerge since 1948 include Ghassan Kanafani's *Men in the Sun*, Emile Habiby's *The Secret Life of Saeed, the Ill-Fated Pessoptimist* and Anton Shammas's *Arabesques*. None of the three can be categorised as 'resistance literature' if an affirmative rhetoric of solidarity and militancy, or of commitment to an overtly identified course of political action, are taken as the indispensable hallmarks of such writing. None features the heroic or militant protagonists, the polemical cast, or the optimistic tone usually associated with 'resistance literature' or indeed with the metropolitan nineteenth-century socialist realist novel. In Kanafani's grim tale, the four Palestinian protagonists remain tragic victims of their situation. In Habiby's *The Pessoptimist*, the main protagonist is a collaborator with the Israeli state. Shammas's *Arabesques*, a radically self-divided novel (temporally split between past and present, spatially divided between the Middle East and the United States, shuffling uneasily between Palestinians inside and outside Israel), is a labyrinthine saga that involves an errant quest for family reunion that finally proves utterly elusive. All three novels are very different in style, but if anything unites them it is the lack of a strong narrative resolution and the absence of any transparent political message.

The point here is not to champion a putative Palestinian modernism at the expense of the Palestinian social realist novel. Nor is it by any means to privilege a disengaged over a committed art since the real question at issue is what constitutes an effective kind of commitment in art. As previously remarked, the exigencies of the Palestinian situation are such that even as there is a decided pressure towards social realism, this drive is often frustrated and goes hand in hand with an essentially modernist sensibility. The exemplary Palestinian novel in this respect, it seems to me, still remains Ghassan Kanafani's *Men in the Sun*. As a committed revolutionary writer of the left, the whole trajectory of Kanafani's short but exceptional career (he was assassinated in 1972, allegedly by the Israeli secret service), was to place his art in the service of national-popular struggle and socialist emancipation. Like many left-wing radical writers, he gravitated more towards a social realist than towards an avant-garde modernist aesthetic. Nonetheless, Kanafani was too searching an intellectual simply to act as cheerleader to either party or people, too rigorously critical to endorse resistance as a sufficient end in itself. His *Men in the Sun* cannot be categorised as either realist or modernist narrative without violence, therefore, because it displays some of the best elements of both. It is said that in the years after World War II, Georg Lukács reversed his earlier dismissal of Kafka as a decadent modernist and celebrated him as a realist. The shift suggests that aesthetic categorisation and historical situation are somehow context-bound, and the political significance of a particular aesthetic form is always contingent on its conditions of production. In Kanafani's short novel, a similar constitutive paradox – one whereby modernist and social realist aesthetic imperatives bleed into each other – can be seen to operate. Although the chapter will focus on *Men in the Sun*, the fundamental predicaments which agitate that novel might also be elucidated in several other major Palestinian novels as well.

## III

Ghassan Kanafani's *Men in the Sun* tells the story of three Palestinian men who suffocate in an empty water-tanker while being smuggled, by a fourth Palestinian, across the border between Iraq and Kuwait.[21] What first strikes one about this novel is the curious discrepancy between its concerns and its setting. All of the principal characters in the tale are Palestinian, and the dilemmas it depicts all stem from the debacle of 1948. Yet despite its *national* focus, the action in *Men in the Sun* is not located in any part of the land of Palestine but takes place instead thousands of miles away on the border between Iraq and Kuwait. Moreover, the tragedy that brings the narrative to conclusion occurs in a space which is quite literally a 'no-place' since the men die in a juridical 'no man's land' between states that defies representation. This 'no-place' must ultimately be read as a figure in the text for Palestine itself – a land that officially disappeared from the map in 1948 and that has existed only in the stubborn imagination of scattered and stateless Palestinians ever since. In Kanafani's text, then, the basic historic predicament of the Palestinian people is inscribed within the narrative as an immanent problematic of representation and form.

Written in 1961 and published in 1963, *Men in the Sun* is set in 1958, exactly a decade after the partition of Palestine. The moment in which the story is set is significant. In 1958 Egypt and Syria had merged into a single state under Nasser to form the United Arab Republic. This was hailed at the time as a momentous event that would speed the creation of the single Arab homeland. When Syria seceded from the merger only three years later, the United Arab Republic collapsed.

These events unleashed an intense debate among Palestinians about the connection between the Palestinian and pan-Arabist struggles, unsettling the prevailing assumption that the liberation of Palestine must await the prior attainment of wider pan-Arab unity, something that now looked increasingly remote and chimerical. Fatah, the first Arab movement with a specifically Palestinian agenda, was formed in Kuwait in 1959. For the Arab Nationalist Movement (ANM), an organisation established mainly by Diaspora Palestinians but with a resolutely pan-Arabist agenda, the dissolution of the United Arab Republic called into question the adequacy of its entire strategy. Some concluded that the failure of the Nasser-led merger made it imperative for the ANM to adopt a more decisively socialist policy within the same pan-Arabist framework. For others, the collapse made it clear that the movement would, however, have to give much greater priority to the Palestinian question. In 1960, the organisation, breaking with previous practice, which had actively discouraged regionalism of any kind, formed its first Palestinian Division. By 1965 it had reversed its previous formulation: where before pan-Arab unity had been considered the essential precondition for the redemption of Palestine, the liberation of Palestine was now declared the necessary precondition for greater Arab unity. Palestine was now declared the means and Arab unity the end.[22]

*Men in the Sun* is a complex narrative that cannot be reduced to an allegorical commentary on these events. The circumstances surrounding the collapse of the United Arab Republic had impelled an urgent critical revaluation of 'the Palestinian question', however, and it is the conceptual crisis generated by this episode, rather than the actual events themselves, that informs *Men in the Sun*. What the collapse of the United Arab Republic had thrown into relief perhaps was the obdurate reality of the nation-state system in the Arab world. For a group such as the ANM whose pan-Arabist strategy called for the transcendence of localised state and national allegiances this lesson in the obduracy of the regional nation-state was a painful one.

This conflict between trans-statist aspirations and the stubborn material reality of states unresponsive to such aspirations is one of the crucial issues that informs Kanafani's novel. Overdetermining that conflict is an even more fundamental issue: the lack of a Palestinian state. If Kanafani's narrative is set thousands of miles from Palestine, this is neither because the issue of the national territory is marginal to his concerns nor because he is concerned solely with the harsh fate of Palestinians in the Diaspora. The immediate absence of Palestine from Kanafani's novel ought to be read rather as a symptom of its most fundamental preoccupation and dilemma: the difficulty of representing a land that has no official existence. The dilemma for Kanafani, that is, is how to convey the predicament of a people whose circumstances seem to render the project of state-building an absolute imperative and yet at the same time exceptionally difficult to achieve.

The story recounted in Kanafani's novel is that of three Palestinian men who have left their refugee camps and make their way to Basra in Iraq where they attempt a desperate bid to have themselves smuggled across the Iraq–Kuwait border. The oldest, Abu Qais, is a peasant evicted from his homeland in 1948. Elderly and fragile, he has been urged by his friends to shake off the stupor in which he has lived since this displacement and has been persuaded to travel to Kuwait where he may be able to find work to provide for his destitute family. The second, Assad, is a young man who has fallen foul of the Jordanian authorities because of his political activities. Duped on his way to Basra by a fellow Palestinian who had promised to help him across the Jordanian border but who then abandoned him inside the frontier, Assad is suspicious that the Iraqi smugglers will do the same. Marwan, a boy of sixteen and the youngest of the three, is bitterly aggrieved with his father who has deserted his mother for a woman of better means, and with his elder brother who has stopped sending remittances to his family after he married in Kuwait. Forced to put aside his dreams of becoming a medical student, he is on his way to Kuwait in search of manual labour so that he may become the family provider.

Too poor to pay the exorbitant rates charged by the professional smugglers, the three migrants strike a deal with a fourth Palestinian, Abul Khaizuran, who promises to smuggle them across the border for a small fee. Since he is a truck-driver for Haj Rida, a prominent Kuwaiti businessman, the lorry, Abul Khaizuran assures them, will not be checked too closely at the border. All the three refugees will have to do is to hide for a few moments in the empty water-tanker while he has his papers cleared at the checkpoints. On the Iraqi side of the border everything goes to plan. At the Kuwaiti checkpoint, though, Abul Khaizuran is delayed much longer than anticipated because a bored border official, who has been told that Abul Khaizuran has been spending his time in Basra with a prostitute, teases the truck-driver about his supposed sexual exploits. Frantic, since he thinks the official may have discovered the shameful secret of his castration during the 1948 war, and because he knows the migrants will stifle if he is detained, Abul Khaizuran presses to have the papers signed as quickly as possible and eventually manages to get away. When the lorry is safely out of sight of the border post, he rushes to open the lid of the tanker only to discover his three compatriots already dead. Smitten with remorse, he plans at first to give the bodies decent burial, but the shock of the tragedy soon dissipates, and Abul Khaizuran decides that it is easier simply to dump the corpses under cover of darkness on a municipal dump outside Kuwait city. This he does but not before he has robbed Marwan's watch and stripped the other bodies of their meagre possessions. The story ends with Abul Khaizuran driving away from the dump, repeatedly demanding of the dead: 'Why didn't you knock on the sides of the tank? Why didn't you bang the sides of the tank? Why? Why? Why?'[23]

*Men in the Sun* is written in a spare, severe, rigorously depersonalised prose scoured of overt commentary of any kind. Despite its terseness, the novel is deceptively rich in realistic detail and manages, by deft detail and allusion, to convey a sense of a much wider Palestinian community extending beyond the immediate compass of the plot. In an insightful reading, Mary Layoun has suggested that there is a contradiction in the work between its stress on the detached, isolated experience of the four protagonists and its simultaneous insistence on the need for communal solidarity. The structure of the novel, Layoun observes, is a rigidly schematic one that divides the tale into six separate segments (or 'chapters'), the opening three of which are named after the three migrants. For Layoun, this compartmentalised structure, which maroons or segregates each of the men within his own section of the narrative, is to be read as a formal expression of the psychological isolation of the men that disables collective agency and thus consigns them to death. Yet, she contends, despite its stress on the inability of the men to surmount their individual isolation, the novel is equally insistent on the communality of their experience – their shared past of displacement and exile, their common death in the dreadful proximity of the tanker. For Layoun, then, there is an inherent contradiciton between the form and the content of Kanafani's novel: at the same time 'as it produces and compartmentalizes the details of its characters' individual lives in the narrative present, the very structure of the narrative insists on, attempts to accomplish by textual fiat, the shared history, the communality, of those same men'.[24]

Just as the temporality of the narrative is constructed in terms of an elaborate series of memories that over-layer past and present, so too each of the sections that introduces the four protagonists can be read in terms of a gradually exfoliating set of concerns centred on the relationship between politics and space. It is no coincidence, as Layoun has suggested, that the novel should begin with Abu Qais, the landless peasant.[25] In this figure, the novel depicts the fate of a whole sector of Palestinian society that was trapped in some kind of class limbo after 1948 since it could no longer be defined as a peasantry (because it lacked land) nor yet as proletarian (since its refugee status impeded its full entry into the state workforce of the host countries). The section to which Abu Qais gives his name opens with a memorably lyrical passage in which the old man lies stretched on the earth listening to what he believes to be its heart pulsating beneath. The sound of the throbbing heartbeat causes him to remember how one of his Palestinian neighbours had mocked this anthropomorphic notion many years before. The neighbour had told him then that it was the reverberations of his own heart that he heard, a suggestion Abu Qais still refuses to accept. Lost in this fantasy, Abu Qais summons himself reluctantly to consciousness and to the realisation that he is stretched not on his own land in Palestine but thousands of miles away on the banks of the Shatt in Iraq. The imagined pulsations of the earth link the two places sensually, and it is only with reluctance that Abu Qais mentally separates one place from the other.

The old peasant's relationship to his lost land is cathected as a form of sexual yearning:

> Every time he breathed the scent of the earth, as he lay on it, he imagined that he was sniffing his wife's hair when she had just walked out of the bathroom, after washing with cold water. The very same smell, the smell of a woman who had washed with cold water and covered his face with her hair while it was still damp.[26]

For him, it is suggested, the earth is not only a source of economic livelihood but the basis on which his whole sense of his position within the larger symbolic order depends. Dislodged from the land, he has now also been cut adrift by economic necessity from wife and family to become both socially and spatially disorientated. Although the peasant's sense of attachment to the earth is invoked in lyrical and sensual terms, it is Abu Qais's inability to maintain proper distinctions between things that is foregrounded throughout this section. He cannot distinguish between the pulsations of the earth and those of his own body. To him, the ground on which he now lies stretched in Iraq is the same organic entity as his lost Palestinian fields. His fantasies of his future in Kuwait and his memories of his lost Palestine continually blend into each other. Overwhelmed by a sense of alien-ation, Abu Qais begins to weep and soon everything 'began to swim behind a mist of tears, the horizon of the river and the sky came to-gether and everything around him became simply an endless white glow. He went back, and threw himself down with his chest on the damp earth which began to beat beneath him again, while the scent of the earth rose to his nostrils and poured into his veins like a flood.'[27] The blurring of river and sky into a flood of tears here marks a failure of outline and of perception, a loss of any clean separation between things as everything merges with everything else. Abu Qais's sense of dislocation is registered with genuine empathy and his sensual response to the landscape may even be read as a critique of the reifica-tion and denaturing of experience that seems to be linked in the novel not only to his displacement from Palestinian soil but to the larger processes of proletarianisation consequent to that upheaval. Never-theless, the fact that Abu Qais sinks down helplessly onto the earth as well as the collapsing together of things into that 'endless white glow' works to counter any romanticisation of his response, and to suggest its inadequacy. The indiscriminate 'white glow' with which this section concludes functions as an ominously proleptic reference to the relentless glare of the sun that will eventually bring Abu Qais and his companions to their fatal end.

This section of *Men in the Sun* must be read, however, not simply as mimetic social commentary, which attempts to describe in faithful detail the condition of the uprooted peasant, but also as an inter-textual critique of a particular kind of Palestinian literary expression that emerged in the wake of the 1948 disaster. The lyrical pathos of Kanafani's writing in this section alludes, that is, to that pervasive sense of nostalgia, melancholy and loss that has been described as a distinctive feature of the Palestinian poetry of exile written in the 1950s and beyond. This poetry – in which the imagery of the rural peasant, the land and the lost house (commonly associated with the Palestinian peasant woman) recurs obsessively – invokes an idealised rural Palestine nostalgically remembered as a lost paradise.[28] Draw-ing on a conventional repertoire of images of flowers, orange groves, olive trees and folk dress, this is a poetry which, as Barbara McKean Parmenter points out, invokes a Palestinian past that not only pre-cedes Zionist colonisation but also the wider disruptions of twentieth-century modernisation and development.[29] For Palestinians, the value of this poetry was that it engaged in a kind of textual rescue of the lost homeland and asserted their continued allegiance to it. As such, it represented an imaginative counter to the Israeli appropriation of the land and it also served to mitigate the sense of alienation experienced by the dispossessed in their exile.

Nevertheless, because this poetic enterprise sought above all to recover and preserve a now vanished world, it tended to be not only rather conventional in technique and imagery but to embalm the landscape of the past in the formaldehyde of memory. As McKean Parmenter notes, whereas 'the Israelis establish their place [in Palestine] by transforming nature – draining swamps, irrigating arid lands, and building cities, Palestinian writers cling [in such poetry] to the original landscape and its relict features for inspiration and support'.[30] Bent on 'making the desert bloom', the Zionist imagination of the landscape, in other words, is tied to a restlessly dynamic rhetoric of colonial improvement and transformation. Dedicated to the preservation in memory of that which had been seized and was now being altered by others, the Palestinian aesthetic, in contrast, is tied to a past-orientated imagery that insists on the changeless or stationary quality of the land and its stubborn resistance to the translations of time and the colonial intruder. The drawback of this aesthetic, however, is its lack of dynamism; the lost landscape can be protected by memory, but it can also be calcified by it; and the resistance to the transformation of the landscape risks hardening into a resistance to the very idea of change itself.

By linking this aesthetic with the exhaustion of Abu Qais, *Men in the Sun* intimates that this poetic discourse, which feminises the land as an object of male desire, is ultimately an insufficient response to the exigencies of the Palestinian situation. The Palestinian landscape invoked in this poetry is a sensual topos of desire, but what is lacking is any real sense of historical causality, any real analysis of the circumstances that contributed to the disaster. Kanafani's novel, then, introjects the stylistic register of the Palestinian poetry of loss, but does so diacritically to assert its inadequacy to the social situation which generates it and to which it addresses itself.

A more consciously politicised conception of space appears to offer itself in this section in the figure of Ustaz Selim, the village schoolteacher whom Abu Qais remembers as he lies dreaming of Palestine on the banks of the Shatt. Recalling the days before his village fell to the Zionists, Abu Qais ponders the arrival of Ustaz Selim from Jaffa and how he had shocked the village elders by refusing to lead them in prayer, telling them that he was a secular teacher and not an imam. The incident that Abu Qais remembers most vividly is one in which he had listened through the open window of the village schoolhouse to Ustaz Selim drilling his students about the source of the Shatt Al-Arab, and chiding one of them for his failure to memorise the details of the geography lesson. Abu Qais remembers how Ustaz Selim had repeated 'a dozen times' the sentence: 'When the two great rivers, Tigris and Euphrates, meet, they form one river called the Shatt al-Arab, which extends from just above Basra to . . .'[31] As he waits, vainly, for his students to complete the sentence, Ustaz Selim becomes increasingly angry. The reference to the Shatt here alludes not only to Abu Qais's present location, but to the expansive dreams of pan-Arab nationalism. For pan-Arabists, the Shatt constituted the eastern boundary of the Arab homeland: in the rhyming slogan of pan-Arab nationalism, broadcast daily on the Voice of the Arabs radio during Nasser's reign, this homeland was to extend from 'the Atlantic Ocean to the Persian Gulf'.[32]

The fact that Ustaz Selim's sentence remains incomplete seems to refer to some larger problem of enclosure. The inability of Abu Qais and the unfortunate student to complete the sentence might suggest that the consciousness of the villagers is simply too rooted in the local to be able to grasp the expansive political vista offered them by pan-Arabism. It might also be read, however, to suggest a tension within pan-Arabism itself. The reference to the Shatt calls to mind the disputed 'Arabness' of this region between Iraq and Iran, and prompts the question as to where exactly the Arab world ends and the Persian one begins. By juxtaposing the problematic 'localisation' of peasant consciousness and the problematic 'universalism' of pan-nationalism in this way, the passage infers that the abstract expansiveness of one may finally be almost as disabling as the parochial limitations of the other. The pan-Arabist vision of Ustaz Selim and the localised vision of Abu Qais may not, then, as some commentators have suggested, encounter each other simply as positive and negative values.[33] While Abu Qais's conception of space is sensual and rooted in the land but is not adequately politicised, Ustaz Selim's imaginative geography is politically motivated but perhaps too little rooted in the material realities of those to whom it is addressed to command an effective response. Instead of privileging an enlightened pan-Arabist conception of space over narrow peasant localism, what Kanafani's text seems to point to is the material difficulty of co-ordinating the different spatial scales of utopian political vision and lived political reality.

The absent term in the first section of *Men in the Sun*, which the second section or 'chapter' will soon press into visibility, is the *state*.

Where Abu Qais's localised vision is too narrowly focused to take much account of the state, Ustaz Selim's expansive pan-Arabism seems to bypass the state altogether by overleaping it in a peremptory and idealised fashion. It is no coincidence, then, that when we come to the section named after Assad, the only one of the migrants with a history of political activism, state boundaries come into prominent focus for the first time and are referred to almost continuously. Expecting to be arrested at any moment by the Jordanian police, Assad had been forced to come to an understanding with Abul-Abd, a lorry-driver delivering a sports car for a 'rich Baghdadi' who had spent the summer in Amman before flying back to Iraq. Promising to smuggle Assad across the Jordanian–Iraqi border for the sum of twenty dinars, Abul-Abd abruptly changes the terms of the agreement when they arrive near the Iraqi frontier. Because Assad is 'a plotter against the state,' the driver argues, his name is sure to be 'registered at all the frontier posts' and 'without a passport or an exit visa' he has no chance of slipping through undetected.[34] Consequently, there is no option but for Assad to make a wide detour through the desert on foot, skirting around the border post, and meeting up again with the lorry on the other side. When Assad reluctantly consents to this, he travels for hours through the scorching desert, finding his way back to the highway only to discover that Abul-Abd has gone on without him. He is later picked up by a Western couple who soon guess what has happened to him and who smuggle him into Iraq. When they learn that Assad is a Palestinian from Ramleh, the male Westerner asks him if he knows Zeita, a small village on the disputed border between Israel and the Jordanian West Bank. He himself, he remarks, had been in Zeita just a few weeks earlier where '[a] little child came up to me and said in English that his house was a few feet beyond the barbed wire'.[35]

In contrast to the narrowly localised or abstractly expansive conceptions of space registered in the preceding section, space in this section is rigorously segmented, and traversed by those who do not belong to the wealthy Western or Arab élite only with great difficulty. It is this compartmentalisation of space that seems to constitute the greatest obstacle to the realisation of Palestinian dreams. Whether it be the refugee child looking forlornly across the barbed wire to his house in Israel, Ustaz Selim's vista of a pan-Arab homeland, or the migrants waiting to find some way across the frontier into Kuwait, it is the border, the ultimate symbol of state sovereignty, that always stands between Palestinians and the materialisation of their dreams.

What the section also highlights, however, is that state borders do not just physically divide space into rigid compartments. They also regulate the flows and contra-flows of goods and people that move across different spaces in complex and variable ways. The ease with which the 'rich Baghdadi' playboy, the Western 'tourists', and Haj Rida, the prominent Kuwaiti businessman, traverse state lines stands out in marked contrast to the onerous journeys of the destitute migrants. Likewise, commodities are moved across state boundaries more easily and more profitably than people are. When Abul Khaizuran spins his story about how he just happens to be in Basra with an empty water-tanker, Assad cuts through his deceptions and tells him: 'It seems to me that Haj Rida and you, sir, are involved in smuggling ... Haj Rida believes that smuggling people on the return journey is a trivial matter, so he leaves it to you – while you in turn leave to him the smuggling of more important things, for a reasonable share of the profits.'[36] What Kanafani's narrative unobtrusively but relentlessly insists on, then, is the way that state borders serve a whole concatenation of economic, juridical, military and other functions, all of which operate in dramatically different ways for different classes or for those with different nationality and political status. For the harassed political activist without state documents, the border is first and foremost a pressing juridical reality constraining his mobility. For the displaced Palestinian child in Zeita, it is an expression of military might materialised in barbed wire. For the impoverished migrants, it is a source of economic exploitation that begins with the exorbitant fees they will have to pay to be smuggled from one state into another, and that will continue even if they do manage to cross the state line in the form of the super-exploitation of their labour as a non-national or alien workforce. Beginning in this section, then, Kanafani's novel underscores the point that state borders constitute a complex and elusive political phenomenon – and not just because they are mostly imaginary lines in the sand. If borders are tricky to negotiate politically, this is because they co-ordinate multiple functions with socially diverse consequences and effects. Accordingly, any political strategy designed to appeal to a wider sense of Arab community will have to be able to come to terms with the way in which the existing state system serves complex, cross-cutting networks of interests. Nevertheless, this is a challenge that will have to be met. As the conclusion of the narrative underscores, to fail to master state borders leads inevitably to disaster.

Starting with its three migrants already arrived in Basra and nervously waiting to be smuggled into Kuwait, *Men in the Sun* might be described as a novel that begins and ends with a border that it never really gets beyond. The construction of time and movement in the narrative is curious in this respect. Insofar as there is any sense of significant movement, the novel reaches back from its temporal 'present,' its 'now'-time, to bring the three protagonists up to that point. There is, however, no corresponding forward movement beyond this, since nothing substantive changes in the lives of the protagonists between their arrival in Basra and their eventual deaths on the border. All that is of consequence to the development of these characters has already happened, therefore, before the narrative proper gets started. The latter part of the tale does involve the relentless forward motion of the truck journeying across the empty desert. But this movement lies outside of what, in Mikhail Bakhtin's terms, we might describe as the 'biographical time' of the protagonists since it 'changes nothing in the life of the heroes, and introduces nothing into their life'.[37] What we have in the second part of the novel, in other words, is mechanical motion without character development, a sterility literalised in the text as a journey across an arid desert that leads only to death. The Palestinian men arrive separately in Basra; their attempt to move collectively forward from there soon comes to an abrupt and horrifying dead end. This inability to get beyond the border represents not so much an individual failure on the part of the migrants as the lack of any available political strategy that might allow them to master political space. The narrative, therefore, is essentially one of stasis and paralysis – in this respect, Kanafani's novel might be described as a sort of social realist *Waiting for Godot*.

If the novel revolves around the tremendous difficulty of mastering public political space, however, it works decisively to close off the idea that a retreat into private domestic space represents a viable alternative. If, as Franco Moretti has argued, one of the functions of the modern European novel is to investigate the conflictual relationship between public and private spheres, to discover whether a balance or compromise can be struck between the two, then Kanafani's novel clearly implies that no such compromise is available.[38] Assad, the fugitive political activist abandoning politics in order to make a new life in Kuwait, is the most obvious example of a wider retreat in the novel from public to private space. What Kanafani's narrative seems to assert, however, is the futility of that retreat: if the Palestinian men cannot master public political space, they cannot escape the consequent sense of crisis by trying to reassert their masculinity in the private, domestic sphere.

It is in the third section of *Men in the Sun*, which introduces the youngest migrant, Marwan, and the driver, Abul Khaizuran, that the thematics of masculine crisis is shifted to the centre of the novel's concerns. From the beginning of this section, the incapacity of the Palestinian men to live up to the ideals of mastery and sufficiency conventionally associated with maleness is underlined. Marwan is an inexperienced youth, a nascent male subject neither capable nor eager to fulfil the responsibilities of adult masculinity prematurely thrust upon him. Browbeaten by the fat Iraqi smuggler who contemptuously dismisses his attempts to bargain down the fee, Marwan fears to lose face and determines that 'he must be more than a man, and show more than courage, or they would laugh at him, cheat him, and take advantage of his sixteen years'. His bid to be 'more than a man', however, badly misfires. When the smuggler dismisses his offer of five dinars, Marwan retorts that he will report him to the police, a threat that simply earns him a sharp blow to the face and the Iraqi picks him up and dumps him unceremoniously in the street outside. Shaken and humiliated, Marwan acknowledges to himself that the threat itself was shameful, and that given the manifest imbalance of force 'any attempt to restore his honour was futile': there is nothing for him to do, he decides, but 'to digest his humiliation'. This need 'to digest his humiliation', to take account of his weakness rather than seeking to disavow it by way of useless threats, may be read as part of a broader insistence in *Men in the Sun* that Palestinians generally must attempt to come to terms with their collective trauma consequent to the catastrophe of 1948. Militant braggadocio and appeals to the Arab state for assistance, it is inferred, are really only attempts to mask a positional weakness that demands instead serious strategic consideration.

As he sits in the street reeling from his blow, Marwan begins to feel an unaccountable sensation of calm. Gradually, he realises that what has allowed him to overcome the shame inflicted on him by the day's events is the fact that he had written a long therapeutic letter to his mother that morning in which he had vented his pent-up feelings of anger and resentment towards his father. His anger stems from the fact that his father had divorced his mother to marry Shafiqa, a woman who owns her own house, an arrangement that allows the old man to escape the destitution of the refugee camps and to attain the security he craved. Rereading his letter in his mind, Marwan is delighted to think that 'he had allowed himself to describe his father as nothing but a depraved beast' and that he had the courage not 'to cross the words out once he'd written them'. As he ponders his familial situation more fully, he is compelled to admit to himself, however, that his feelings towards his father are not so clear-cut as his disgusted description in the letter would suggest. Though convinced that his father 'had certainly done something horrible'[39] when he abandoned his family, Marwan nonetheless understands his father's need for security, and even his desire to escape the endless burden of providing for the family – something Marwan himself is none too happy to have inherited. Moreover, he feels that his elder brother Zakaria shares some of the blame for his father's wretched behaviour. After all, he tells himself, it was only when Zakaria got married in Kuwait and stopped sending remittances to his family in Jordan that his father finally abandoned hope and deserted them.

The Oedipal overtones of this father–son conflict are evident, though the paternal failures that recur all across the novel suggest that the crisis depicted here is collective rather than simply individual. The loss of homeland in 1948 is identified with a loss of manhood and with a failure of the paternal function that throws familial relations into disarray. This in turn provokes a crisis on the part of the younger males, Assad and Marwan, concerning their insertion into the discredited masculine order of things. Trying to shield his mother from the mortification of a second desertion, Marwan has kept from her his knowledge that the reason why the usual remittances no longer come from Kuwait is that Zakaria has got married and started a family of his own. Guarding this knowledge as though it were a shameful secret, Marwan is astonished when Abul Khaizuran guesses the truth of his family situation almost as soon as they are introduced. When Marwan asks the lorry-driver how he could know of Zakaria's marriage, the latter replies: 'One doesn't have to be a genius to understand. Everyone stops sending money to their families when they get married or fall in love.'[40] Marriage here acquires a distinctly negative valence: stripped of affective aura, it does not serve the usual function of affirming or reproducing the social order; on the contrary, it appears as a shoddy compromise with the way of the world, as something always at cross-purposes with a commitment to one's own immediate blood-relations.

The same hostility to the idea of conventional heterosexual domesticity finds even more overt expression in Assad's story. The money his uncle loans Assad in order to leave Jordan is given on the understanding that when he finds a job in Kuwait Assad will marry Nada, the uncle's daughter. Assad bitterly resents the fact that his uncle should have attached this condition to the loan:

Who told him that he wanted to marry Nada? Just because his
father had recited the Fatiha with his uncle when he and Nada
were born on the same day? His uncle considered that was fate.
Indeed he had refused a hundred suitors who had asked for
his daughter's hand and told them she was engaged. O God of
devils! *Who told him that he, Assad, wanted to marry her? Who told
him he ever wanted to get married?* Here he was now reminding
him again. He wanted to buy him for his daughter as you buy a
sack of manure for a field.[41]

The disgust Assad expresses at the prospect of an arranged marriage
modulates into a more generalised disgust with the idea of marriage
per se and with a sense that one's life has been predetermined or
dictated in advance, stripped of individual choice or decision. As the
reference to the first sura of the Quran suggests, the future marked
out for Assad has been determined not only by his actual father but
also in the name of the symbolic father. The ratification of the dictate
of the actual father in the name of the symbolic father attests that the
paternal order which Assad resents is essentially a social rather than a
purely personal or psychological matter – the law of the father acquires
the character of an impersonal fate, an imposition, decreed from the
moment the child is born. Fathers and marriages in the novel, then, are
both negatively marked. Marriages appear only as shoddy economic
arrangements: the desertion of Marwan's father for the security of
Shafiqa's house, Zakaria's abandonment of his own family once he
marries, the marriage that his uncle would impose on Assad. Likewise,
the paternal generation associated with the 1948 debacle may be old
and rather pathetic like Abu Qais or Marwan's father, or more sinister
like Abul-Abd or Abul Khaizuran, but there are no positive images of
fatherhood in the text.

*Men in the Sun* is a totally male-dominated novel, then, but it is also
one that displays a distinct unease with the whole construction of the
masculine order of things. It is a narrative replete with fallen fathers
and with sons that bitterly resent having to take up the paternal legacy
and who display a marked hostility (apparently shared by the text
itself) to any attempt to insert them into the conventional familial and
sexual system. The masculine crisis referred to here finds its exemplary
figure in Abul Khaizuran who has been castrated as a consequence
of an explosion in the 1948 war, but it is imperative to note that his
emasculation is only the most exemplary instance of a wider sexual
crisis that also extends to include the other characters.

The most striking feature of *Men in the Sun*, however, is not
its representation of historical trauma in terms of a crisis of male

sexuality – such associations, as Kaja Silverman and others have pointed out, are quite conventional.[42] But while Kanafani deploys the stock figure of the emasculated or castrated male, he, much more unusually, makes no attempt to shore up the masculine crisis he depicts. *Men in the Sun*, that is, marshals none of the usual defensive mechanisms to ward off the horror of the spectacle of male castration. It makes no move to re-establish the status quo at the end by producing some potent male figure that might serve – like the recuperated Yonatan in Amos Oz's *A Perfect Peace* for instance – as a model for a restored masculinity. On the contrary, *Men in the Sun* never resolves the crisis in masculinity it sets in motion, it sustains and amplifies the correlation of masculinity and castration until the very end.

*Men in the Sun*, this suggests, cannot be read as a narrative that simply deploys the stock figure of the castrated male as a symbol for the loss of political power in an unreflective or uncritical way therefore. Progressing from one spectacle of male sexual crisis to another, the novel demands to be read, rather, as a deliberate attempt to work through the logic of that crisis so that it must be faced up to and not evaded or peremptorily shored up. It is in its treatment of the two anatomically mutilated figures in the text that the narrative's treatment of the spectacle of male castration is most forcefully developed. These two figures are Shafiqa, the Palestinian amputee for whom Marwan's father deserts his original family, and Abul Khaizuran, the castrated Palestinian driver.

In order to understand the relationship between these two physically mutilated figures in the narrative, we can usefully refer in more detail at this point to Kaja Silverman's observations on the relationship between historical trauma and male castration. According to Silverman, the attributes of mastery and sufficiency normatively associated with maleness require the male subject to see himself, and the female subject to recognise and desire him, only through images of unimpaired masculinity. Hence, she argues, the 'dominant fiction' of a particular society, by which she means that delicate balance between its established master narratives and the impression of reality needed to sustain their credibility, urges both male and female subjects to deny all knowledge of male castration by believing in the commensurability of penis and phallus, of symbolic and actual father. Under conditions of acute historical trauma, however, it can become impossible to sustain such belief in the self-sufficiency of the male or in the commensurability of penis and phallus. Masculinity, in other words, is normally constructed by denying male castration, a denial tenuously sustained by attributing castration solely to female subjectivity. The reactions attributed by Freud to the male subject at the sight of the female genitalia are explicable in this context. According to Freud, the sight of the female genitalia offers an alarming spectacle to the male subject, uncomfortably reminding him of the prospect of his own castration, threatening him with the loss of the penis and, by extension, of his property, status and power. On the other hand, the spectacle is also consoling because it confirms for the male subject that this dreaded prospect has not actually been visited upon him; he can reassure himself that this fate has been inflicted on the female only. When, as in situations of historical catastrophe, the male subject is forced to confront his own castration, the spectacle of his own lack, his automatic reaction is to deflect that spectacle by hysterically projecting it onto the female.[43]

Through the figures of Shafiqa and Abul Khaizuran, *Men in the Sun* stages this conventional masculine response to the spectacle of male castration, but does so only to stress its inadequacy, to intimate that this is simply a self-deceiving reflex that diverts attention from the deeper crisis. As Marwan reminisces on his father's desertion of his mother, he recalls how his father's new wife, Shafiqa had had her right leg 'amputated at the top of the thigh' during the Zionist bombardment of Jaffa in 1948. Some time after they had been evicted from Palestine, Shafiqa's father had bought her a house with funds donated by a charity. When he had gone to visit his father before setting off for Kuwait, Marwan had found himself luridly obsessed by the spectacle of Shafiqa's deformity, wondering to himself 'where her thigh ends?' The mixture of prurient fascination and revulsion which he feels recalls Freud's account of the way in which the male subject responds to the sight of the female genitalia. Marwan's outrage that his father should have divorced his mother 'to marry that deformed woman'[44] can be read, then, as a defensive reaction which betrays his inclination to project the disgust he feels for the moral weakness of his father onto Shafiqa's physical disability.

Associated as it is in the text with the dismemberment of Palestine in 1948, and with the consequent breakdown of conventional familial order, Shafiqa's amputated leg functions as the sign of a castration anxiety that has its roots in male concerns about patrimony and legitimate succession. When these castration anxieties manifest themselves initially in Kanafani's narrative by way of Shafiqa's amputation, it seems as if the narrative is working to contain what are essentially male anxieties by projecting the castration onto the female body. As the narrative develops, however, it turns out that the spectacle of Shafiqa's mutilation serves only as a proleptic lead in to the more centrally positioned and powerfully invoked spectacle of Abul Khaizuran's castration. The Shafiqa episode, that is, is staged in the text as a kind of interpretative temptation initially offered to the reader only to be thoroughly demolished later since subsequent events demonstrate that castration is by no means a specifically female phenomenon.

Though present in the text only in the form of a repressed memory reluctantly recalled, the event of Abul Khaizuran's castration, also incurred in the 1948 national catastrophe, is at the emotional and thematic centre of *Men in the Sun*. Into that episode is compressed a powerful sense of the pain and rage and helpless impotence suffered as a consequence of the partition and loss of Palestine. Preoccupied with his own bitter thoughts about marriage as they journey across the desert towards Kuwait, Assad innocently asks Abul Khaizuran if he has ever been married. Jolted by the question which releases a torrent of repressed memories:

> Abul Khaizuran shook his head, then he narrowed his eyes to meet the sunlight which had suddenly struck the windscreen. The light was shining so brightly that at first he could see nothing. But he felt a terrible pain coiled between his thighs. After a few moments he could make out that his legs were tied to two supports which kept them suspended, and that there were several men surrounding him. He closed his eyes for a moment, and then opened them as wide as he could. The circular light above his head hid the ceiling from him and blinded him. As he lay there, tied firmly in that strange fashion, he could only remember one thing which had happened to him a moment before, and nothing else. He and a number of armed men were running along when all hell exploded in front of him and he fell forward on his face. That was all. And now, the terrible pain was still plunging between his thighs and the huge round light was hanging over his eyes and he was trying to see things and people, narrowing his eyes as much as he could. Suddenly a black thought occurred to him and he began to scream like a madman. He couldn't remember what he said then, but he felt a hand covered with a slippery glove placed over his mouth with a violent movement. The voiced reached him as though it were coming through cotton:
> 'Be sensible. Be sensible. At least it's better than dying.'...
> ... Each time he was asked, casually, 'Why haven't you got married?' the same feeling of pain plunging between his thighs came back to him, as though he were still lying under the bright round light with his legs suspended in the air.[45]

This passage offers a graphic dramatisation of the way in which historical trauma is lived as a felt experience of male castration. The whole structure of the episode suggests that this castration is experienced as an enforced insertion of the male into an appallingly supine and 'feminised' position. Strapped down on the bed, his legs suspended in the air and splayed apart in what appears like a grim inversion of the position classically associated with the female subject about to give birth, the text positions Abul Khaizuran in what is to him a 'monstrously' feminine posture. The abject sense of lack and exposure associated in the male imagination with this position rebounds with doubled force against the male subject. Whereas a woman lying in this way might be giving birth, Abul Khaizuran's occupancy of the same position simply underscores his sterility.[46]

Whenever he contemplates his castration, Abul Khaizuran feels himself the object of a relentless, humiliatingly probing gaze – figured in the text as that blinding arc of light that glares down on him from the ceiling of the operation theatre. This relentless stare is also gendered in the text because Abul Khaizuran remembers that when the castration was being performed: 'There was a woman there, helping the doctors. Whenever he remembered it his face was suffused with shame.'[47] It is this exposure of his lack to a female gaze that represents the crowning humiliation for Abul Khaizuran. This is best explained in terms of Silverman's argument that the dominant fiction calls on both male and female subjects to deny all knowledge of male castration. For Silverman, the sense of masculine mastery rehearsed in the dominant fiction requires women to avert their eyes, as it were, to any suggestion that men might be scarred by the same lack as they.[48] Accordingly, she contends, it is not anatomical lack per se so much as woman's refusal to continue to go along with the fiction of unimpaired masculinity that constitutes the severest threat to conventional masculinity. The fact that Abul Khaizuran's castration was exposed to a woman's gaze, therefore, suggests that it is not just the physical act of castration itself so much as the woman's refusal to avert her eyes, to pretend it never happened, that inspires the male's deepest terror. The dismemberment of his homeland in 1948 – the event to which this emasculation is tied – involves not only a loss of territory, then, but of masculine status and dignity. The loss of national homeland, Kanafani's text implies, involves not simply the physical dispersal of a society but the collapse of the 'dominant narrative' or symbolic order that had structured its whole sense of its social world. Hence that impotent sense of dislocation and disorientation that is the generalised condition of all the male Palestinians depicted in the novel.

The topos of the emasculated male discussed here recurs with some considerable frequency in Palestinian narrative. All of Kanafani's works, from the extremely moving early short story 'The Land of Sad Oranges' to later novels such as *Return to Haifa*, involve difficult relationships between fallen fathers, humiliated by history, and their acutely ambivalent sons. In Halim Barakat's *Days of Dust*, set during the 1967 war, the hero of the novel, Ramzi, is a young Palestinian professor who conducts an affair with Pamela, an American woman, during the six days of the war. On the fourth day, Pamela reads to Ramzi from the Old Testament about a Canaanite king who had agreed to allow his daughter to marry a son of Jacob, the Israelite. Jacob had stipulated that the marriage could proceed only if the Canaanite men agreed to be circumcised like the Israelites. When the Canaanites were helpless in pain after their mass circumcision, the Israelites seized the opportunity to take captive their women and children and steal their lands. Ramzi draws the obvious parallel: the Israelites of old resemble the modern Israelis who are now inflicting a similar catastrophe on the Palestinians. In another version, the family in Sahar Khalifeh's novel *Wild Thorns* is encumbered by a cantankerous old father who can live only with the support of a kidney-machine, the upkeep of which is financed by a son who secretly works on a construction site in Israel. The conclusion of the narrative builds towards a moral dilemma in which that son will have to choose whether to save his incapacitated father or to allow him to die in order to release the rest of the family from his bondage.[49]

What distinguishes *Men in the Sun*, then, is not its depiction of the historical trauma of the loss of Palestine as a crisis of male sexuality but its stubborn refusal to summon the usual defences against this crisis. Faced with a catastrophic situation – the novel seems to suggest – there is a natural tendency to shrink in horror from the event, to seek for some sort of escape from an overwhelmingly hostile and seemingly hopeless environment when what is really called for is a lucid registration of the catastrophe. The meaning of the catastrophe, in short, needs to be diagnosed before it can be overcome.

In *Men in the Sun*, the moral and emotional failure to come to terms with the historical loss of Palestine and the consequent collapse of the traditional symbolic order is staged as a refusal to come to terms with the fact of male castration. Abul Khaizuran exemplifies this panicked attempt to flee the scene of that trauma in a useless bid to escape its consequences:

> No, he couldn't consent, even after ten years, to forget his tragedy and get used to it. He couldn't even accept it when he was under the knife and they were trying to convince him that it was better to lose one's manhood than one's life. O God of devils! They don't even know that, they don't know anything, and then take it on themselves to teach people everything. Hadn't he accepted it, or was he incapable of accepting? From the first few moments he had decided not to accept; yes, that was it. Moreover he couldn't entirely picture what had happened, and so he had fled from the hospital instinctively and blindly, before he had completely recovered. It was as though his flight could bring things back to normal again.[50]

Abul Khaizuran's whole life has become one continuous flight in a desperate attempt to evade the tragedy that has befallen him. But fleeing, of course, is precisely what all of the men in *Men in the Sun* are doing. Given the link between flight and the refusal to confront the spectacle of male castration clearly developed in the passage cited above, we can see why the decision of the three Palestinian migrants to flee with Abul Khaizuran must inevitably prove disastrous.

In terms of the logic of the text, to travel with Abul Khaizuran is to succumb to blind and hysterical panic or to search for delusory silver linings in Kuwait. It is to lack the fortitude necessary to take proper strategic stock of one's position, including the weaknesses of that position. 'Flight' in *Men in the Sun* must be read, then, as more than just physical retreat. It can take many forms: the search for individual economic salvation in Kuwait; the desire to abandon the seemingly hopeless world of politics for the refuge of marriage and family; reliance on the Arab state élites to come to the rescue; even the melancholy seductions of pessimism and despair. Something more than simply a critique of Palestinian emigration or movement away from the land of Palestine is at issue then. The ideologeme of 'flight' in Kanafani's novel must be read to refer to any kind of panicky or peremptory political strategy not firmly grounded in an objective and dispassionate structural appraisal of the political disabilities incurred by Palestinians after 1948.

It is the veritably Adornean rigour with which it insists on the need to come to terms with a condition of acute historical crisis, a condition to which it offers neither solutions nor consolations, that makes

*Men in the Sun* such an austerely powerful text. The connection between the partition of Palestine and the act of male castration in the
narrative implies that without a territory there can be no real future
for Palestinians as a nation. Yet the narrative is no less emphatic in
its insistence that no strategy capable of effecting the recovery of the
Palestinian homeland as yet exists. Nostalgic yearnings for the lost
paradise of the past or the narrowly local vision associated with the
old peasant Abu Qais will not help the Palestinians. The pan-Arabism
identified with Ustaz Selim appears to offer a more expansive political alternative, but the noble ideal of pan-Arab unity is everywhere
overwhelmed in the text by the constant reference to the crude reality
of state borders, and to the manifold processes of state repression and
inter-Arab exploitation.

The Arab world depicted in *Men in the Sun* is a dystopian world
criss-crossed with Israeli, Jordanian, Lebanese, Iraqi and Kuwaiti borders. Created by the European imperial powers to secure their own
neo-imperial interests in the Middle East, these frontiers divide the
Arab world into state-defined units and national economies that take
little account of the economic and political needs, or even the population distribution, of the Arab people. Thus, as Saree Makdisi has
observed, the small oil-rich states of the Gulf, with their tiny populations, have to import most of their skilled workforces from other Arab
countries, while the bulk of their capital outflow is directed not to the
Arab world but to the more developed capital markets of Europe, East
Asia, and the US. At the same time, the other Arab states are in need
of capital, have few natural resources and high unemployment rates,
and depend on remittances from expatriate labourers. Hence 'there is
a grossly disproportionate distribution of wealth and resources in the
Arab world, and, consequently, not only a great deal of inefficiency
(not to mention injustice) but an absurd lack of cooperation and co-
hesiveness, and hence an often self-inflicted weakness with regard
to the global economy.'[51] It is this general condition that Kanafani's
novel struggles to make visible. In the vision of inter-Arab division
and exploitation offered here, it is clear that the dilemmas of the
Palestinians are rooted not alone in Zionism but also in the oppressive
nature of this wider Middle Eastern state system.

While the ANM, to which Kanafani was connected when *Men in
the Sun* was written, may have correctly diagnosed this neo-colonial
state order as key to the wider problems of the region, the novel's
relentless insistence on state borders suggests that this state system,
however malign, cannot be bypassed simply by appeal to common

Arab sentiment. A successful socialist strategy, the text seems to imply, must be anchored in the uneven development of capital in the region, not merely in subjective sentiment or utopian aspiration. The pan-Arabism to which the ANM aspires, the novel intimates, cannot simply override the state. The road to the universal cannot bypass the local or the national sphere; for a wider regional strategy to be effective, the struggle must be materially embedded in the place-specific demands and concerns of various exploited classes. The universal, in other words, must emerge, dialectically, through the co-ordination of locally embedded struggles, not through some Olympian attempt to transcend them. The problem, however, for socialists such as Kanafani is that the case against the humanly destructive chaos of the market, and the state system on which it depends, is strongest precisely where socialism's reach has always been weakest: at the level of the global system as a whole.

*Men in the Sun*, then, confirms no political strategy, not even the left-wing pan-Arabism to which Kanafani himself gave his allegiance. Yet neither does it settle for a resigned cynicism, which simply accepts with a shrug that the ways of the world are bad and that there is nothing other than corruption. The novel concludes with a quite specific repudiation of passivity and fatalism in the question asked of the three migrants who died silently in the belly of the empty water-tanker: 'Why didn't you knock on the sides of the tank? Why didn't you bang the sides of the tank? Why? Why? Why?' These words, it must also be noted, however, are spoken by Abul Khaizuran, and they suggest that the victims are now being blamed for their own deaths simply because they did not resist. But what effective strategy of resistance was available to them? What kind of resistance is it that the text calls for here? For resistance of any kind, which would at least be better than none at all? The fact that the ideologeme of 'flight' is associated in the text with precipitate ill-considered responses to the weakness of one's condition does not warrant such a reading. If there is an aporia, an indissolvable antinomy, at the heart of *Men in the Sun*, it is that the novel demands a kind of strategic resistance it is unable to name.

In this context we can begin to appreciate how painfully apt the central metaphor in *Men in the Sun* is for the predicament it purports to express. In the image of that empty water-tanker with its cargo of suffocating refugees stalled on a border in the desert between one state and another, Kanafani manages to express something essential about the dilemmas confronting Palestinian nationalism. At its simplest, the image must be read to suggest that it is imperative for Palestinians to come to terms with the question of state borders and the wider Middle Eastern state system they incarnate. A direct trajectory can be traced in *Men in the Sun* from the historical trauma of the partition of Palestine in 1948 to the deaths of the fleeing Palestinian migrants who meet their sorry fate on the Iraq–Kuwait border. It is no accident that it is on this border, site of another historically controversial partition – that which severed the small state of Kuwait from Iraq to serve the oil-interests of the imperial powers – that Kanafani has his migrants meet their desperate end. Attempting to flee the disaster of one partition, the Palestinian protagonists discover that catastrophe lies once more in wait for them.

Even if Kanafani's novel cannot articulate the kind of resistance that it demands, its remarkable achievement is to have formally embodied the predicament it attempts to elaborate. As described here, the fundamental crisis in *Men in the Sun*, imaged as a crisis of male castration, is one which has its origins in the loss and partitioning of Palestine in 1948 and in the subsequent difficulty of mastering political space that follows from that traumatic event. On the one hand, *Men in the Sun* attempts to give expression to the Palestinian longing for national form but, at the same time, it sternly insists on the intractable obstacles that must be overcome if that dream is ever to be realised. According to Benedict Anderson, the novel constructs the imaginary space of the nation by means of a picaresque *tour d'horison* which weaves together diverse spaces – villages, cities, hospitals, monasteries, prisons – into a clearly bounded whole.[52] For *Men in the Sun*, the partition of the land of Palestine and the subsequent dispersal of the Palestinian people means that a self-enclosed spatial continuum of this kind, one that would encompass the totality of Palestinian existence, cannot be materialised. The two primary chronotopes, to use Mikhail Bakhtin's terms, in Kanafani's narrative are the road and the border. The road, according to Bakhtin, 'is a particularly good place for random encounters. On the road ("the high road"), the spatial and temporal paths of the most varied people – representatives of all social classes, estates, religions, nationalities, ages – intersect at one spatial and temporal point. People who are normally kept separate by social and spatial distance can accidentally meet; any contrast may crop up; the most various fates may collide and interweave with one another.'[53]

If the road figures so prominently in *Men in the Sun* it is no doubt because, in the absence of the achieved enclosure of the nation-state, it offers the best means available to Kanafani to 'resolve' the practical difficulty of bringing together in a single time-space the spatially dispersed and socially stratified Palestinians who normally live in conditions that do not allow for unmediated contact between one scattered locale and another. The open road, then, functions as a compensatory substitute for the enclosure of the nation-state, but it is precisely because it is *only a substitute* that it is marked in *Men in the Sun* with such negative connotations – it leads away from Palestine and towards death. In the kind of novel Anderson has in mind, the journey serves as a metaphor for connection; it is the journey along the road that weaves together the various locales of the nation into an imaginatively enclosed continuum. In Kanafani's narrative, however, the road, the journey, appears not as a metaphor for connection, opportunity, mobility or the chance for adventure, but as a featureless line stretching into infinity, offering only what Bakhtin described in another context as 'enforced movement through space'.[54]

The road, the border, that phantom space between two state borders where the men are asphyxiated, the desert itself: these all operate in *Men in the Sun* as space degree-zero, as the antithesis of national space. If these figures dominate *Men in the Sun*, it is because Kanafani's narrative, unable to summon into existence the fullness of a self-enclosed national space, can only summon into being its antithesis, the signs of its absence: the anti-place of the desert, the 'no-place' between two state borders, or the road and the border – that is, lines, spatial figures without breadth or dimension. The apprehension that the Palestinian condition was resistant to the kinds of novelistic representation that might apply to achieved nation-states does not, however, cause Kanafani to abandon the ambition to give expression to the longing for national form. On the contrary, the remarkable achievement of *Men in the Sun* is to retain that ambition even if 'Palestine' can only appear here as a negative topology, a 'no-place' etched into the narrative by the signatures of its invisibility.

When Kanafani's novel first appeared, it provoked a welter of protest from its Arab readers. The bleakness of its conclusion struck a raw nerve with an audience that found Kanafani's 'pessimism' intolerable. As Mary Layoun has remarked: 'Given the rhetoric generated by the Arab states and the traditional Palestinian leaders about the Palestinian situation, the conclusion of *Rijāl fī al-shams* [*Men in the Sun*] seemed ignominious if not heretical. Images of the Palestinians' triumphant return on the shoulders of their Arab brothers or at least of resistance until death were preferable.'[55] When a Syrian film *al-Makhdu'un* (*The Deceived*), based on *Men in the Sun*, was made in 1972, the conclusion of the original narrative was altered to eliminate some of its more unsettling, anti-state elements.

As Layoun observes, the usual explanation of the 'pessimism' of *Men in the Sun* is that the novel was written at a time when an official Palestinian resistance movement had yet to be established. Concomitantly, the altered ending of the film version of the novel is explained by the fact that after the establishment of the PLO and the emergence of the various Palestinian guerrilla movements, the bleakness of Kanafani's novel had become 'glaringly incongruous'.[56] This explanation has its merits because it suggests that the modernist anguish that informs Kanafani's text, like the anguish of European modernism as identified by Theodor Adorno, is ultimately rooted in an objective loss of revolutionary momentum.[57] When that momentum resurfaces, and new possibilities appear on the political horizon, a new kind of art, less tied to the determinate negation of what had seemed an intractably dystopian empirical reality, may also emerge with it.

Nevertheless, this conception of things risks trivialising Kanafani's achievement. It does so because it conceives the dilemmas and the anguished soul of the novel as symptoms of a time (before the 'real' resistance and new hope emerged with the guerrilla units) and not of an enduring system (the colonial and neo-colonial state order in the Middle East). The emergence of the new Palestinian resistance under the PLO was undoubtedly a development of enormous significance, but in the end that movement, like its predecessors, could not overcome the constraints and pitfalls of the Middle Eastern state system. For Adorno, despite their ostensibly apolitical nature, modernist works, such as those of Kafka and Beckett especially, must be defended as authentically political works of art because in dismantling illusion they explode art from the inside, whereas proclaimed commitment only subjugates art from the outside, hence only illusorily. The 'implacability' that marks the works of Kafka and Beckett, on the other hand, he comments:

> compels the change of attitude which committed works merely demand. He over whom Kafka's wheels have passed, has lost for ever both any peace with the world and any chance of consoling himself with the judgment that the way of the world is bad; the element of ratification which lurks in resigned admission of the dominance of evil is burnt away.[58]

It is on this basis that one can distinguish the ending of Kanafani's novel from the entropic endings and resigned diminuendos earlier identified in Northern Irish novels such as Mac Laverty's *Cal* or in Israeli ones such as Oz's *A Perfect Peace*. For Kanafani's novel does not at all acquiesce with what already is or despair of resistance: on the contrary, it demands resistance, but stipulates that it must be based on an unflinching analysis of the objective conditions of the Palestinian situation. It refuses to settle for anything less or to trade in this stern demand for any consolation. Since, for the Palestinians, the need for effective resistance is as imperative today as when *Men in the Sun* first appeared in 1963, the challenge of Kanafani's earliest and most 'pessimistic' novel still retains its currency. Seen in this light, the howls of protest that greeted *Men in the Sun* on its initial publication are the surest signs of its success. The pained Arab and Palestinian readers of the novel are compelled to confront their own political emasculation, to see their unhappy condition as the product of their own internal divisions – this as a necessary precondition to any movement forward from there.

But the challenge of Kanafani's novel also goes beyond this. If Kanafani's readership found the conclusion of *Men in the Sun* intolerable, this is because it may rightly have intuited that the novel demands that Palestinians contemplate not merely their own political paralysis but the even more dreadful spectre of their ultimate disappearance as a nation. By the end of the novel all three Palestinian migrants are dead, and only Abul Khaizuran, rendered sterile by his catastrophe, remains. This threat of national extinction is the real terror provoked by the ignominious dumping of the three Palestinian protagonists on the Kuwaiti dump while Abul Khaizuran pilfers Marwan's broken watch – a metaphor for the termination of Palestinian time. 'Pessimism' is a totally inadequate term, however, to express what is involved in this act of imagination. If Kanafani demands that his Palestinian readership contemplate the prospect of its own disappearance as a nation, its possible consignment to the dust-heap of history, this is 'because averting the unthinkable seems to require us imaginatively to entertain it'.[59] To counter the possibility of such an ignominious ending, Kanafani requires that his readership disavow the very disavowal that dismisses this fate as 'unthinkable'. The wager of *Men in the Sun*, then, is that nothing less than the courage to contemplate the possibility of their own erasure from history can steel the determination necessary for Palestinians to avert that fate.

## IV

In *After the Last Sky*, Edward Said writes: 'Wherever we Palestinians are, we are not in our Palestine, which no longer exists.'[60] It has been argued in this chapter that it is because of this condition of national homelessness that the novel can seem so important in the Palestinian context – even if the form cannot always deliver what is expected of it. In other words, the novel has offered Palestinians a medium through which they might conceive the 'tacit Utopia' of their still-to-be-realised collectivity – what Adorno once described as 'the fragile Utopia of reconciliation in an image'.[61] Until they secure that homeland, the condition of the refugee, banging against the iron walls of the state, will remain paradigmatic of all Palestinians.

The Irish socialist leader James Connolly once remarked that Ireland without its people meant nothing to him. Connolly's remarks were aimed at those conservative Irish bourgeois nationalists who, making a fetish of territory, cared more about liberating the land than the people who worked it. For Connolly, the goal of liberating national territory was vitally important because it was a necessary precondition to a higher end – so that its people might be free. But bourgeois nationalists tended to make territorial sovereignty an end in itself. In Palestine today, one could argue, the danger Connolly warned against in Ireland, threatens to come to pass: since the signing of the Oslo Accord, the emancipation of the Palestinian people has been subordinated to the liberation of whatever stretches of land the Israelis can be persuaded are no longer imperative to their own needs. It is, ironically, those who suffered most in 1948 and 1967, those who became stateless refugees, who may be sacrificed to this territorial imperative. Already their right in principle to return to Palestine has been compromised by relegating the issue to the 'final status' negotiations where it will be bargained and bartered over alongside such issues as borders and the fate of Jerusalem. Their tragedy is thereby reduced to a legal and technical dispute over repatriation and compensation; something that inevitably diminishes the larger human significance of the 1948 and 1967 exoduses and their manifold human consequences. In this context, Kanafani's *Men in the Sun* exerts an undiminished critical power. Expressing a critique tied neither to a moment in time nor to a site-specific location but to a system, his novel permits no real forgetting of the bitter human anguish and trauma that attends the stateless condition.

It is this, too, perhaps that makes Kanafani's work not only a Palestinian classic but a contemporary contribution to 'world literature' as well. The wisdom of the contemporary moment has it that with the fall of the Berlin Wall and the lifting of the Iron Curtain humanity is now on the threshold of a new global era. New modes of commerce and finance, new communications technologies, new multicultural ethnoscapes, we are told, are finally creating the conditions that will deliver a borderless world. Currently, much of the intellectual community in the West and elsewhere seems utterly in thrall with this millennial euphoria. The word 'border' has become one of the great academic buzzwords of recent times; 'border-crossing' a term used by cultural critics and multinational corporations alike to describe all sorts of supposedly transgressive acts. In this sanitised currency, the complex material reality of state borders is volatilised.[62]

Contrary to the conventional wisdom of the times, there is compelling evidence to suggest that current globalising processes are not in fact 'hollowing out' the state or rendering the whole idea of national community redundant. Some states are indeed compelled by globalising processes to relinquish traditional functions, but the same processes also encourage all states to intensify control over other operations – not least the policing and surveillance of those countless millions that global capital has rendered destitute and stateless.[63] Some analysts rightly warn that where nation-states have not managed to build strong bonds between majority and minority communities, the new globalising currents have the potential to render such bonds even more brittle. Even if the established identifications with the nation-state are under some stress in the present climate, however, broader emancipatory political communities of identification have yet to emerge – given socialism's low-tide at present such prospects seem indeed to have receded. Like the readers of novels, the world, however, has a quite unquenchable and commendable desire for happy endings. But in the dark climate of our times Kanafani's novel, with its insistence that we remember the stateless trapped in deserts that never bloom, issues a telling reminder that happy endings cannot be gifted to us: they have to be won.

# Notes

## Introduction

1 For some speculations on South Africa, see A. J. Christopher, 'South Africa: the case of a Failed State Partition', *Political Geography* 13 (1994), 123–36.

2 On the German cultural controversies attending reunification, see Stephen Brockmann, *Literature and German Reunification* (Cambridge University Press, 1999). These debates are discussed in more detail in Chapter Two.

3 An early case for repartition in Northern Ireland was made by Consevative MP, Julian Critchley, in his pamphlet *Ireland: a New Partition* (London: Bow Publications, 1972). The fullest case was made by Liam Kennedy in his *Two Ulsters: a Case for Repartition* (Belfast: The Author/Queen's University, 1986). Though contemplated apparently as a 'doomsday scenario' by some loyalist paramilitaries, the repartition idea has never enjoyed widespread support in any quarter in Ireland. For a more comprehensive discussion of repartition, see John Whyte, *Interpreting Northern Ireland* (Oxford: Clarendon Press, 1996), 226–30.

4 A useful comparative analysis of the diplomatic negotiations leading up to partition in several British colonies is T. G. Fraser, *Partition in Ireland, India and Palestine: Theory and Practice* (London: Macmillan, 1984).

5 Robert Schaeffer, *Warpaths: the Politics of Partition* (New York: Hill and Wang, 1990).

6 On the distinction between colonies of settlement and colonies of exploitation (or administration), see George Fredrickson, *The Arrogance of Race: Historical Perspectives on Slavery, Racism, and Social Inequality* (Middletown: Wesleyan University Press, 1985), 216–35.

7 Donald Harman Akenson's *God's Peoples: Convenant and Land in South Africa, Israel and Ulster* (Ithaca: Cornell University Press, 1992) is an extended study of what Akenson sees as an Old Testament culture of covenanting shared by Israeli Zionists, Ulster Unionists and

Afrikaners. For these peoples, he argues, the territories they have inherited are granted by divine charter and anything that might be interpreted as a surrender of that God-given inheritance can be conceived, therefore, as a blasphemous breach of faith with that contract. The study is suggestive, and the Biblical language of convenanting, exile in the wilderness and repelling the gentile enemy has certainly played an important role in the articulation of both modern Unionism (the Paisleyite version is a recent case in point) and Zionism. Akenson's work tends, however, to conceive of this element of the cultures concerned in essentialist and a-historical fashion, and to privilege its importance over the more secular elements and interests at work in both Unionism and Zionism.

8 There is substantive debate in Indian historiography on partition as to whether, had wiser counsel prevailed, the Indian National Congress and the Muslim League might have arrived at some sort of rapprochement concerning greater regional autonomy and more decentralised state structures that might have averted partition. This thesis is developed in Ayesha Jalal, *The Sole Spokesman: Jinnah, the Muslim League and the Demand for Pakistan* (Cambridge: Cambridge University Press, 1994).

9 Benedict Anderson, 'Long-Distance Nationalism', in *The Spectre of Comparisons: Nationalism, Southeast Asia and the World* (London: Verso, 1998), 58–74.

10 See Gene Bassett, 'Who Said There's Nothing to Evolution?' (*Pittsburgh Press*, 8 February, 1974). The image is reprinted in L. Perry Curtis Jr., *Apes and Angels: the Irishman in Victorian Caricature*, revised edition (Washington: Smithsonian Institute Press, 1997), 178.

11 On republican representations of the Palestinian struggle in wall murals, see Bill Rolston, *Politics and Painting: Murals and Conflict in Northern Ireland* (London: Associated University Press, 1991), 38–9, 80, 94–5.

12 For a more extended analysis of this film, see Ella Shohat, *Israeli Cinema: East/West and the Politics of Representation* (Austin: University of Texas Press, 1989), 58–76.

13 Some comparative analyses that examine the Irish and Israeli–Palestinian situations include Hermann Giliomee and Jannie Gagiano (eds.), *The Elusive Search for Peace: South Africa, Israel and Northern Ireland* (Cape Town: Oxford University Press, 1990); Ian S. Lustick, *Unsettled States: Britain and Ireland, France and Alegeria, Israel and the West Bank-Gaza* (Ithaca: Cornell University Press, 1993); and Akenson, *God's Peoples*.

14 Cited in Fraser, *Partition in Ireland, India and Palestine*, 15.

15 Tudor, cited in Keith Jeffrey, 'Introduction,' in Keith Jeffrey (ed.), *'An Irish Empire'?: Aspects of Ireland and the British Empire* (Manchester: Manchester University Press, 1996), 10–11.

16 On the concept of the 'interregnum,' see Antonio Gramsci, 'State and Civil Society', in *Prison Notebooks*, trans. Quintin Hoare and Geoffrey Nowell-Smith (New York: International Publishers, 1971) 210–70, and especially 275–6 where these remarks appear. For a recent application

of the concept to Northern Ireland, see Richard Kirkland, *Literature and Culture in Northern Ireland since 1965: Moments of Danger* (London: Longman, 1996).

17 Some of these studies include Aijaz Ahmad, *In the Mirror of Urdu: Recompositions of Nation and Community, 1947–1965* (Shimla: Indian Institute of Advanced Study, 1993); Susie Tharu, 'Rendering Account of the Nation: Partition Narratives and Other Genres of the Passive Revolution', *The Oxford Literary Review* 16 (1994), 69–91; Urvashi Butalia, *The Other Side of Silence: Voices from the Partition of India* (London: Penguin Books, 1998); and the articles collected in Ritu Menon (ed.), 'Special Topic: the Partition of the Indian Sub-Continent', *Interventions: International Journal of Postcolonial Studies* 1 (1999).

## 1. Ireland, Palestine and the antinomies of self-determination in 'the badlands of modernity'

1 Tom Nairn, *The Break-Up of Britain*, second edition (London: Verso, 1977); Partha Chatterjee, *Nationalist Thought in the Colonial World: a Derivative Discourse* (Minneapolis: University of Minnesota Press, 1986) and *The Nation and its Fragments: Colonial and Postcolonial Histories* (Princeton: Princeton University Press, 1993); Miroslav Hroch, *Social Preconditions of National Revival in Europe: a Comparative Analysis of Patriotic Groups among the Smaller European Nations* (Cambridge: Cambridge University Press, 1985); Anthony D. Smith, *The Ethnic Origins of Nations* (London: Basil Blackwell, 1986); James M. Blaut, *The National Question: Decolonizing the Theory of Nationalism* (London: Zed Press, 1987); Homi Bhabha (ed.), *Nation and Narration* (London: Routledge, 1990); Eric J. Hobsbawm, *Nations and Nationalism Since 1780: Programme, Myth, Reality* (Cambridge: Cambridge University Press, 1990); Benedict Anderson, *Imagined Communities: Reflections on the Origin and Spread of Nationalism*, revised edition (London: Verso, 1991); Etienne Balibar and Immanuel Wallerstein, *Race, Nation, Class: Ambiguous Identities* (London: Verso, 1991); Ernest Gellner, *Nations and Nationalism*, third edition (Ithaca: Cornell University Press, 1991); Basil Davidson, *The Black Man's Burden: Africa and the Curse of the Nation-State* (Oxford: James Currey Ltd., 1992). Liah Greenfeld, *Nationalism: Five Roads to Modernity* (Cambridge: Harvard University Press, 1992); *The Break-Up of Britain* deals with Northern Ireland, but Nairn, in a crudely mechanistic way, attributes partition to regional cleavages caused by uneven capitalist development. Breuilly's discussion of partition appears in John Breuilly, *Nationalism and the State* (Manchester: Manchester University Press, 1982), 175–82.

2 Anderson, *Imagined Communities*, 114. My emphasis.

3 Ibid., 115.

4 On modern African borders, see A. I. Asiwaju (ed.), *Partitioned Africans: Ethnic Relations Across Africa's International Boundaries, 1884–1984* (London: C. Hurst, 1985) and Paul Nugent and A. I.

Asiwaju (eds.), *African Boundaries: Barriers, Conduits and Opportunities* (London: Printer Publishers, 1996). On Latin America, see Alistair Hennessy, *The Frontier in Latin American History* (London: Edward Arnold, 1978).

5 In his latest work, Anderson addresses some of the shortcomings discussed here. See 'Majorities and Minorities', in Benedict Anderson, *The Spectre of Comparisons: Nationalism, Southeast Asia and the World* (London: Verso, 1998), 318–30.

6 The literature here is too extensive to list, but useful general studies include the following. On Ireland: Michael Laffan, *The Partition of Ireland, 1911–1925* (Dundalk: Dundalgan Press, 1983); Au ten Morgan, *Labour and Partition: the Belfast Working Class, 1905–1923* (London: Pluto Press, 1990); Terry Cradden, *Trade Unionism, Socialism and Partition* (Belfast: December Publications, 1993); Mary Harris, *The Catholic Church and the Foundation of the Northern Irish State* (Cork: Cork University Press, 1993); Paul Bew, *Ideology and the Irish Question: Ulster Unionism and Irish Nationalism 1912–1916* (Oxford: Clarendon Press, 1994) and Eamonn Phoenix, *Northern Nationalism, Nationalist Politics, Partition, and the Catholic Minority in Northern Ireland, 1840–1940* (Belfast: Ulster Historical Foundation, 1994). On Israel–Palestine: Edward Said, *The Question of Palestine* (New York: Vintage Books, 1980); Avi Shlaim, *The Politics of Partition: King Abdullah, the Zionists, and Palestine, 1921–1951* (Oxford: Oxford University Press, 1990); Ilan Pappé, *The Making of the Arab-Israeli-Conflict, 1947–1951* (London: I. B. Tauris, 1994); Itzhak Galnoor, *The Partition of Palestine: Decision Crossroads in the Zionist Movement* (Albany: State University of New York Press, 1995); Yossi Katz, *Partner to Partition: the Jewish Agency's Partition Plan in the Mandate Era* (London: Frank Cass, 1998). On India: Penderel Moon, *Divide and Quit: an Eye-Witness Account of the Partition of India* (Oxford: Oxford University Press, 1961); Ayesha Jalal, *The Sole Spokesman: Jinnah, the Muslim League and the Demand for Pakistan* (Cambridge: Cambridge University Press, 1985); Mushirul Hasan (ed.), *India's Partition: Process, Strategy, and Mobilization* (Delhi: Oxford University Press, 1993).

7 Stanley Waterman, 'Partition and Modern Nationalism', in Colin H. Williams and Eleonore Kofman (eds.), *Community Conflict, Partition and Nationalism* (London: Routledge, 1989), 117–32, 117.

8 D. L. Horowitz, *Ethnic Groups in Conflict* (Berkeley: University of California Press, 1985), 588–9.

9 For a more extensive discussion which situates the contemporary division of Bosnia in the context of earlier episodes in Ireland, India and Palestine, see Radha Kumar, *Divide and Fall?: Bosnia in the Annals of Partition* (London: Verso, 1997).

10 Michael Mann's 'The Dark Side of Democracy: the Modern Tradition of Ethnic Cleansing', *New Left Review* 235 (1999), 18–45, offers a remarkable account of the role of population transfer and ethnic cleansing in the construction of the modern state.

11 Perry Anderson, 'Diary', *London Review of Books* 20:18 (17 Oct. 1996), 28–9.

12 Ernest Gellner, 'Nationalism and Politics in Eastern Europe', *New Left Review* 189 (1991), 127–34, 128.

13 The idea that nationalism becomes more murderous as it moves eastwards across Europe and Asia and away from Western Europe and the United States is commonplace, and is reiterated by some leading theoreticians of nationalism such as Hans Kohn, Elie Kedourie and Ernest Gellner. For an incisive critique of both the 'return of the repressed' conception of nationalism and of the manichean division between civic and ethnic nationalisms, see Rogers Brubaker, 'Myths and misconceptions in the study of nationalism', in John A. Hall (ed.), *The State of the Nation: Ernest Gellner and the Theory of Nationalism* (Cambridge: Cambridge University Press, 1998), 272–306. For Brubaker, the weakness of the manichean division between civic and ethnic nationalism is that if ethnic nationalism is interpreted narrowly, to imply an emphasis on descent, biology or race as the grounds of nationality, then there is very little ethnic nationalism in existence since from this perspective an emphasis on common culture has to qualify as a form of civic nationalism. On the other hand, if ethnic nationalism is interpreted broadly, as ethno*cultural*, while civic nationalism is interpreted narrowly, as involving an acultural conception of citizenship, the problem is just the opposite: civic nationalism gets defined out of existence, and virtually all nationalism has to be considered as ethnic or cultural.

14 Reginald Coupland, *Palestine Royal Commission Report*, Cmd 5479 (1937). Cited in T. G. Fraser, *Partition in Ireland, India and Palestine: Theory and Practice* (London: Macmillan, 1984), 131.

15 *Palestine Royal Commission Report*, 117. Cited in Fraser, *Partition*, 133.

16 The category of Britishness as used here clearly does not include Ulster Unionists who are clearly deemed by Coupland to be 'Northern Irish'.

17 Breuilly, *Nationalism and the State*, chapter 7. The term 'collaborator system' as Breuilly uses it refers to the creation of institutions in the colonial-state that secure special political rights for a particular group. For Breuilly, it is not the mere existence of sub-national communities as such but rather 'the structure of the collaborator system which is of paramount importance in shaping both an effective territorial nationalist and cultural sub-nationalist movement prior to the creation of an independent state' (183).

18 Fraser's *Partition in Ireland, India and Palestine* offers some useful insights into British attitudes to partition in these various regions.

19 For an important critique of this contemporary tendency to subsume nationalisms into a single category, see Neil Lazarus, *Nationalism and Cultural Practice in the Postcolonial World* (Cambridge: Cambridge University Press, 1999), 68–143.

20 See Erica Benner, *Really Existing Nationalisms: a Post-Communist View from Marx and Engels* (Oxford: Clarendon Press, 1995), 8.

21 Ibid., 226.

22 Ibid., 8.

23 For more comprehensive discussions, see Galnoor, *Partition of Palestine* and Katz, *Partner to Partition*.

24 In Ireland, the North Eastern Boundary Bureau *Handbook* established the new southern Irish state's official view of Ulster Unionists. It classified Unionists as 'a religious minority... which has been able through use of assiduous outside forces to ... insist on cutting off from the nation not only its own adherents, but a large minority whose traditional allegiance was to the nation as a whole' (North Eastern Boundary Review, *Handbook of the Ulster Question*, vi. Cited in John McGarry and Brendan O'Leary, *Explaining Northern Ireland: Broken Images* (Oxford: Blackwell, 1995), 433, note 94). The official Palestinian attitude to Israeli Zionists is expressed in the 1964 Palestinian Charter where in Article 18 Judaism is described as a 'revealed religion' and not as a nationality.

25 Partha Chatterjee, 'Religious Minorities and the Secular State: Reflections on an Indian Impasse,' *Public Culture* 8 (1995), 11–39. For a more extended discussion of liberalism and group rights, see Will Kymlicka's *Liberalism, Community, and Culture* (Oxford: Clarendon Press, 1989) and *Multicultural Citizenship: a Liberal Theory of Minority Rights* (Oxford: Clarendon Press, 1995).

26 Unlike Israeli Zionists, Unionists did not claim a state of their own, and wanted to remain within the multinational United Kingdom. Many Unionists would deny, on this basis, that Unionism ever had anything in common with other movements for national liberation or self-determination. Nevertheless, the practical effect of partition was to grant them their own devolved sub-state, which they controlled in their own interests. In his analysis of Irish partition Michael Laffan argues that 'Ulster Unionists had always stressed their British citizenship and denied they were part of an Irish nation or even one of two separate Irish nations. Yet their tactics of trying to gain as much territory as possible without endangering their long-term security, of trying to "rescue" outlying minorities heavily outnumbered by adherents of a rival group or people, were identical to those being employed by Yugoslavia, Romania, or any of the other nation states whose frontiers were decided at this very time in the peace treaties of 1919–20. However much they may have loathed the idea, Ulster Unionists conformed to a pattern of continental European nationalism' (Laffan, *Partition of Ireland*, 68).

27 Liberal theories on national self-determination are quite varied. Some specifically exclude the wish to preserve cultural identity as legitimate grounds for the establishment of an independent state. See, for example, A. H. Birch, 'Another Liberal Theory of Secession', *Political Studies* 32 (1984), 596–602. Whereas Birch assumes that a minority has no right to secede unless it is materially oppressed by the existing state, Harry Beran argues that any (self-defined) minority in any state has the right to vote to secede, provided the seceding group is willing in its turn to extend the same right to any other (self-defined) minority within the proposed secessionist territory. These rights can only be exercised, however, if the would-be state does not violate

certain conditions: it must not create an enclave within an existing state; it must not occupy a centre that is economically or militarily essential to the existing state; and so on. See Harry Beran, 'A Liberal Theory of Secession', *Political Studies* 32 (1984), 21–31. David Miller critiques Beran's theory on the basis of its impracticality and arbitrariness in his *On Nationality* (Oxford: Clarendon Press, 1995), 110–12. Miller's work contains a sophisticated discussion of national self-determination, which takes as its starting point that secession should be given serious consideration only when an established state contains two or more groups with distinct and irreconcilable *national* (and not merely ethnic) identities. Where granting it limited political autonomy within the existing state cannot adequately protect a minority nationality, Miller suggests that it has in principle the right to secede. But the implementation of this principle is subject to certain restrictions. If the territory demanded by the seceding minority contains in turn its own minorities with nationalities radically incompatible with those of the seceding group, then this would simply recreate on a smaller scale the very problem the secession was supposed to eliminate. In such case, there is good case for blocking the original secession. The essential thing here is to note that for Miller the governing principle is to discover the optimum political conditions that can secure national identities, not simply the will of majorities. Hence he argues that in cases where no redrawing of boundaries can implement that principle fully, solutions that fall short of traditional statehood must be accepted. Essentially, he argues, this will require a constitutional settlement that creates a representative institution for the people in question and assigns to it legislative and executive powers over matters essential to its identity and material welfare. See his *On Nationalities*, 81–118.

28 David McDowell, *The Palestinians: the Road to Nationhood* (London: Minority Rights Publications, 1995), 24.
29 Said's remarks appear as part of a bitter exchange with Michael Walzer. For the full exchange, see 'Appendix B' in William D. Hart, *Edward Said and the Religious Effects of Culture* (Cambridge: Cambridge University Press, 2000), 187–99.
30 See V. I. Lenin, *Questions of National Policy and Proletarian Internationalism* (Moscow: Progress Publishers, 1967), 60. Lenin's emphasis.
31 On the colonialist nature of the Zionist enterprise, see Gershon Shafir, *Land, Labor, and the Origins of the Israeli-Palestinian Conflict, 1882–1914* (Cambridge: Cambridge University Press, 1989) and Edward Said, *The Question of Palestine*. See also Chapter Four.
32 On the social origins of Palestinian nationalism among the élite classes, see Muhammad Y. Muslih, *The Origins of Palestinian Nationalism* (New York: Columbia University Press, 1988). On the Palestinian peasantry and nationalism, see Ted Swedenburg, 'The Role of the Palestinian Peasantry in the Great Revolt (1936–1939),' in Ilan Pappé (ed.), *The Israeli/Palestinian Question: Rewriting Histories* (London: Routledge, 1999), 129–67.

33 On the role of Unionist paramilitary organisations in the establishment of the Northern Irish State, see Michael Farrell, *Arming the
Protestants: the Formation of the Ulster Special Constabulary and the Royal
Ulster Constabulary* (Dingle: Brandon Publishers, 1983). For a brief account of the role of Zionist paramilitary organisations in the establishment of Israel, see Ilan Pappé, *The Making of the Arab-Israeli Conflict*,
50–56. For a comparative account of British security and policing policy in Ireland and Palestine, see Tom Bowden, *The Breakdown of Public
Security: the Case of Ireland: 1916–1921 and Palestine 1936–1939* (London:
Sage, 1977).

34 The literature on the dispossession of the Palestinian population in
1948 is vast and controversial. Key works include Benny Morris,
*The Birth of the Palestinian Refugee Problem, 1947–1949* (Cambridge:
Cambridge University Press, 1987) and Nur Masalha, *Expulsion
of the Palestinians* (Washington: Institute of Palestinian Studies,
1992).

35 On the Palestinians inside Israel, see Elia Zuriek, *The Palestinians in
Israel: a Study in Internal Colonialism* (London: Routledge and Kegan
Paul, 1979).

36 For astute analyses of the several strands of contemporary Ulster loyalist and Unionist attitudes in recent decades, see the essays in Peter
Shirlow and Mark McGovern (eds.), *Who Are 'The People'?: Unionism, Protestantism and Loyalism in Northern Ireland* (London: Pluto
Press, 1997). On populist loyalism and the 'peace process,' see Alan
Finlayson, 'Loyalist Political Identity After the Peace', *Capital & Class*
69 (1999), 47–75.

37 Arthur Aughey, 'Recent Interpretations of Unionism', *Political Quarterly* 61 (1990), 188–99, 194. My emphasis. Some leading examples
of 'New Unionist' analysis are collected in John Wilson Foster (ed.),
*The Idea of the Union: Statements and Critiques in Support of the Union
of Great Britain and Northern Ireland* (Vancouver: Belcouver Press,
1995).

38 See Liam O'Dowd, '"New Unionism", British Nationalism and the
Prospects for a Negotiated Settlement in Northern Ireland', in David
Miller (ed.), *Rethinking Northern Ireland: Culture, Ideology and Colonial-
ism* (London: Longman, 1998), 70–93.

39 John Wilson Foster, 'Strains in Irish Intellectual Life', in Liam O'Dowd
(ed.), *On Intellectuals and Intellectual Life in Ireland: International, Comparative and Historical Contexts* (Belfast: Institute of Irish Studies & Royal
Irish Academy, 1996), 71–97, 86.

40 O'Dowd, '"New Unionism", British Nationalism,' 89.

41 Article 3, *Agreement Reached in the Multi-Party Negotiations*, 1998.

42 The account of the Agreement outlined here is based quite closely,
both in argument and phrasing, on Brendan O'Leary's 'The Nature
of the British-Irish Agreement', *New Left Review* 233 (1999), 66–96. My
conclusions differ in some respects to O'Leary's; he has little to say
about class struggle or the way in which class and national struggles
in Northern Ireland are intertwined.

# Notes to pages 44–55

43 For a more extended discussion, see Denis O'Hearn, Sam Porter and Alan Harpur, 'Turning Agreement to Process: Republicanism and Change in Ireland', *Capital & Class* 69 (1999), 7–25.

44 For a succinct account of Israeli settlement activity in the West Bank and Gaza, see McDowell, *The Palestinians*, 81–91.

45 This critique is developed not only by Palestinian dissenters to the Oslo Agreement but also by some seasoned Israeli commentators as well. The most detailed Palestinian critique in English is Edward Said's *Peace and its Discontents: Gaza-Jericho 1993–1995* (London: Vintage, 1995). For an Israeli critique, see Meron Benvenisiti, *Intimate Enemies: Jews and Arabs in a Shared Land*, (Berkeley: University of California Press, 1995). See also Norman Finklestein, 'Whither the "Peace Process"', *New Left Review*, 218 (1996), 138–50, and Graham Usher, *Palestine in Crisis: the Struggle For Peace and Political Independence after Oslo* (London: Pluto Press, 1995).

46 For a short account of these laws, see McDowell, *Palestinians*, 43–5.

47 For accounts of the history of the idea of a bi-national democratic state in Palestinian thought, see Muhammad Muslih, *Towards Coexistence: an Analysis of the Resolutions of the Palestinian National Council* (Washington: Institute for Palestinian Studies, 1990), and Alain Gresh, *The PLO: the Struggle Within: Towards an Independent Palestinian State*, trans. A. M. Berrett (London: Zed Books, 1985).

## 2. Estranged states: national literatures, modernity and tradition, and the elaboration of partitionist identities

1 Ernest Gellner, *Nations and Nationalism* (Ithaca: Cornell University Press, 1983), 57. My emphasis.

2 For a comprehensive overview of Gellner's theory of nationalism, see Brendan O'Leary, 'Ernest Gellner's Diagnoses of Nationalism: a Critical Overview, or, What is Living and What is Dead in Ernest Gellner's Philosophy of Nationalism?', in John A. Hall (ed.), *The State of the Nation: Ernest Gellner and the Theory of Nationalism* (Cambridge: Cambridge University Press, 1998), 40–88.

3 Benedict Anderson, *Imagined Communities: Reflections on the Origin and Spread of Nationalism*, revised edition (London: Verso, 1991).

4 Cairns Craig, *The Modern Scottish Novel: Narrative and the National Imagination* (Edinburgh: Edinburgh University Press, 1999), 9.

5 Sarah Corse, *Nationalism and Literature: the Politics of Culture in Canada and the United States* (Cambridge: Cambridge University Press, 1997), 18–33.

6 Webster, cited in Corse, *Nationalism and Literature*, 28.

7 Ibid.

8 Ibid., 29.

9 Tom Nairn, *The Break-Up of Britain: Crisis and Neo-Nationalism*, second edition (London: Verso, 1981), 339.

10 On this topic, see Saree Makdisi, *Romantic Imperialism: Universal Empire and the Culture of Modernity* (Cambridge: Cambridge University Press, 1998), especially 190, note 35.

234

11 For a more elaborate discussion, see Benedict Anderson, 'Majorities and Minorities', in *The Spectre of Comparisons: Nationalism, Southeast Asia and the World* (London: Verso, 1998), 318–30.

12 See Johannes Fabian, *Time and the Other: How Anthropology Makes its Object* (New York: Columbia University Press, 1983).

13 Friedrich Meinecke, *Cosmopolitanism and the National State*, trans. Robert B. Kimber (Princeton: Princeton University Press, 1970). On Meinecke's concept of the *Kulturnation*, see Stephen Brockmann, *Literature and German Reunification* (Cambridge: Cambridge University Press, 1999), 6–10.

14 On the circumstances that condition tendencies towards divergence or convergence in partitioned societies, see Yung-Hwan Jo and Stephen Walker, 'Divided Nations and Reunification Strategies', *Journal of Peace Research* 6 (1972), 247–59 and Stanley Waterman, 'Partitioned States', *Political Geography* 6 (1987), 151–70.

15 See James Mellis, 'Writers in Transition: the End of East German Literature?', in Derek Lewis and John McKenzie (eds.), *The New Germany: Social, Political and Cultural Challenges of Unification* (Exeter: University of Exeter Press, 1995), 220–42, 221.

16 David Bathrick, *The Powers of Speech: the Politics of Culture in the GDR* (Lincoln: University of Nebraska Press, 1995), 43–4. Other works in English that discuss the roles of literature in the two Germanys include: Keith Bullivant, *The Future of German Literature* (Oxford: Berg, 1994); Friedricke Eigler and Peter C. Pfeiffer (eds.), *Cultural Transformations in the New Germany: American and German Perspectives* (Columbia: Camden House, 1993); Stuart Parkes, *Writers and Politics in West Germany* (New York: St. Martin's Press, 1986); and Arthur Williams, Stuart Parkes and Roland Smith (eds.), *German Literature at a Time of Change 1989–1990: German Unity and German Identity in Literary Perspective* (Bern: Peter Lang, 1991).

17 Alison Lewis, 'Unity Begins Together: Analyzing the Trauma Of German Unification', *New German Critique* 64 (1995), 135–59, 155. Matters were somewhat less symmetrical, though, than this suggests. The East German state considered fascism a by-product of capitalism rather than a specifically German phenomenon, thus universalising the problem. It also insisted that as a socialist society it, unlike the West, had eliminated the preconditions on which fascism depended. The Federal Republic associated fascism with the Third Reich and 'Hitlerism', thus construing it as a political rather than economic or cultural phenomenon. But because the West claimed to be the only legitimate successor state to the Third Reich, it had more problem in distancing itself from the fascist past, and was compelled to reckon more with that legacy, however narrowly defined.

18 On German constitutional history, see Peter Pulzer, 'The Citizen and the State in Modern Germany', in Eva Kolinsky and Wilfried van der Will (eds.), *The Cambridge Companion to Modern German Culture* (Cambridge: Cambridge University Press, 1998), 20–43.

19 Brockmann, *Literature and German Reunification*, 25.

20 Cited in Brockmann, *Literature and German Reunification*, 32.

21 Cited in Brockmann, *Literature and German Reunification*, 29–30.
22 Brockmann, *Literature and German Reunification*, 71.
23 On Irish cultural nationalism and the Literary Revival, see: Seamus Deane, *Celtic Revivals: Essays in Modern Irish Literature, 1880–1980* (Winston-Salem: Wake Forest University Press, 1985); Terry Eagleton, *Heathcliff and the Great Hunger: Studies in Irish Culture* (London: Verso, 1995); John Wilson Foster, *Fictions of the Irish Literary Revival* (New York: Syracuse University Press, 1987); and Declan Kiberd, *Inventing Ireland: the Literature of the Modern Nation* (London: Jonathan Cape, 1995).
24 On the different evolutions of national literature in the United States and Canada, see Corse, *Nationalism and Literature*.
25 On Unionist culture since partition, see Gillian McIntosh, *The Force of Culture: Unionist Identities in Twentieth-Century Ireland* (Cork: Cork University Press, 1999).
26 *The Irish Times*, 26 January 1926. Cited in Clare O'Halloran, *Partition and the Limits of Irish Nationlism: an Ideology Under Stress* (Dublin: Gill and Macmillan, 1986), 11.
27 Flan Fitzgerald, 'A Week by the Lagan', in *The Catholic Bulletin* 13 (1923), 13. Cited in O'Halloran, *Partition*, 11.
28 The ratification of partition in terms of this essentialist cultural paradigm finds its most elaborate expression in M. W. Heslinga, *The Irish Border as a Cultural Divide* (Assen: van Gorcum, 1962).
29 Hewitt, cited in John Wilson Foster, *Colonial Consequences* (Dublin: Lilliput Press, 1991), 278.
30 For contrasting views on Ulster literary regionalism, see McIntosh, *Force of Culture*, 180–219; Patrick Walsh, '"Too Much Alone": John Hewitt, Regionalism, Socialism, and Partition', *Irish University Review* 29 (1999), 341–57; Tom Clyde, 'A Stirring in Dry Bones: John Hewitt's Regionalism', in Gerald Dawe and John Wilson Foster (eds.), *The Poet's Place: Ulster Literature and Society: Essays in Honour of John Hewitt, 1907–1987* (Belfast: Institute of Irish Studies, 1991), 249–58; and Edna Longley, 'Progressive Bookmen: Politics and Northern Protestant Writers since the 1930s', *Irish Review* 1 (1986), 50–7.
31 Explaining his own response to Ulster regionalism, Roy McFadden has observed: 'I suspected that the Ulster Regionalist idea could be used to provide a cultural mask for political unionism or a kind of local counter-nationalism ... In a late conversation, Hewitt confessed that his concept of Ulster had omitted that part of it west of the Bann. In truth, the Hewitt region did not extend beyond the familiar home counties of Antrim and Down' ('No Dusty Pioneer: A Personal Recollection of John Hewitt,' in Dawe and Wilson Foster (eds.), *The Poet's Place*, 176).
32 Longley, 'Progressive Bookmen', 56.
33 For more comprehensive accounts of the Northern state's responses to partition, see Rex Cathcart, *The Most Contrary Region: the BBC in Northern Ireland, 1924–1984* (Belfast: Blackstaff Press, 1984) and Martin McLoone, 'The Construction of a Partitionist Mentality: Early Broadcasting in Ireland', in Martin McLoone (ed.), *Broadcasting in a Divided Community: Seventy Years of the BBC in Northern Ireland*, (Belfast:

Blackstaff, 1996), 20–34. On the evolving character of modern Unionist identity, see James Loughlin, *Ulster Unionism and British National
Identity Since 1885* (London: Pinter, 1995).

34 Terence Brown's *Ireland: A Social and Cultural History, 1922–1985*
(London: Fontana, 1990) remains the standard authority on cultural
developments in the Irish Free State, later Republic.

35 Francis Mulhern, *The Present Lasts a Long Time: Essays in Cultural Politics*
(Cork: Cork University Press, 1998), 22.

36 For more comprehensive discussions, see Liam O'Dowd (ed.), *On In-
tellectuals and Intellectual Life in Ireland: International, Comparative, and
Historical Contexts* (Belfast: Institute of Irish Studies & Royal Irish
Academy, 1996).

37 See, for example, Thomas Kinsella, 'Introduction', in *The New Oxford
Book of Irish Verse* (London: Oxford University Press, 1986); Terence
Brown, *Ireland's Literatures: Selected Essays* (Mullingar: Lilliput, 1988),
203–22; and Richard Kirkland, *Literature and Culture in Northern
Ireland Since 1965: Moments of Danger* (London: Longman, 1996), 53–84.

38 See Seamus Deane (general editor),*The Field Day Anthology of Irish Writing*, 3 vols. (Derry: Field Day Publications, 1991).

39 Phenomena such as the rock-band U2, numerous Irish boy bands such
as 'Boyzone' and 'Westlife,' and the dance-extravaganza *Riverdance*,
which have all attained massive commercial success at a global level,
signal this wider shift.

40 A classic study is Shlomo Avineri's *The Making of Modern Zionism:
the Intellectual Origins of the Jewish State* (London: Weidenfeld and
Nicolson, 1981).

41 Chaim Rabin, *A Short History of the Jewish Language* (Jerusalem: The
Jewish Agency, 1973), 69.

42 Sue Wright (ed.), *Language and the State: Revitalization and Revival in
Israel and Eire* (Clevedon: Multilingual Matters, 1996).

43 With the establishment of the State of Israel in 1948, Hebrew became the
national language, and easily dominated the other official language,
Arabic. Arabic is the language of instruction in Arab and Druze schools
and is taught in Jewish schools. While not official, English is the de
facto second language of speakers in both Arabic and Hebrew, and a
required language for all Jewish and Arab schools and the universities.

44 Wright (ed.), *Language and the State*, 19.

45 Standard works in English on Modern Hebrew literary history include Simon Halkin, *Modern Hebrew Literature* (New York: Schocken,
1970); Leon I. Yudkin, *1948 and After: Aspects of Israeli Fiction* (Manchester: University of Manchester, 1984); Gershon Shaked, *Modern
Hebrew Fiction* (Bloomington and Indianapolis: Indiana University
Press, 2000).

46 On Zionism's settlement ideologies, see Baruch Kimmerling, *Zionism and Territory: the Socio-Territorial Dimensions of Zionist Politics*,
(Berkeley: University of California Press, 1983).

47 For accounts of Zionist conceptions of the Diaspora Jew, see Sander
Gilman, *Jewish Self-Hatred: Anti-Semitism and the Hidden Language
of the Jews* (Baltimore: Johns Hopkins University Press, 1986) and

Paul Breines, *Tough Jews: Political Fantasies and the Moral Dilemma of American Jewry* (New York: Basic Books, 1991).

48 See Aharon Kellerman, 'Settlement Myth and Settlement Activity: Interrelationships in the Zionist Land of Israel', *Transactions of the Institute of British Geographers* 12 (1996): 363–78, and Kimmerling, *Zionism and Territory*, 86–7 and 201–4.

49 On Zionists and South Africa, see Ran Greenstein, *Genealogies of Conflict: Class, Identity and State in Palestine/Israel and South Africa* (Hanover: University Press of New England, 1995).

50 For a short overview of Israeli literature since the 1960s, see Brian Cheyette, 'Israel', in John Sturrock, (ed.), *The Oxford Guide to Contemporary Writing* (Oxford: Oxford University Press, 1996), 238–49.

51 On Arab Jewish immigration to Israel and Israeli assimilation policy, see Tom Segev, *1949: the First Israelis*, trans. Arlen Neal Weinstein (New York: Free Press, 1986). On Zionism and Sephardi Jews in Israel, see Ella Shohat, *Israeli Cinema: East/West and the Politics of Representation* (Austin: University of Texas Press, 1989) and G. N. Giladi, *Discord in Zion: Conflict between Ashkenazi and Sephardi Jews in Israel* (London, Scorpion Publishing, 1990) and Shlomo Swirska, *Israel: the Oriental Majority*, trans. Barbara Swirski (London: Zed Books, 1989).

52 Ella Shohat, *Israeli Cinema*, 4.

53 Ibid., 119.

54 These remarks by Ben-Gurion and Abba Eban are cited in Shohat, *Israeli Cinema*, 116–17.

55 On the fate of Iraqi Jewish writers in Israel, on which this summary borrows, see Nancy E. Berg, *Exile from Exile: Israeli Writers from Iraq* (New York: State University of New York, 1996).

56 Ammiel Alcalay, *After Jews and Arabs: Remaking Levantine Culture* (Minneapolis: University of Minnesota Press, 1993), 237–8.

57 Edward Said, *The Politics of Dispossession: the Struggle for Palestinian Self-Determination 1969–1994* (London: Chatto & Windus, 1994), 119.

58 For a more elaborate account, see Ami Elad-Bouskila, *Modern Palestinian Literature and Culture* (London: Frank Cass, 1999).

59 Nadine Gordimer, 'Art and the State in South Africa', *The Nation* (24 December 1983), 657.

60 On Korean literature, see Paik Nack-Chung, 'Commitment to Overcoming Division in Korean Fiction of the 1980s', *Korea Journal* 28 (1988), 4–15, 14.

61 For a striking instance of the more general pattern described here, see Edward W. Said, 'Return to Palestine Israel', in *The Politics of Dispossession*, 175–99.

62 For a more comprehensive analysis of Jews as represented in recent Palestinian literature, see Elad-Bouskila, *Modern Palestinian Literature and Culture*, chapter 5.

63 Carol Bardenstein, 'Threads of Memory and Discourses of Rootedness: Of Trees, Oranges and the Prickly-Pear Cactus in Israel/Palestine', *Edebiyât* 8 (1998), 1–36, 2–3.

64 Paik Nack-chung has argued that in a sense all modern Korean literature is partition literature since division is a historical fact that has had

major consequences for all Koreans. For Paik, whether an individual literary work explicitly raises the problem of division is of minor importance since national conflicts always encompass much that is not specifically nationalist: competing visions of the good society, alternative models of modernisation, and so on. Hence, literary works or genres that isolate state borders as a single issue will usually only distort social reality with damaging artistic and political consequences. See Paik Nack-chung, 'Commitment to Overcoming Division in Korean Fiction', 6.

### 3. 'Fork-tongued on the border bit': partition and the politics of form in contemporary narratives of the Northern Irish conflict

1 Seamus Heaney, 'Whatever You Say Say Nothing,' *North* (London: Faber and Faber, 1975), 57–60.
2 On the history and politics of the Irish border, see Liam O'Dowd, *Whither the Irish Border?: Sovereignty, Democracy and Economic Integration in Ireland* (Belfast: CRD Pamphlet Series, 1994). My analysis of the Troubles owes much to O'Dowd's many works on the topic.
3 I am referring here to the practice described by Benedict Anderson whereby the map of the nation-state is reduced to a logo or pure sign, and made infinitely reproducible, available for transfer to posters, official seals, letterheads and textbook covers. See Benedict Anderson, *Imagined Communities: Reflections on the Origin and Spread of Nationalism*, revised edition (London: Verso, 1991), 170–8.
4 On the idea of the island in English nationalism, see Gillian Beer, 'The Island and the Aeroplane: the Case of Virginia Woolf', in Homi K. Bhabha (ed.), *Nation and Narration* (London: Routledge, 1990), 265–90.
5 Paul Fussell, *Abroad: British Literary Travelling Between The Wars* (Oxford: Oxford University Press, 1980), 33–4.
6 For a more extended discussion, see Colm Ryan and Liam O'Dowd, 'Restructuring the Periphery: State, Region and Locality in Northern Ireland', in G. Day and G. Rees (eds.), *Regions, Nations, and European Integration* (Cardiff: University of Wales Press, 1991), 193–209.
7 Liam O'Dowd, Bill Rolston, and Mike Tomlinson, 'From Labour to the Tories: The Ideology of Containment in Northern Ireland,' *Capital and Class* 18 (1982), 72–90.
8 John Whyte, *Interpreting Northern Ireland* (Oxford: Clarendon Press, 1990), 202.
9 For a more elaborate discussion, see Joseph Ruane and Jennifer Todd, *The Dynamics of Conflict in Northern Ireland: Peace, Conflict and Emancipation* (Cambridge: Cambridge University Press, 1996).
10 All history writing is inherently revisionist. In Ireland, however, 'revisionism' has come to refer specifically to a variegated but identifiable intellectual current that came to prominence during the Northern Troubles. While the term is primarily associated with Irish historiography, revisionism has exerted a powerful influence on most disciplines in the humanities and the social sciences. For more

comprehensive discussions, see Ciaran Brady (ed.), *Interpreting Irish History: the Debate on Historical Revisionism* (Dublin: Irish Academic Press, 1994).

11 Liam O'Dowd, 'Intellectuals and the National Question in Ireland', in Day and Rees (eds.), *Regions, Nations, and European Integration*, 125–39.

12 These figures are cited in Austen Morgan, *Labour and Partition: the Belfast Working-Class, 1905–1923* (London: Pluto Press, 1991), 301–3.

13 See Clare O' Halloran, *Partition and the Limits of Irish Nationalism: an Ideology under Stress* (Dublin: Gill and Macmillan, 1987), xiv.

14 Ibid.

15 This concept of trauma is developed in the remarkable reading of Freud's work in Jean Laplanche, *Life and Death in Psychoanalysis*, trans. Jeffrey Melham (Baltimore: Johns Hopkins University Press, 1976).

16 Ian Lustick makes a convincing case for the intrinsic connection between these in his *Unsettled States, Disputed Lands: Britain and Ireland, France and Algeria, Israel and the West Bank-Gaza* (Ithaca: Cornell University Press, 1993), 441.

17 Georg Lukács, 'Observations on the Theory of Literary History,' cited in Franco Moretti, *Signs Taken for Wonders: Essays on the Sociology of Literary Forms* (London: Verso, 1980), 10. Theodor Adorno, *Aesthetic Theory*, trans. C. Lenhardt (London: Routledge & Kegan Paul, 1984), 327.

18 In his survey of novels on the Northern situation published since 1969, Bill Rolston observes that 'one common theme is that the problem of violence in the North of Ireland derives from Republicans'. 'By comparison', he writes, 'loyalists appear infrequently, and even then often as shadowy figures in the wings'. See Bill Rolston, 'Mothers, Whores and Villains: Images of Women in the Novels of the Northern Ireland Conflict', *Race & Class* 1:31 (1989), 41–57, 41.

19 Stanley Baldwin, *On England: and Other Addresses* (Harmondsworth: Penguin Books, 1926), 218.

20 Scott, cited in Brian Hollingworth, 'Completing the Union: Edgeworth's *The Absentee* and Scott the Novelist', in J. H. Alexander and David Hewitt (eds.), *Scott in Carnival* (Aberdeen: Selected Papers from the Fourth International Scott Conference, Edinburgh, 1991), 503–4.

21 Baldwin, *On England*, 218.

22 Doris Sommer, *Foundational Fictions: the National Romances of Latin America* (Berkeley: University of California Press, 1991).

23 Ibid., 24.

24 Nancy Armstrong, *Desire and Domestic Fiction: a Political History of the Novel* (Oxford: Oxford University Press, 1987).

25 Joan Lingard, *Across the Barricades* (London: Penguin Books, 1988, [1972]), 48. The romance-across-the-divide genre must be seen against the background of increasing communal divergence in the period. Official reports found that between August 1969 and February 1973 a total of between thirty and sixty thousand people, between nearly 7 and 11 per cent of the Belfast population, were forced to leave their homes to move into more exclusively Catholic or Protestant neighbourhoods. Estimates indicate that over 80 per cent of those forced to move were

Catholic. Recent census data showed that by 1992 only about 7 per cent
of the Northern population lived in areas with roughly equal numbers
of Catholics and Protestants. See Fionnuala O'Connor, *In Search of a
State: Catholics in Northern Ireland* (Belfast: The Blackstaff Press, 1993),
160–9.

26 Joan Lingard, *Hostages to Fortune* (London: Puffin Books, 1976), 86.

27 Ibid., 30. Lingard's emphasis.

28 The discursive formation to which Lingard's novels are closest is that
strand of liberal Unionism Jennifer Todd describes as 'Ulster British'.
Lingard's novels seem to anticipate the 'New Unionist' discourse discussed in Chapter One. See Jennifer Todd, 'Two Traditions in Unionist
Political Culture', *Irish Political Studies* 2 (1987), 1–26.

29 Michael Denning, *Cover Stories: Narrative and Ideology in the British Spy
Thriller* (London: Routledge & Kegan Paul, 1987), 15–22, 39–41.

30 Ibid., 2, 13–14.

31 On the links between contemporary cinematic thrillers about the
North and older traditions of representing Ireland on screen, see
John Hill's 'Images of Violence', in Kevin Rockett, Luke Gibbons
and John Hill, *Cinema and Ireland* (London: Croom Helm, 1987),
147–93.

32 Bernard Mac Laverty, *Cal* (London: Penguin Books, 1983). For the purposes of this study, I will concentrate my analysis on the novel rather
than the film.

33 Ibid., 154.

34 Ibid., 37.

35 Ibid., 110.

36 Ibid., 145.

37 Ibid., 39.

38 Ibid., 34.

39 Ibid., 114.

40 Ibid., 111.

41 Ibid., 130, 108.

42 Ibid., 138, 39, 89, 124.

43 Ibid., 154, 134.

44 For a more extended account of the way in which Julia Kristeva brings
together the writings of Freud and René Girard in her analysis of the
symbolic logic of the state, on which the account here borrows, see
John Lechte, *Julia Kristeva* (London: Routledge, 1990), 148–53.

45 Georg Lukács, *The Historical Novel*, trans. Hannah and Stanley Mitchell
(Lincoln: Univerity of Nebraska Press, 1983 [1962]), 37.

46 *The Crying Game* won an Academy Award for best original screenplay of 1993, by which time it had grossed over sixty million dollars
for Miramax. As well as referring to the film version, I will refer to
Neil Jordan's screenplay, *The Crying Game* (London: Vintage, 1993).
All quotes are from this edition.

47 Rebecca Bell-Metereau, *Hollywood Androgyny* (New York: Columbia
University Press, 1993), 284.

48 Slavoj Zizek, 'From Courtly Love to *The Crying Game*', *New Left Review*
202 (1993), 95–108, 107.

49 Judie Wheelwright, 'Opening the Borders', *New Statesman and Society* (30 October 1992), 35.

50 See René Girard's theory of mimetic desire in *Deceit, Desire, and the Novel: Self and Other in Literary Structure*, trans. Y. Freccero (Baltimore: Johns Hopkins University Press, 1965), 1–53.

51 Stephen Tifft, 'The Parricidal Phantasm: Irish Nationalism and the *Playboy* Riots', in Andrew Parker, Mary Russo, Doris Sommer and Patricia Yaeger (eds.), *Nationalisms and Sexualities* (London: Routledge, 1992), 313–32, 321.

52 Slavoj Zizek has argued that it is 'totally misleading' to read *The Crying Game* in this way since 'in the very sphere of privacy where the hero had hoped to find a safe haven, he is compelled to complete an even more vertiginous revolution in his most intimate personal attitudes'. While this is true to a point, it ignores the ways in which the conventionally gendered structure of the relationship between Fergus and Dil remains largely intact despite the fact that it is not heterosexual. Zizek's interpretation takes little account of the treatment of Irish politics in the film and none whatever of the figure of Jude, the film's only woman character and its most prominent IRA representative. Zizek, it seems, *has* to leave Jude out to make his argument work. Zizek, 'From Courtly Love to *The Crying Game*', 107.

53 Jordan, *The Crying Game*, 45.

54 Laura Mulvey, 'Visual Pleasure and Narrative Cinema', *Screen* 3:16 (1975), 6–18.

55 Jordan,*The Crying Game*, 50.

56 Afro-American feminist critic bell hooks confirms this. Her instinctive response to this scene, she notes, was that: 'Because I considered Jude to be first and foremost a fascist, I did not initially see her death as misogynistic slaughter.' bell hooks, *Outlaw Culture: Resisting Representations* (London: Routledge, 1994), 61.

57 Wheelwright, 'Opening the Borders,' 35.

58 Jordan, *The Crying Game*, 12.

59 René Girard, *Violence and the Sacred*, trans. Patrick Gregory (Baltimore: Johns Hopkins University Press, 1977). For Girard, cyclical processes of violence can only be halted when the contending parties accept the neutrality of the law.

60 See, for example, Joe Craig, John McAnulty and Paul Flannigan, *The Real Irish Peace Process* (Belfast: Socialist Democracy, 1998).

61 Joseph Ruane, 'Conflict Management vs. Conflict Resolution: an Emancipatory Approach to the Northern Ireland Conflict', *Irish Journal of Sociology* 4 (1994), 51–66, 61.

## 4. Agonies of the potentates: journeys to the frontier in the novals of Amos Oz

1 McDowell, *The Palestinians*, 24. Writing on the Suez War, the historian Simha Flapan contends that the Israeli establishment was willing to contemplate a greatly enlarged Israel should circumstances permit. 'In preparing for the war with French leaders Guy Mollet and

Christian Pineau', he writes, 'Ben-Gurion had proposed an outright partition of Jordan. The West Bank was to be given to Israel; the East Bank, to Iraq. In exchange, Iraq would sign a peace treaty with Israel and undertake to absorb the Palestinian refugees' (Simha Flapan, *The Birth of Israel: Myth and Realities* (London: Croom Helm, 1987), 51.

2 For a more comprehensive discussion of these developments, see Baruch Kimmerling, 'Boundaries and Frontiers of the Israeli Control System: Analytical Conclusions', in Baruch Kimmerling (ed.), *The Israeli State and Society*, (Albany: State University of New York Press, 1989), 265–84.

3 The works of the New Historians referred to here include: Tom Segev, *1949: the First Israelis* (New York: The Free Press, 1986); Benny Morris, *The Birth of the Palestinian Refugee Problem, 1947–1949* (Cambridge: Cambridge University Press, 1987) and *Israel's Border Wars, 1949–1956: Arab Infiltration, Israeli Retaliation, and the Countdown to the Suez War* (Oxford: Clarendon Press, 1993); Simha Flapan, *The Birth of Israel*; Avi Shlaim, *Collusion Across the Jordan: King Abdullah, the Zionist Movement, and the Partition of Palestine* (Oxford: Oxford University Press, 1989); Ilan Pappé, *Britain and the Israeli–Arab Conflict, 1948-1951* (New York: Macmillan, 1988) and *The Making of the Arab–Israeli Conflict, 1947–1951* (London: I. B. Tauris, 1992). There are some interesting methodological parallels between Irish and Israeli 'revisionisms'. Both set out to 'demythologise' popular nationalist history or 'mythology' and have championed a positivistic professional history as a counter to the self-delusions of popular nationalist history. Where partition is concerned, both Irish and Israeli revisionists deal almost exclusively with 'high' history and in neither case has there been any extended attempt, as there has been in India for example, to study partition 'from below'. But there are also important differences between the two. The Israeli revisionists have accepted the usefulness of the settler-colonial paradigm to explain Israeli history whereas the various strands of Irish revisionism have been distinctly hostile to any colonialist conception of Irish history.

4 Baruch Kimmerling, *Zionism and Territory: The Socio-Territorial Dimensions of Zionist Politics* (Berkeley: University of California Press, 1983); Gershon Shafir, *Land, Labor, and the Origins of the Israeli-Palestinian Conflict, 1882–1914* (Cambridge: Cambridge University Press, 1989); Uri Ram, *The Changing Agenda of Israeli Sociology: Theory, Ideology, and Identity* (Albany, NY: State University of New York Press, 1995).

5 Ella Shohat, *Israeli Cinema: East/West and the Politics of Representation* (Austin: University of Texas Press, 1989) and Ammiel Alacaly, *After Jews and Arabs: Remaking Levantine Culture* (Minneapolis: University of Minnesota Press, 1993).

6 On contemporary Israeli intellectual debates, see Laurence J. Silberstein, *The Postzionism Debates: Knowledge and Power in Israeli Culture* (London: Routledge, 1999).

7 This description appears on the dust-jacket of Amos Oz, *In the Land of Israel*, trans. Maurice Goldberg-Bartura (New York: Vintage Books, 1984).

8 Amos Oz, *Israel, Palestine and Peace* (London: Vintage, 1994), 17.

9 For a very different account to Oz's, see Norman Finkelstein, *The Rise and Fall of Palestine: a Personal Account of the Intifada Years* (Minneapolis: University of Minnesota Press, 1996), 86–7.

10 See Amos Oz, *Israel, Palestine and Peace*, 116. The article was originally printed in *The Guardian* (1 September 1993), trans. Amos Oz and Ora Cummings.

11 On settlement myths and the frontier in Israeli society, see Aharon Kellerman, 'Settlement Myth and Settlement Activity: Interrelationships in the Zionist Land of Israel', *Transactions of the Institute of British Geographers* 12 (1996), 363–78.

12 The most famous American example is Frederick Jackson Turner *The Frontier in American History* (New York: Holt, Reinhart and Winston, 1962). Turner's thesis, developed in 1893, was adapted to the British Empire by Lord Curzon who chose 'Frontiers' as his theme for the Romanes Lectures in Oxford in 1904. See Lord Curzon, *Frontiers* (Oxford: Clarendon Press, 1907). See also Linda Colley, *The Significance of the Frontier in British History* (Austin: University of Texas Press, 1995).

13 For a more detailed discussion, see Kimmerling, 'Boundaries and Frontiers of the Israeli Control System', 265–84.

14 John McClure, *Late Imperial Romance* (London: Verso, 1994).

15 Ibid., 10.

16 Amos Oz, *Elsewhere, Perhaps*, trans. Nicholas de Lange (London: Fontana Paperbacks, 1989), 16. First published in Hebrew under the title *Makom aher* in 1966.

17 Ibid., 295.

18 Ibid., 11, 12.

19 Theodor Herzl, *The Jewish State: an Attempt at a Modern Solution to the Jewish Question*, trans. Sylvia d'Avigdor and Israel Cohen (New York: American Jewish Emergency Council, 1946), 96.

20 Chaim Weizmann, Colonial Office [CO] 733/297/75156/11/Appendix A. Extract from Weizmann's speech, 23 April 1936. Peel Commission Report.

21 McClure, *Late Imperial Romance*, 8, 3.

22 Oz, *Elsewhere, Perhaps*, 11.

23 Ibid., 324.

24 Ibid., 87.

25 Ibid., 43.

26 Ibid., 102.

27 Ibid., 153.

28 Ibid., 226.

29 Ibid., 236.

30 In his compelling essay on modern anti-Semitism, Moishe Postone argues that all forms of racism attribute potential power, usually of a sexual or commercial character, to the hated Other, but that the power attributed to Jews is much greater than that ascribed to other scapegoated groups. What distinguishes the power imputed to the Jews in modern anti-Semitism, he suggests, is that it is mysteriously

intangible, abstract and universal. In the anti-Semitic imagination, Jewish power is not 'rooted' but hidden and abstract; hence the frequency with which it is linked to international conspiracy, whether capitalist or socialist. Thus, for Postone, 'a careful examination of the modern anti-Semitic worldview reveals that it is a form of thought in which the rapid development of industrial capitalism, with all its ramifications, is personified and identified as the Jew. It is not merely that Jews were considered to be owners of money, as in traditional anti-Semitism, but that they were to be held responsible for economic crises and identified with the range of social restructuring and dislocation resulting from rapid industrialisation.' See Moishe Postone, 'Anti-Semitism and National Socialism', in Anson Rabinbach and Jack Zipes (eds.), *Germans and Jews Since the Holocaust* (New York: Holmes and Meier, 1986), 302–14, 306. The sinuously elusive Siegfried, and his association with international capital and consumerism, recall the discursive tropes identified by Postone.

31 For more comprehensive analyses of this transition, see Baruch Kimmerling, 'Boundaries and Frontiers of the Israeli Control System', 265–84, and Nira Yuval-Davis, 'The Current Crisis in Israel', *Capital and Class* 22 (1984), 5–15.

32 On Israel's 'borders of destiny', see Jay Y. Gonen, *A Psychohistory of Zionism* (New York: Mason-Chartier, 1975), 193–4.

33 Oz, *Elsewhere, Perhaps*, 283.

34 Ibid., 173.

35 Ibid., 326, 325.

36 Ibid., 331.

37 On colonial settler writing, see Elleke Boehmer, *Colonial and Postcolonial Literature: Migrant Metaphors* (Oxford: Oxford University Press, 1995) 213–22.

38 Oz, *Elsewhere, Perhaps*, 126.

39 Ibid., 102.

40 Ibid., 95.

41 Ibid., 268.

42 Alcalay, *After Arabs and Jews*, 42.

43 On Kahane and the wider rise of right-wing maximalist Zionism in Israel after 1967, see Ehud Sprinzak, *The Ascendance of Israel's Radical Right* (Oxford: Oxford University Press, 1991).

44 See, for example, Amos Oz, *In the Land of Israel*, 103–53.

45 Oz, *Elsewhere, Perhaps*, 42–3.

46 Amos Oz, *A Perfect Peace*, trans. H. Halkin (London: Vintage, 1993). First published in Hebrew as *Menuhah ha-or* (Tel Aviv: Am Oved Publishers, 1982).

47 Ibid., 132.

48 Ibid., 205, 208.

49 Ibid., 267.

50 Ibid., 204, 205.

51 The narrative structure will be familiar to many from American movies on Vietnam. See, for example, Susan Jeffords, *The Remasculinization of America: Gender and the Vietnam War* (Bloomington: Indiana

University Press, 1989) and Kaja Silverman, *Male Subjectivity at the Margins* (London: Routledge, 1992).

52 The number of Palestinians massacred in Deir Yassin is disputed, some recent scholars putting the figure at 120, most at around 250. What is not disputed is the brutality involved. As one recent work puts it, after their successful assault on the village 'the Jewish fighters killed many of the remaining men, women, and children, and raped and mutilated others. Those not killed immediately were paraded through Jerusalem and then sent to the city's Arab sector.' Cited in Baruch Kimmerling and Joel S. Migdal, *Palestinians: the Making of a People* (Cambridge, Mass.: Harvard University Press, 1993), 151–53, 151.

53 Oz, *A Perfect Peace*, 133, 124.

54 Ibid., 125.

55 Ibid., 125–6.

56 Ibid., 133.

57 Ibid., 127, 137.

58 Ibid., 130, 139.

59 See Neil Asher Silberman and David Small (eds.), *The Archaelogy of Israel: Constructing the Past, Interpreting the Present* (Sheffield: Sheffield Academic Press, 1997).

60 This has been argued in recent times by Joan Peters in *From Time Immemorial: the Origins of the Arab–Jewish Conflict over Palestine* (New York: Harper & Row, 1984). For a coruscating critique of Peters's work, see Norman Finkelstein, *Image and Reality of the Israeli–Palestine Conflict* (London: Verso, 1995), chapter 2.

61 Oz, *A Perfect Peace*, 135.

62 Carol Bardenstein, 'Threads of Memory and Discourses of Rootedness: of Trees, Oranges and the Prickly-Pear Cactus in Israel/ Palestine', *Edebiyât* 8 (1998), 1–36. See Susan Slyomovics, *The Object of Memory: Arab and Jew Narrate the Palestinian Village* (Philadelphia: University of Pennsylvania Press, 1998); W. J. T. Mitchell, 'Holy Landscape: Israel, Palestine, and the American Wilderness', *Critical Inquiry* 26 (2000), 193–223; Edward Said, 'Invention, Memory and Place', *Critical Inquiry* 26 (2000), 175–92.

63 Oz, *A Perfect Peace*, 129–30.

64 Yerach Gover, *Zionism: the Limits of Moral Discourse in Israeli Hebrew Fiction*, (Minneapolis: University of Minnesota Press, 1994), 54.

65 Oz, *A Perfect Peace*, 135.

66 John Noyes, *Colonial Space: Spatiality in the Discourse of German South West Africa 1884–1915* (Chur: Harwood Academic Publishers, 1992), 182–215.

67 Oz, *A Perfect Peace*, 270.

68 Ibid., 271.

69 Ibid., 328.

70 Ibid., 334.

71 Ibid., 323.

72 Ibid., 333.

73 Ibid., 330.

74 McClure, *Late Imperial Romance*, 13.

75 Richard Slotkin, *Gunfighter Nation: the Myth of the Frontier in Twentieth-Century America* (New York: Atheneum, 1992), 351–2. On affinities between American and Israeli perceptions of the frontier, see W. J. T. Mitchell, 'Holy Landscape: Israel, Palestine, and the American Wilderness', 193–223.
76 Oz, *A Perfect Peace*, 347.
77 Ibid., 354, 353.
78 Ibid., 368.
79 Ibid., 372, 373.
80 Ibid., 355.
81 Ibid., 364.
82 Oz, *Israel, Palestine and Peace*, 77.
83 Franco Moretti, *Atlas of the European Novel, 1800–1900* (London: Verso, 1998), 35. Emphasis in original.
84 Ehud Ben Ezer, 'Between Romanticism and the Bitterness of Reality: the Arab Question in Our Literature', [Hebrew] *Shdemot* 46 (Spring 1972), 12. Cited in Gilead Morahg, 'New Images of Arabs in Israeli Fiction', *Prooftexts* 6 (1986), 147–62.
85 Morahg, 'New Images of Arabs in Israeli Fiction', 150.
86 The phrase appears in an essay on Cruise O'Brien in Christopher Hitchens, *Prepared for the Worst: Selected Essays and Minority Reports* (London: Chatto and Windus, 1989), 40–52, 51.

### 5. The meaning of disaster: the novel and the stateless nation in Ghassan Kanafani's *Men in the Sun*

1 For more comprehensive discussions on the development of Palestinian national strategy since 1948, see Muhammad Muslih, *Toward Coexistence: an Analysis of the Resolutions of the Palestinian National Council* (Washington: Institute for Palestine Studies, 1990) and Alain Gresh, *The PLO: the Struggle Within: towards an Independent Palestinian State*, trans. A. M. Berrett (London: Zed Books, 1985).
2 Barbara Harlow, 'Palestine or Andalusia: the Literary Response to the Israeli Invasion of Lebanon', *Race & Class* 2:24 (1984), 40. My emphasis.
3 Ibid., 41.
4 This interview appears as the 'Afterword' in Fadwa Tuqan, *A Mountainous Journey: An Autobiography*, trans. Olive Kenny (London: The Women's Press, 1990), 203.
5 This formulation borrows on Cairns Craig's eloquent development of the relationship between novel and nation in his *The Modern Scottish Novel: Narrative and the National Imagination* (Edinburgh: Edinburgh University Press, 1999), 9.
6 Anton Shammas, *Arabesques*, trans. Vivian Eden and Anton Shammas (London: Penguin, 1990), 146.
7 Said's essay appears as the 'Afterword' to the English translation of Elias Khoury's novel *Little Mountain*, trans. Maia Tabet (London: Collins Harvill, 1990), 139–40.
8 Ibid., 140, 142.

9 Jean Franco, *An Introduction to Spanish-American Literature* (Cambridge: Cambridge University Press, 1969), 56.

10 Franco Moretti, 'Conjectures on World Literature', *New Left Review* 1 (2000), 54–68.

11 Antonio Candido, 'Literature and Underdevelopment', in *On Literature and Society*, trans. Howard S. Becker (Princeton: Princeton University Press, 1995), 119–41, 127.

12 Cited in John Kenny, "No Such Genre': Tradition and the Contemporary Irish Novel,' in P. J. Matthews (ed.), *New Voices in Irish Criticism* (Dublin: Four Courts, 2000), 51.

13 See James Clifford, 'On Ethnographic Allegory', in James Clifford and George E. Marcus (eds.), *Writing Culture: the Poetics and Politics of Ethnography* (Berkeley: University of California Press, 1986), 115, and Edward Said, *Culture and Imperialism* (London: Vintage, 1994), 273.

14 Fredric Jameson, *The Political Unconscious: Narrative as a Socially Symbolic Act* (Ithaca: Cornell University Press, 1981), 102.

15 Edward Said, 'Arabic Prose and Prose Fiction since 1948', Introduction to Halim Barakat, *Days of Dust*, trans. Trevor Le Gassick (Washington: Three Continents Press, 1974), ix–xxxiv, xv.

16 Elleke Boehmer, 'Endings and New Beginning: South African Fiction in Transition', in Derek Attridge and Rosemary Jolly (eds.), *Writing South Africa: Literature, Apartheid and Democracy, 1970–1995* (Cambridge: Cambridge University Press, 1998), 43–56, 46.

17 Franco Moretti, 'Modern European Literature: a Geographical Sketch', *New Left Review* 206 (1994), 98.

18 Benita Parry, 'Some Provisional Speculations on the Critique of "Resistance Literature"', in Elleke Boehmer, Laura Chrisman and Kenneth Parker (eds.), *Altered States?: Writing and South Africa* (Sydney: Dangaroo Press, 1994), 11–24, 15.

19 Neil Lazarus, 'Modernism and Modernity: T. W. Adorno and Contemporary White South African Literature', *Cultural Critique* 5 (1986–87), 131–55, 139.

20 Martin Jay, *Adorno* (Cambridge, Mass.: Harvard University Press, 1984), 130–31. Cited in Lazarus, 'Modernism and Modernity', 139.

21 Ghassan Kanafani, *Men in the Sun and other Palestinian Stories*, trans. Hilary Kilpatrick (Washington DC: Three Continents Press, 1983). Originally published as *Rijal fi al-shams* (Beirut: Dār al-Muthallath, 1963).

22 For a more extended account, see Walid Kazziha, *Revolutionary Transformation in the Arab World* (London: Croom Helm, 1975).

23 Kanafani, *Men in the Sun*, 56.

24 Mary Layoun, *Travels of a Genre: the Modern Novel and Ideology* (Princeton: Princeton University Press, 1990), 202.

25 Ibid., 190.

26 Kanafani, *Men in the Sun*, 9.

27 Ibid., 15.

28 For a more detailed commentary on the way in which the lost land is linked to images of women, see Susan Slyomovics, *The Object of Memory: Arab and Jew Narrate the Palestinian Village* (Philadelphia: University of Pennslyvania Press, 1998), chapter 6.

29 Barbara McKean Parmenter, *Giving Voice to Stones: Place and Identity in Palestinian Literature* (Austin: University of Texas Press, 1994), 43. See also A. L. Tibawi, 'Visions of Return: the Palestinian Arab Refugee in Arabic Poetry and Art', *Middle East Journal* 17 (1963), 507–26; Adnan Mohammad Abu-Ghazaleh, 'The Impact of 1948 on Palestinian Arab Writers: the First Decade', *Middle East Forum* 2–3:46 (1970), 81–92, and Hanan Mikhail Ashrawi, *Contemporary Palestinian Literature Under Occupation* (Bir Zeit: Bir Zeit University Press, 1976).

30 Parmenter, *Giving Voice to Stones*, 79.

31 Kanafani, *Men in the Sun*, 10.

32 My discussion here draws on Muhammad Siddiq's *Man is a Cause: Political Consciousness and the Fiction of Ghassan Kanafani* (Seattle: University of Washington Press, 1984), 9–17.

33 Ibid., 17.

34 Kanafani, *Men in the Sun*, 17.

35 Ibid., 21.

36 Ibid., 35.

37 M. M. Bakhtin, *The Dialogic Imagination: Four Essays*, trans. Cary Emerson and Michael Holquist (Austin: University of Texas Press, 1981), 90.

38 Franco Moretti, *The Way of the World: the Bildungsroman in European Culture* (London: Verso, 1987), 79.

39 Kanafani, *Men in the Sun*, 22, 23, 25.

40 Ibid., 28.

41 Ibid., 19–20. My emphasis.

42 See Kaja Silverman, 'Historical Trauma and Male Subjectivity', in *Male Subjectivity at the Margins* (London: Routledge, 1992), 52–151. Silverman's thesis is that in situations of acute historical trauma, the male's normative identification with power and privilege is so threatened that it can no longer be sustained, with the result that the male finds himself confronted with the spectacle of castration that is conventionally ascribed only to women.

43 Silverman, *Male Subjectivity at the Margins*, chapters 1 and 2.

44 Kanafani, *Men in the Sun*, 26, 29, 25.

45 Ibid., 37–38.

46 In Sahar Khalifeh's *Wild Thorns*, trans. Trevor LeGassick and Elizabeth Fernea (New York: Olive Branch Press, 1989), the hero, Adil, compares the pain of an implicitly masculinised Palestinian resistance to female labour pains and concludes: 'Some of us get high on the resistance. Some of us on the glories of warfare. And we get high on kidney pains, yes, they really hurt, even worse than birth pangs. But labour pains are at least followed by a birth. We have kidney pains while you go into labour and then blame us for not giving birth. What are we supposed to give birth to?' (68).

47 Kanafani, *Men in the Sun*, 47.

48 Silverman, *Male Subjectivity at the Margins*, 42.

49 The father as a problematical figure is not confined to narative fiction. In *A Mountainous Journey: an Autobiography*, Fadwa Tuqan writes that when her father died in 'the 1948 debacle' her 'tongue was freed' and

she began to write 'quite voluntarily, and without outside coercion' the patriotic poetry that he had vainly solicited from her while he still lived (113). Raja Shehadah's *Samed: Journal of a West Bank Palestinian* (New York: Adama Books, 1984) also repeatedly returns to the author's difficult relationship with his father. At one point, Shehadeh writes of how the spectacle of a group of rather pathetic West Bank elders fawning over an Israeli official outraged him, and he comments angrily that Palestinian culture is one 'so geared to paternalism that it hardly matters who does the ordering' (29). It is interesting to note in this context Declan Kiberd's observation that in the literature of the pre-state period, when the struggle for Irish independence seemed stalled, the classic texts of the nationalist cultural renaissance are full of inadequate, unreliable or absent fathers. See Kiberd, *Inventing Ireland: the Literature of the Modern Nation* (London: Jonathan Cape, 1995), 380–95.

50 Kanafani, *Men in the Sun*, 38.

51 Saree Makdisi, '"Postcolonial" Literature in a Neocolonial World: Modern Arabic Culture and the End of Modernity', *Boundary 2* 22:1 (1995), 85–115, 95.

52 Benedict Anderson, *Imagined Communities: Reflections on the Origin and Spread of Nationalism*, revised edition (London: Verso, 1991), 30.

53 Bakhtin, *The Dialogic Imagination*, 243.

54 Ibid., 105.

55 Layoun, *Travels of a Genre*, 187.

56 This explanation for the 'pessimism' of *Men in the Sun* is offered in Hilary Kilpatrick, 'Tradition and Innovation in the fiction of Ghassan Kanafani', *Journal of Arabic Literature* 7 (1976), 53–64.

57 Adorno's evaluation of modernism, and the seemingly inordinate emphasis he put on the role of the critical intellectual, was premised, as Neil Lazarus observes, on his belief that the Marxist attempt to change the world had miscarried and the European proletariat was no longer even a force for progress. Because the European masses had been pacified, the burden of opposing a totally administered world had passed to the critical intellectual and it was in this context also that modernism's negativity revealed itself as critical and hence progressive. See Neil Lazarus, 'Modernism and Modernity', 131–55.

58 Theodor Adorno, 'Commitment', in Fredric Jameson (ed.), *Aesthetics and Politics* (London: Verso, 1988), 177–95, 191.

59 The phrase appears in Stephen Connor's *The English Novel In History, 1950–1995* (London: Routledge, 1996), 201.

60 Edward Said, *After the Last Sky: Palestinian Lives* (New York: Pantheon Books, 1986), 11.

61 Theodor Adorno, *Aesthetic Theory*, trans. C. Lenhardt (London: Routledge and Kegan Paul, 1984), 350, 228.

62 See Masao Miyoshi, 'A Borderless World?: From Colonialism to Transnationalism and Decline of the Nation-State', *Critical Inquiry* 19 (1993), 726–51.

63 See David Harvey, *Spaces of Hope* (Edinburgh: Edinburgh University Press, 2000).

# Index

# Index

# Index

# Index

Walser, Martin, 61, *No Man's Land*, 63
Walsh, Patrick, 236n.30
Waterman, Stanley, 19, 229n.7, 235n.14
Webster, Noah, 53, 234n.6
Weizmann, Chaim, 151, 244n.20
Wheelright, Julie, 130, 138, 242n.49, 242n.57
Whyte, John, 100, 226n.3, 239n.8
Williams, Arthur, 235n.16
Williams, C., and Kofman, E., 229n.7
Wolf, Christa, 63, 64
Woods, Vincent, *At the Black Pig's Dyke*, 77
Wright, Sue, 237n.42, 237n.44

Yeats, W. B., 67, 104
Yehoshua, A. B., 83, 90, 144, 183
Yemen, 83
Yiddish, 80–1; *see also* Zionism
Yizhar, S., 82
Yudkin, Leon I., 237n.45
Yugoslavia, 2, 3, 21, 27, 37, 97

Zach, Nathan, 83
Zionism, colonial settler character, 4–5, 6–7, 81, 143–4, 147–8, 163–4, 232n.31; and imperialism, 5, 7–8, 37, 38, 92, 151; and Irish nationalism, 6–7; compared to Ulster loyalism, 7, 226–27n.7; and self-determination 29–40; and partition of Palestine, 30; and Holocaust, 37, 170–1; origins, 80, 92; and Yiddish, 80–1, 85; role of kibbutz, 82; Ashkenazi hegemony, 83–5, 91; treatment of Sephardi Jews, 84–5; and anti-semitism, 156, 162, 170–1, 244–5n.30; and Diaspora, 156, 161–2; immigration and expansion, 161–2; and archaeology, 169. *see also* Hebrew Revival, Israel; Oslo Accord; Oz, Amos; partition
Zizek, Slavoj, 130, 241n.48, 242.n52
Zuriek, Elia, 233n.35